*Christopher Durang
Explains It All for You*

Also by Christopher Durang

A History of the American Film
The Marriage of Bette and Boo
Laughing Wild

Christopher Durang Explains It All for You

SIX PLAYS BY

CHRISTOPHER DURANG

Grove Press
New York

Published simultaneously in Canada
Printed in the United States of America

Library of Congress Cataloging-in-Publication Data

Durang, Christopher, 1949–
Christopher Durang explains it all for you : six plays / by
Christopher Durang
p.   cm.
ISBN-10: 0-8021-3232-4
ISBN-13: 978-0-8021-3232-1
I. Title.
PS3554.U666A6   1990
812'.54—dc   90-36867

Grove Press
an imprint of Grove/Atlantic, Inc.
841 Broadway
New York, NY 10003

Distributed by Publishers Group West

www.groveatlantic.com

06 07 08 09 10   20 19 18 17 16 15 14 13 12 11

To Stephen, Wendy, and Elizabeth;
and
to my mother's sense of humor

Contents

Introduction

First there is the solar system.

Within the solar system is the earth. Near the earth is the sun. Apparently Copernicus was right, and the earth does revolve around the sun. Thus the Catholic Church was wrong to make Galileo recant and, according to Brecht, Galileo's recanting foreshadowed the lack of scientific responsibility that led to the discovery of the atom bomb and the general misuse of atomic power.

Also nearby is the moon.

My earliest memories are as a gleam in my father's eye. My father fought in World War II and landed on Normandy Beach on D day. After that he returned to New Jersey, where he met my mother.

In 1948 I recall being inside my mother's womb. Freud was right about its soothing, secret qualities. Jung was correct about the various symbols and the collective unconscious.

My birth on January 2, 1949, I have repressed. (Repression is a gift from God, and we must honor it as such.) I was born in Montclair Hospital, Dr. Nathan Ram the doctor in attendance. Harry Truman was president. I was circumcised, presumably by Dr. Ram, and baptized, presumably by a priest. My parents and their families were very Catholic. This was to influence my writing and my digestion.

I liked rocking chairs, and was a well-behaved child. I recall in my crib understanding from my mother that it was wrong to hold an Eeyore doll between my legs. My mother, like the Catholic Church, had no interest in whether the Eeyore was consenting or not; some things are wrong because they are wrong.

My parents fought a great deal, sometimes when driving cars, and this was fairly harrowing. I was encouraged by my mother and by her sister Marion to pray to God that the arguing would stop, and that Russia would be converted to Catholicism, and that my mother would give me brothers and sisters. My parents eventually divorced, Russia has not to my knowledge converted, and my mother suffered through three still-births. As Sister Mary Ignatius points out, all our prayers *are* answered, it's just that sometimes the answer is no.

I wrote my first play in the second grade of Our Lady of Peace School. It was more or less plagiarized from the *I Love Lucy* episode where Lucy has a baby, and was two pages long. Eisenhower was now president. My parents were too lazy to build a fallout shelter in our basement, so we would have to trust in prayer to protect ourselves from nuclear attack.

I was taught by nuns until seventh grade, when I switched to an all-boys Catholic prep school taught by very intelligent and nice Benedictine priests. I briefly attempted to be a juvenile delinquent and smoked Marlboros for about a month but stopped, as I was very short and looked silly.

The school was on the grounds of a monastery, and my junior and senior years I spent a few weekends joining in the daily routine of the monastery. Prayers, then breakfast, then prayers, then lunch, then prayers, then dinner, then prayers, then sleep. I found the predictability quite attractive. I was going to join the monastery right after high school, but they said I should wait. And then I just stopped believing in all those things, and I never did join the monastery. I became a depressed undergraduate.

I went to non-Catholic Harvard. I had written plays all during high school, but in college dried up. My daily routine eventually degenerated into skipping my classes, sleeping all day, cleaning bathrooms (my term-time job), and going to the movies. This obsessive movie-going eventually inspired *A History of the American Film*. The bathroom cleaning hasn't inspired anything as of yet.

Sophomore year I saw my first psychiatrist, who, I later learned, was actually a priest. (No, I'm not making that up.) A subsequent psychologist was very helpful, and my senior year I snapped out of my depression some and put on *The Greatest Musical Ever Sung*, a giddy travesty I'd written presenting the Gospels as a musical comedy (the Blessed Mother sang "The Dove That Done Me Wrong"; the Transfiguration was sung as "Everything's Coming Up Moses"). Collegiate admittedly, but then I was, after all, in college. The show was popular, but also caused a bit of a stir among those who found it offensive, including a Jesuit priest teaching at Harvard who wrote the *Harvard Crimson* calling me "a pig trampling in a sanctuary."

Putting on this play, I recaptured the exhilaration I'd known in high school of an audience responding to something I'd written. I started to write again, and the play that came out was the first one in this collection, *The Nature and Purpose of the Universe*.

The title came from a momentary misunderstanding. By my senior year (1971) the universities had become exhausted with trying to figure out how to cope with sit-ins and take-overs and non-negotiable demands. One morning I discovered a booklet under my door that Harvard put out trying, poignantly, to define how it saw its role; the booklet was entitled "The Nature and Purpose of the University," but I, in a moment of blurry-eyed existentialism, thought it said "The Nature and Purpose of the Universe."

The impetus for the play was the suffering of a friend of my mother's—a lovely woman, age twenty-five, who had five children and an alcoholic brute of a husband. She had asked the local parish priest, a nice and admirable man in most respects, if she could perhaps use birth control to protect herself in case her husband raped her in a drunken rage; the priest thought about it over dinner, then said no. The husband did force himself on her, and she had a sixth child. Although the play is not about the chains of child-bearing, it *is* about a life filled with nothing but pain and disappointment, and how the Catholic Church sometimes fosters a masochistic acceptance of this (offer it up, Christ suffered, this is *your* cross to bear, you'll be rewarded in the next life).

However, the noteworthy thing about the play for my so-called development is the utter glee of its tone; I cackled aloud as I wrote it. During my religious days I viewed suffering with great compassion and concern as something Christ wished me to alleviate. Then without religion I found suffering (mine, others', the concept of) totally paralyzing, and spent my college days obsessively spouting depressing movie quotes at baffled dinner companions—"I am worn out with grief and fatigue" (Godard's *Band of Outsiders*), I'd say over salad. Or "My life is an empty place; what are you going to do about it?" (Pinter and Clayton's *The Pumpkin Eater*) over veal cutlet. Or "Between grief and nothing, I'd choose nothing" (Godard's *Breathless*) over coffee.

But then as I started to write *Nature and Purpose*, suddenly the extremity of suffering made me giddy, and I found the energy and distance to *relish* the awfulness of it all. This "relish" is something that audiences do not always feel comfortable with, and I find that some people, rather than simply disliking my work, are made furious by it.

This play was my application to Yale School of Drama—that, and the letter calling me a pig.

I was accepted, and the summer before I went to Yale I wrote *'dentity Crisis* after reading and sympathizing with schizophrenic case histories reported by R. D. Laing and A. Esterson in *Madness, Sanity and the Family.* " 'dentity," by the way, is the word "Identity" with the "I" missing, but no one ever gets this and usually thinks the play has something to do with dentistry, so I guess it's actually a bad title.

The play has the same sort of gleeful tone as *Nature and Purpose.* Its theme of a strong-minded person (often crazy) imposing his or her will over a weaker person (potentially sane and often a child; in this case, loony Edith Fromage over her daughter, Jane) is a recurring one in my writing and in my past, and probably has reached a sort of peak in the portrait of Sister Mary Ignatius and her attempts to make her students accept what she sees as the only truth.

I went to Yale with a tentative sense of confidence, hoping to find encouragement, which I found, especially from Howard Stein, then dean of playwriting, and most especially from Robert Brustein, then dean of the school and artistic director of the adventurous Yale Repertory Theatre.

The first draft of *Titanic*, the third play in this collection, came from an exercise Howard Stein asked us to do: write a scene on a train with a man smoking a cigar, and a woman asking him to stop. My train was also a boat, and not much was said about cigars, though a lot was said of white bread, mirrors, and marmalade.

I continued writing *Titanic* in Jules Feiffer's class (he thought he was a bad teacher, but he was very good), and cut out a section where the *Titanic* docked at Port Authority Bus Terminal in New York. Feiffer, who liked the play, said it was a pre-pubescent temper tantrum of children learning about their parents' "doing it" (and I added the phrase "pre-pubescent temper tantrum" to a line of Victoria's), but I think the play is probably too messy to be thematically enclosed. It clearly has to do with children's anger at parents (they kill them, after all), with parents manipulating and seducing their children, and with a certain fear of and disgust with sex. (Some days I still think sex is fearful and disgusting, but perhaps God means it to be that way.) In any case, even though the play is sort of a mess, I think it's a funny and evocative mess, and I'm happy to have it in print.

Upon graduation, I hung around New Haven for a year acting in two shows at Yale Rep (including Albert Innaurato's and my *The Idiots Karamazov*), then doing odd jobs. I finally faced going to New York in the fall of 1975.

My first two plays seen in New York were *The Nature and Purpose of the Universe* and *Titanic*, both done as 11 P.M. late shows off-off-Broadway. The first was a nice, sturdy success. The second, *Titanic*, was a sort of cult success off-off in the murderous, pre–Manhattan Plaza West 43rd Street, and an excellent cast featured my two favorite actor-classmates from Yale, Kate McGregor-Stewart and Sigourney Weaver. The play moved to a commercial run off-Broadway where I received the harshest reviews I hope I will ever get. In retrospect, the moved production was too fast and frenetic, I allowed myself to be bullied into making some bad cuts (which removed a kind of texture of craziness), and the otherwise good direction did lack a certain double edge of farce and sadness that I keep trying to find. For instance, if Victoria says, "I have always longed for a solution" with a true and felt sadness, something more peculiar and surprising happens to the play than if it's all pace, pace, pace.

But, most of all, the play was not a mainstream play, and the idea that we had Walter Kerr come to it (happily, he chose not to review it) is hilarious.

The closing of *Titanic*, or "the sinking of," as most critics quipped predictably, found me with no money and not a little taken aback by the fury of some of the reviews. Martin Gottfried, then on the *New York Post* and a known enemy of Brustein's, marveled that I had received an M.F.A. from Yale; and Ross Wetzsteon of the *Village Voice* complained that the play was against family and society— something that the *Village Voice* would not usually complain of, it seemed to me—and unkindly psychoanalyzed me as hating and fearing women; this last was inaccurate as well as unkind—I hate and fear people, regardless of gender.

Immediately following the semi-debacle of *Titanic*, I found much success with *A History of the American Film*. The play began at the invaluable O'Neill National Playwrights Conference, and went on in 1977 to have a triple premiere (three separate productions) at the Hartford Stage Company, the Mark Taper Forum in Los Angeles, and the Arena Stage in Washington, D.C.

The next year was taken up with preparing the play for Broadway. Unfortunately, things didn't come together on Broadway as well as they had in the regionals. My rewrites went off kilter, the ANTA Theatre was much too large for us, and though the *New York Times* review was good, the other reviews were cranky and harsher on the show than I felt it deserved, flawed though it was.

Anyway, the next year was depressing. I found it was hard to write—I kept imagining what various critics might say about some piece I'd start; and my mother was dying of cancer. She'd had a long history with the disease, starting with breast cancer in 1973, seeming remission, then a tumor on the hip in 1976. Failed treatments and pain and more tumors and operations went on for three more years; her prognosis was basically hopeless, but the disease moved at an ambiguous pace—depending on the speed with which the bone cancer spread, she could live anywhere from six months to five years to possibly more. Her last weeks were as Diane describes in *Sister Mary Ignatius*, and she died on March 10, 1979.

My mother tried to use her Catholic religion to help her face death and find some comfort. Alas, it did not work for her, though it did work for one of her sisters, for whom watching my mother's impending death was a painful but nonetheless religiously understandable event—she was simply on her way to God.

I had not consciously thought about the teachings of the Catholic Church for some years, and watching my mother try to grasp on to religion triggered in me recollections of the doctrines I had been taught.

For starters, I was nostalgic for belief, since it offered comfort; and yet I was also made angry by the illogic of the Church's muddy teachings on how suffering fits into God's Grand Plan. From thoughts on suffering, I moved on to remember the dizzying intricacies of some of the dogma—limbo, the Immaculate Conception, mortal and venial sin, papal infallibility, etc. Because ten years had passed since I'd thought about all this, I felt like a tourist in my own past, and what I'd accepted as a child and forgotten about as a young adult now seemed on a new viewing as the sincere ravings of a semi-lunatic.

The last year of my mother's life I began *Sister Mary Ignatius Explains It All for You*, the fifth play in the collection; I wrote the second half a few months after she died. The play was in no way written "because" my mother died. It was written partially in giddy recall (who can believe we once believed in limbo?), and partially in anger (the Church's teachings on sex have done nobody any good). And it's also written from a basic, and disappointed, nonbelief—for even when one ignores and forgives the sillier rules that have been made up by generations of Irish and Italian men who thought they heard God whispering in their ears, what still remains is the Church's presentation of a paternal, watching-over-us Good Shepherd whose supposed power and concern for us simply does not correlate with the facts of human suffering. God knows [*sic*] that I'm not the first person to think these thoughts. Still, when the myth of the Good Father in heaven is taught as fact and ingrained in you from early childhood, to realize much, much later that this is untrue is, frankly, very disappointing.

That *Sister Mary Ignatius* has become my one commercial success in New York to date is an unanticipated pleasure. It was first done off-off-Broadway by Curt Dempster's Ensemble Studio Theatre as part of its annual one-act marathon, and was directed by Jerry Zaks, who proved himself a master at balancing its comedy and seriousness. From this production the actress Elizabeth Franz and I both won 1980 Obie awards. Elizabeth's superb portrayal, funny but murderous, pig-headed but always illuminated by what seems to be a true faith, has been an indispensable contribution to the play and to its reception. And in 1981 Andre Bishop and his Playwrights Horizons produced *Sister Mary Ignatius* off-Broadway, again with Jerry Zaks and Elizabeth Franz, this time with a curtain raiser, *The Actor's Nightmare*.

Ever since *Sister Mary's* success at Ensemble Studio Theatre, I had been trying to come up with another one act to precede it and make it a full, and thus more marketable, evening. I felt this curtain raiser should be more light-hearted than *Sister Mary*, should not have a woman as its main character, and, if it mentioned religion at all, should express some of my nostalgia for the comfort of religion rather than my bitterness over its disappointments. From this came *The Actor's Nightmare*, written specifically to double-cast with *Sister Mary* and written after waking up from a nightmare. The nightmare in question wasn't really an actor's nightmare (dreaming you have to act in a play you've never rehearsed), though I've certainly had those dreams. Anyway, the mere fact of having a bad dream reminded me that I had, on and off, considered doing something with this recurring actor's fear. Of all my characters, George Spelvin most recognizably has my diction (I am very polite in life—all that Catholic training—if not in my writing), and I had a highly enjoyable time this summer playing the role for two weeks while the excellent Jeff Brooks was on vacation. I did, however, attend four rehearsals.

Beyond Therapy, the final play in this collection, was written on a commission from the Phoenix Theatre. I wrote it during an odd period of self-discipline (not yet repeated) during which I stopped eating cookies and cake, jogged daily around the reservoir, and then wrote for several hours after my run. In the evenings I would take heavy drugs and pick up prostitutes.

When I wrote this play, my friends were all turning thirty. Most of them were seeing psychiatrists, they all talked about relationships (me too, me too), and they all worried about not being married yet. So the play is about "relationships," and also how psychology and psychobabble hinder and help us.

I had two excellent productions of the play, the first off-Broadway at the Phoenix in January 1981, directed by Jerry Zaks and starring Sigourney Weaver and Stephen Collins, the second on Broadway in May 1982, directed by John Madden and starring Dianne Wiest and John Lithgow. The script was rewritten and, I feel, improved for the Broadway version. However, the critical response to the play both times was extremely mixed, especially confusing the second time around, since the positive side of the mix seemed to consider the play a nearly complete success, while the negative side seemed to consider the play pretty much a fizzle.

The most significant complaints about the play have been that Bruce and Prudence are boring compared to their lunatic therapists, and that the play is a series of sketches not a play. Although it is possible that the naysayers are right and the play is unsatisfying, my present belief after watching audiences enjoy these two very good productions is that some critics are unwilling to accept the stylization of some of the comedy. For instance, Bruce's behavior in the first scene, weeping repeatedly and blurting out marriage proposals, is exaggerated past what it would be in a *situational* comedy about the same character, though he still acts out of a recognizable psychology, in my opinion, if not Walter Kerr's.

Furthermore, faced with this stylized, "heightened" comedy (found especially in the two therapists' characters), some critics seem unwilling to go along with me when I switch to a more realistic comic mode and actually ask the audience to feel for Prudence's plight, particularly in scene four when Bruce and Prudence meet for the second time and actually start to hit it off a little, and at the end when Bruce and Prudence feel regretful that though they hit it off a little, it still isn't quite enough. Switching tone from lunatic comedy to momentary seriousness or ruefulness is something that continues to interest me, and I intend to keep trying to do it, and if the critics won't come along, well then, as Andrew in *Beyond Therapy* would say, fuck 'em.

So where was I? There's the solar system, the sun, the moon, the stars. I went to drama school with Meryl Streep; once she complimented me on a blue shirt I was wearing. Outside the universe, where we go after death, is heaven, hell, and New Jersey. New Jersey has the highest cancer rate in the nation, second only to that nice spot in Nevada where they tested an atom bomb near where they filmed the terrible movie *Genghis Khan*, and years later many of the movie's participants (John Wayne, Susan Hayward, technicians, et al.) died of cancer. The square root of 1089 is 33. There are two pints in a quart. There is a very loud amusement park right outside my present lodgings. My sophomore year roommate at Harvard had a poster by Sister

Corita on the wall. Sister Corita, for those of you who don't know or who have repressed her memory, was a "with-it" nun of the sixties who painted cheery, upbeat, inspirational religious art, things like "God Is Love" in bright crayon scrawl, or the Wonder Bread yellow dot logo used as a cutesy representation of the Eucharist (Wonder Bread . . . get it?). In any case, this particular poster of hers was just her crayon scrawl, and it said: "To believe in God means knowing that all the rules will be fair, and that wonderful surprises are in store. . . ." This poster irritated me greatly in college. Where is Sister Corita now? The square root of 9801 is 99. 4 × 7 = 28. The French word for window is *la fenêtre*. I don't know the Italian for window, or ceiling. Critics sometimes complain that I have trouble ending my plays. This is nonsense. #$%!!2357&:::::::::::::::::::::::::::::

Christopher Durang
August 1, 1982
New York City

The Nature
and Purpose
of the Universe

The Nature and Purpose of the Universe was presented by the Direct Theatre at the Wonder Horse Theatre in New York on February 21, 1979. The production was directed by Allen R. Belknap, setting by Jonathan Arkin, lighting by Richard Winkler, costumes by Giva Taylor. The cast was as follows:

RONALD, an agent of God	Jeff Brooks
ELAINE MAY ALCOTT, an agent of God	Caroline Kava
STEVE MANN	Tom Bade
ELEANOR MANN	Ellen Greene
DONALD MANN	Ethan Phillips
ANDY MANN	Eric Weitz
GARY MANN	Chris Ceraso
COACH GRIFFIN	Robert Blumenfeld
RALPH	T. A. Taylor
FATHER ANTHONY HEMMER	T. A. Taylor
THE POPE	Robert Blumenfeld

(The roles of Ralph and Father Hemmer, and of Coach Griffin and the Pope, may be doubled.)

A "radio play" version of the play was presented by the Direct Theatre in September 1975, directed by Allen R. Belknap and Yannis Simonides. Due to the "radio" concept, there was more doubling among the men's roles. The cast of this version was as follows:

RONALD, an agent of God	Justin Rashid
ELAINE, an agent of God	Lynnie Godfrey
STEVE MANN	James Nisbet Clark
ELEANOR MANN	Anne De Salvo
ANDY, COACH, FATHER HEMMER	David Wilborn
DONALD, RALPH	Nick Mariano
GARY, THE POPE	Lars Kampmann

(The non-radio version requires two women, seven men. The radio version requires two women, five men.)

SETTING

There are two ways to set this play.

The first is to set it recognizably in the messy middle-class home of Eleanor and Steven Mann. Kitchen area, kitchen table and chairs stage right; living area with TV and small sofa center stage; desk and chair of living area stage left. (This presumes a fairly wide stage. With a narrower stage, the TV center area and desk left area can be merged into one area; the sofa can become a chair.)

This home is not presented too realistically. For instance, though Eleanor should have a frying pan, she should have no stove; it's better that she mime using one. And in the scenes set outside the home, there should be no attempt to actually change the set. For instance, the school scene of Miss Mansfield's office should be placed at the desk in the house (with center stage and stage right blacked out). The nightclub in Iceland can be the kitchen table with a cloth thrown over it (or even no cloth); if snow should fall, it falls in the kitchen.

Because Ronald sets the scene in his narration, the audience is fairly willing to accept the change of scenes without actual set alteration; and thematically there is something appropriate in all of the scenes taking place in the home.

The other alternative is to split the stage two thirds, one third. The right two thirds is the Mann home; you need the kitchen, living area—the kitchen table and chairs, a TV, an

3

armchair or sofa. The stage left one third would be "Ronald and Elaine's area," an all-purpose area outside the home where Ronald and Elaine go about their "agent of God" business. The area would need a sturdy table and two chairs. The table, with prop additions at the designer's discretion, would be made to represent Sister Annie's office; the office of Miss Mansfield; the table in the nightclub in Iceland; and the sacrificial table at the end of the play. The Pope's speaking in Weehawken would also be set there. Throughout the play, whichever set you use, there should be a chair stage left for Ronald to sit in and watch the action whenever he is not in a scene or is not addressing the audience.

SCENE: *A kitchen–living room setting, not too elaborate and flexible enough to accommodate easy changes. A few chairs, a kitchen table set for breakfast. Cereal boxes and the like.*

> *Enter* RONALD, *an agent of God. He is dressed neatly in a suit and tie, or perhaps in a tuxedo. On his arm is* ELAINE, *another agent of God; she is dressed in an attractive red or black evening gown. They walk toward the audience, smiling as if inviting them to an especially elegant social event.*

RONALD: The Nature and Purpose of the Universe. Chapter One. It was an ordinary Tuesday morning, much like any other Tuesday morning.

> (ELAINE *now exits, having completed her greeting function.*)

> The frost was on the pumpkin and a nip was in the air. It was an ordinary Tuesday morning, much like any other Tuesday morning. Steve and Eleanor Mann were just getting up. Eleanor was still crying softly into her bathrobe because her oldest son was a dope pusher, and her middle son was a homosexual and wore purple scarves, and her youngest son had recently lost his penis in a strange McReilly's reaper accident.

> (RONALD *goes and sits in his chair left, out of the action. He watches. Enter* ELEANOR *and* STEVE MANN. ELEANOR *looks bedraggled, and carries a frying pan and spatula; she stands by the kitchen*

table and scrambles eggs; she cries softly into a dish towel. Stove, eggs not necessary. STEVE, *in a suit, sits at the table, reading a newspaper and drinking coffee. For a while there's just the scrambling, the reading, the quiet crying.*)

STEVE: Eleanor! Why are you crying? You just got up.

ELEANOR: Oh, Steve, I don't understand it. Not any of it. Our house is worth forty-five thousand dollars. Where did it all start to go wrong?

(*Enter* DONALD, *about twenty-five, seedy and vicious.*)

DONALD: Hey, Mom, where's my spare hypodermic?

ELEANOR: Oh, Steven. Speak to your son.

STEVE: I saw it in the hall closet.

DONALD: God damn it.

(*He exits. Enter* ANDY, *about fourteen, wearing short pants with a large white bandage covering the crotch of his pants.*)

ANDY: Good morning, Mom. Good morning, Dad.

(ELEANOR *looks at him and, overcome with grief, cries into a dish towel.*)

STEVE: Good morning, son. How's the boy?

ANDY: Okay.

(*Enter* DONALD.)

DONALD: God damn it! The needle's not there! Now where is it? One of you must have taken it. Who was it?

ELEANOR (*sobbing*): Oh, Donald, why must we live like this?

DONALD (*hurls her to the ground*): Shut up, you stupid drudge! Did you throw my hypodermic out? Did you, you slut? Slattern! Trollop! Tramp!

ELEANOR: Steven! Don't let him treat me this way!

STEVE: Donald, have a little patience with your mother please.

DONALD: You threw the needle out, didn't you, bitch? (*He kicks her.*)

ELEANOR (*screams*): You shouldn't take drugs! You shouldn't sell drugs! We'll all be arrested!

ANDY: We need more sugar, Mom, for the cereal.

DONALD: What do you know? You're going to pay me for that needle and I'm going to kill you if you take any of my things ever again! (*He kicks her. She screams.*)

ELEANOR: Steven!

STEVE: Don't despair, Ellie. Have faith. God provides.

ELEANOR: I know, but look what He's provided!

STEVE (*furious*): Don't you dare to talk against God, you whore of Babylon. (*He kicks her.*) Do you want the children not to believe in God?

ELEANOR: Oh, Steve, please! Let me finish making the eggs.

STEVE: What sort of example is that?

ANDY: We don't believe in God, Dad. Ever since that earthquake in Peru.

STEVE: You see what you've done, Pig?

ELEANOR: I didn't cause the earthquake! Oh, Steve. Let me finish the eggs.

DONALD: Hurry up, I'm hungry.

(*The sons and father go calmly back to eating;* ELEA-NOR *gets up from the floor, cries into the dish towel, and starts scrambling the eggs again. There is silence except for the eggs and her whimpering.*)

STEVE (*after a while*): Eleanor, don't snivel. It's depressing.

ELEANOR: I'm sorry, Steven.

(*Enter* GARY, *the middle son, dressed entirely in purple.*)

GARY: Good morning, Dad. Good morning, Donald. Good morning, Andy. (*He kisses his father and brothers on the cheek.*)

ELEANOR: Don't you say hello to your mother?

GARY (*chilly, doesn't like her*): How are you, Eleanor?

ELEANOR: Oh, Gary. Gary, Gary.

(GARY *starts to nuzzle* ANDY's *shoulder, and then kiss behind his ears.* ELEANOR, *after a bit:*)

Gary, stop it! Your brother has no genitals! Leave him alone.

(DONALD *kicks over the table.*)

DONALD: Can we have no peace in the morning? Is there no civilization left anywhere in this stupid house? What kind of town is this? What kind of people are these? (*He hurls his mother to the ground.*)

ELEANOR: Steven, help me! Help!

(Enter RONALD. *Action freezes. Then actors exit, except for* RONALD.*)*

RONALD: The Nature and Purpose of the Universe. Chapter Two. It was an ordinary Tuesday morning, just like any other Tuesday morning. There was much for Eleanor to do. There was the cleaning to do, and the beds to be made, and the meals to be prepared so that she could keep home nice for her men. Andy went off to school, Gary off for a short cruise in the park, Steve went off to his job, and Donald went off to scrape and save, pimp and push. God assigns my friend Elaine to impersonate a next-door neighbor who upsets Eleanor.

*(*RONALD *sits in his chair. Enter* ELEANOR *with a vacuum cleaner.* ELEANOR *tries to turn the vacuum on, but it won't work. She starts to cry.)*

ELEANOR *(on her knees)*: Oh, please, God, please let my vacuum cleaner work. Please. And I promise I won't complain about my sons. Just please let my household appliances work. I don't care about the electric tooth-brush, but I need the vacuum cleaner and the washing machine and the *(she sobs)* refrigerator. Oh, please God! Please! Let my car start again and I promise I'll pick up hitchhikers even if they beat me with chains because I know that some of them are your angels sent in disguise to test me, I know this, my husband Steve tells me it's so, and he's much more religious than I am. I'm just an unworthy woman. Oh, God, help me.

(Enter ELAINE MAY ALCOTT, *dressed as a housewife. She drags a little girl behind her. The little girl is ap-*

*parently entirely unconscious. The little girl is best
played by a doll.*)

ELAINE (*furious*): Don't you ever answer your door bell,
Mrs. Mann? Do you always ignore your neighbors?

ELEANOR: Oh, Mrs. Ackerman, I'm sorry. I didn't hear the
bell. Can I get you coffee or . . . What's the matter with
your daughter?

ELAINE: Well might you ask, Mrs. Mann. I found her in the
bathroom this morning, passed out next to the john,
and I found this hypodermic stuck in her little arm.
(*She whips hypodermic out of her purse.*) See this,
Mrs. Mann?

ELEANOR: Oh, Mrs. Ackerman, how horrible!

ELAINE: Horrible, she says. You hear that, God? The dope
pusher's mother is horrified. (ELAINE *jabs* ELEANOR's
arm with the hypodermic.)

ELEANOR (*screams*): Oh, my God, you've punctured me.

ELAINE (*mimicking*): Oh, my God, you've punctured me.
Damn right I've punctured you. What about my
daughter? Do you know how much weekly allowance
we have to give Caroline to feed her habit? Fifty dollars
a week. You hear that, Mrs. Mann? We have to pay my
hophead daughter fifty dollars a week, all of which goes
to your hateful, sick son.

ELEANOR: Oh, Mrs. Ackerman.

ELAINE: Your family is the bane of Maplewood, Mrs. Mann.
My husband has been attacked in the garage by your
pansy son twice now, and just last week we found your
little son's penis in our driveway. My little Bobby was
going to use it for fish bait until I took it away from him.

Do you think I like to live in this atmosphere of sickness, Mrs. Mann? Do you think I want to live near your horrible family?

ELEANOR: Oh, Mrs. Ackerman, I know how you must feel. But do you think we might possibly have my son's penis back?

ELAINE: Certainly not! I put it right down the garbage disposal. I don't want your family's private parts hanging around my kitchen. (ELAINE *jabs* ELEANOR *with the hypodermic again.*)

ELEANOR: Mrs. Ackerman, please. I'm bleeding.

ELAINE: Bleeding, she says. You hear that, God? My little daughter Caroline is OD'ing and Mrs. Mann is complaining about a few punctures. (*Screaming.*) What about my daughter? I want some reparation. Reparation, Mrs. Mann!

ELEANOR: Oh, Mrs. Ackerman, what can I say?

ELAINE: Give me your color TV! I want your color television.

ELEANOR: Oh no, please. Donald would beat me. He watches TV all the time.

ELAINE: I don't care what he does. I just know that I'm taking your television set or I'm calling the police.

ELEANOR: Please, please, Mrs. Ackerman.

(ELAINE *picks up the television set.*)

ELAINE (*shouting*): KEEP YOUR HORRIBLE FAMILY AWAY FROM ME, DO YOU HEAR? Do you hear?

(She exits with television, leaving little CAROLINE *behind.)*

ELEANOR: There, there, Caroline, it's all right.

(Enter RONALD. *Action freezes, then actors exit.)*

RONALD: The Nature and Purpose of the Universe. Chapter Three. It was an ordinary Tuesday morning, but oh God, thought Eleanor, what has happened over the years? All my hopes dashed, she thought, all my illusions crushed. I remember how happy I was in high school, playing the lead in a Chekhov play. What one was it, I wonder? And while Eleanor thought these despairing thoughts, she did the wash and baked a cake. And while Eleanor prayed to God, God was busy communicating a message to Steven about the New Pope. God's instrument on earth is again my friend Elaine May Alcott, whom God this time assigns to masquerade as Sister Annie De Maupassant, the radical nun of Bernardsville.

*(*RONALD *sits. Enter* ELAINE *dressed as a nun. Since* ELAINE *has little time to change costumes, her costumes should be minimal. In this case, a nun's veil.* ELAINE *sits at a desk, blesses a cigarette, then smokes it. Enter* STEVE.*)*

ELAINE: How do you do, Mr. Mann? I am Sister Annie De Maupassant, the radical nun of Bernardsville.

STEVE: I have heard much of your reputation, Sister.

ELAINE: And I of yours, Mr. Mann. I am told that you are one of the most thoughtful and brilliant of Catholic laymen within a radius of five dioceses. The Jesuits speak well of you.

STEVE: I am humbled by your thinking well of me.

ELAINE: But enough of this small talk. We are here on more important matters. Something is awry in Rome. The Pope is not the proper Pope. He is a fraud. He is not the Deity's choice.

STEVE: Sister Annie De Maupassant, what can this mean? You mean Pope Paul is not a proper Pope?

ELAINE: Pope Paul is a false Pope. He speaks with the Papal wee wee.

STEVE: As bad as that?

ELAINE: I fear so.

STEVE: What must be done?

ELAINE: In a few weeks Pope Paul is coming to New Jersey to bless the air in Weehawken. God has communicated to me that we must spirit him away, reveal him as a fraud, and instate the true Pope in his proper place. Only then will the Church be able to gain its rightful and dominant place in the world.

STEVE: Sister Annie De Maupassant, you may certainly depend on me.

ELAINE: God bless the laity! Thank you, Mr. Mann, I knew I could. My agents will get in touch with you soon. Simply continue your life as you normally would, stay close to the sacraments, and make ready for the Holy Spirit.

STEVE: Sister Annie De Maupassant, I have one question. Has God perhaps revealed to you who the true Pope is?

ELAINE: Yes, Mr. Mann, He has.

STEVE: Who is it to be?

(ELAINE *stands on her desk.*)

ELAINE: Mr. Mann, it is I, Sister Annie De Maupassant, who is the true and only Pope. (*She throws a handful of glitter into the air and stamps her foot in triumph. Then she opens her mouth and lets out a high, continuous shrieking sound, while her tongue flies in and out of her mouth. She places her hand on her throat, in surprise, as if she has no control over the noises she is making. The noises stop, and she speaks.*) Bonjour, Jean. Comment ça va? Auf wiedersehen. Oh my God, I'm speaking in tongues. (*She shrieks again, her tongue going in and out; it's a gibberish sound, half sung, half screamed. Then she speaks again.*) Moo goo gai pan. (*Swedish:*) Yo. Inga Swenson gunnar cheese. (*Shrieks again. Has* STEVE *help her exit. Then while she is exiting:*) Flores, flores para los muertos.

(*She and* STEVE *exit.* RONALD *addresses the audience again.*)

RONALD: The Nature and Purpose of the Universe. Chapter Four. The sun hit its zenith shortly after noon that day, just as Gary and his new friend scuttled behind a bush in the park. It was a Tuesday like any other Tuesday, except that Eleanor got a call from Andy's junior high school principal. It seems that Andy had upset his athletic teacher. God assigns Elaine to play the role of the principal's secretary, and the athletic coach plays himself.

(RONALD *retires to his seat. Enter* ELAINE, COACH GRIFFIN, *and* ANDY. ELAINE *sits at a desk, ripping up papers and/or shooting rubber bands into the air.*

ANDY's *shirt is off, and* COACH GRIFFIN *is whipping him on the floor. Enter* ELEANOR, *carrying a full laundry basket.*)

ELEANOR: Oh, dear, oh, dear. What is the matter?

ELAINE: I'm sorry to interrupt your busy day, Mrs. Mann, but we have a little problem here. (*Offers her hand, gracious.*) I'm Miss Mansfield, Mr. Watson's secretary. Mr. Watson is on sabbatical this semester, and in his absence I have complete power. (*Looking around room, cheerfully awed.*) I don't know what to do with it all, really.

ANDY (*being whipped*): Mommy!

ELAINE (*charming*): Oh, I'm sorry. Coach Griffin, please don't inflict any more corporal punishment on Master Mann right now. (*To* ELEANOR:) Discipline is a delicate thing. Mrs. Mann, I'm going to be frank. We've all been worried about Andrew in school lately.

COACH: I won't have no boy without a male organ in my gym class.

ELEANOR: That seems to me prejudiced.

COACH: If he doesn't have an organ, he should be on the girls' side. I'm not having no girl in my gym class.

ELAINE (*smiles*): You see our problem.

ELEANOR: Well, I guess there's nothing I can say. Can Andrew be exempted from gym?

COACH: Certainly not.

ELAINE: We have our rules.

ELEANOR: Well I guess he'll have to have gym with the girls then.

COACH: Damn right.

ELAINE (*pleased*): I'm glad that's settled.

COACH: And he can't wear an athletic supporter either.

ELEANOR: I'm sure he wouldn't want to, Coach Griffin. Mr. Griffin, I only hope that someday you are mangled by a McReilly's reaper, and then I hope you shall have more sympathy for people without organs.

ELAINE: Please, let us remain ladies and gentlemen.

ELEANOR: Might I go now?

ELAINE: I'm afraid we have another complaint to deal with, from the Mothers' Cake Committee of the PTA. I have here a letter from Mrs. Samuel Fredericks which I must read to you. (*Reciting:*) Dear Miss Mansfield, I am shaken . . .

ELEANOR: Where is the letter?

ELAINE (*smiles*): I've committed it to memory. Dear Miss Mansfield, I am shaken and upset. At our otherwise successful Mothers' Cake Sale at the children's playground the other day, our festivities were disturbed by the actions of a certain young man who my daughter says was Andrew Mann. This young boy had the temerity to approach our Mothers' Cake Counter where he proceeded to undo his pants and to expose himself to the baking mothers present. We were all appalled. There was nothing there. New paragraph. Now, Miss Mansfield, I am as much in favor of charity and kindness as the next mother, but enough is enough! I have been sick to my stomach all day, and expect to be so for much of tomorrow. Surely there must be a fit punishment for this crime, Miss Mansfield, for as our prisons attest, crime is encouraged by leniency. I leave this matter in your capable hands. Sincerely, Mrs. Samuel Fredericks, 31 Club Drive, Maplewood. (*Pause.*) Have you anything to say, Andrew?

ANDY (*softly*): I hate school.

ELAINE: All children think they hate school. No, my task is to do the right thing, to perpetrate the correct punishment. So I've decided that to symbolize the ungentlemanly nature of Andrew's behavior he will be required to wear girls' clothing for one month, at which time I will reconsider his case.

ELEANOR (*concerned*): Do you think that that will help him realize the wrongness of his action?

ELAINE: I don't know. But if he doesn't expose himself again, I shall feel we have succeeded. (*Lowering her voice.*) Exhibitionism of a sexual nature must be checked early, Mrs. Mann. Repression is a gift from God, and we must honor it as such.

ELEANOR: I worry that such punishment might be harmful.

ELAINE: Well, time will tell. Oh, and, by the way, Mrs. Mann, I'm afraid that Mrs. Fredericks requested that you return your PTA membership card and that your car be denied use of the school parking lot. Since parents are frequently partly to blame for the failings of their children, I think that this is only just. Thank you for coming, Mrs. Mann. I've enjoyed meeting you.

ELEANOR: Miss Mansfield, I can only apologize from the depth of my heart to you, and to you, Coach Griffin, for the pain and anguish my son Andrew has given you.

And I only hope that never again will I be made to feel as embarrassed and humiliated by a member of my family, and I beg you all to forgive me.

(*She exits with her wash.*)

ANDY: Mommy!

(COACH *whips him again,* ELAINE *rips papers, perhaps all in rhythm. Enter* RONALD. *Action freezes, actors exit.*)

RONALD: The Nature and Purpose of the Universe. Chapter Five. It was an ordinary Tuesday afternoon, just like any other Tuesday afternoon, and Donald was doing so well that he had no more rooms to send his girls to, so he brought Crystal home. God assigns my friend Elaine to play Crystal.

(*Exits. Enter* ELEANOR, *still with the wash. Enter* DONALD *and* ELAINE, *who is dressed as a prostitute.*)

DONALD: Now look, Mom, there's no more room in the city so Crystal's gonna meet her trick here, and she's gonna use your room.

ELEANOR: Oh, Donald, please.

DONALD: Look, can it, bitch. (*He pushes her slightly.*) I'm going to watch some . . . WHERE'S THE TV?

ELEANOR: Oh Donald!

ELAINE: Jesus.

DONALD: Where is the friggin' television?

ELEANOR: Donald, your language. (*He pushes her to the ground.*)

DONALD (*hissing*): Where is it?

ELEANOR: Mrs. Ackerman took it in reparation.

DONALD: Who is Mrs. Ackerman?

ELEANOR: She lives down the street. You sell her little daughter drugs.

DONALD: Your story better be true. I'll be back.

(*Exits*)

ELAINE (*cheap dame voice*): Your son's very violent.

ELEANOR: It was that year we lived in Union that did it. Donald used to be such a quiet boy, but the other children were so rough in Union. He had to learn how to defend himself. They used to fight with Coke bottles and power saws.

ELAINE (*getting on the ground next to her*): You know, if you didn't have such dishpan features, you could be almost attractive, honey.

ELEANOR: Oh, dear God.

(ELAINE *inches closer.*)

ELAINE: Have you ever made it with another woman?

ELEANOR: *Life* magazine was right! You are all lesbians!

ELAINE: Hey, come on, relax.

ELEANOR: Get away from me! Steve! Donald! Where are you?

(ELAINE *tackles* ELEANOR. ELEANOR *screams. Enter* COACH GRIFFIN. ELAINE *is on top of* ELEANOR.)

COACH: Hey what's going on? Which one of you is Crystal?

ELAINE (*points to* ELEANOR): She is.

ELEANOR: No, I'm not.

ELAINE: See ya later, Crystal.

(COACH GRIFFIN *picks up* ELEANOR, *carries her out as she screams. Enter* RONALD.)

RONALD: Hello, Elaine. How are you?

ELAINE: All right. Excuse me. I've got to go change.

(*Exits.*)

RONALD: The Nature and Purpose of the Universe. Chapter Six. It no longer seemed an ordinary Tuesday to Eleanor. Coach Griffin's hot sweating body came down upon her with the force of a thousand violins. The sun was like a hot pomegranate. Coach Griffin did degrading things to Eleanor, some of them very athletic. At the end of three hours, he kicked her very hard with his boot.

(*Exits. Enter* ELEANOR, *worn, and* COACH GRIFFIN.)

COACH: That was lousy. That was among the worst I've ever had. Boy, you're lousy. You can tell Donald if he thinks I'm paying you for that, he's crazy. I should be paid for putting up with you, you aging slob.

(*He spits on her, kicks her, exits.*)

ELEANOR: Oh, God, please let this day come to a close. Please! (*She sinks to the floor weeping.*)

(*Enter* RONALD. RONALD *should be very sincere in the next scene.*)

RONALD: Excuse me. Your door was open. I'm the Fuller Brush Man.

ELEANOR: Please, please, leave me alone. I can't stand any more.

RONALD (*takes her face in his hands*): Eleanor, let me look at you.

ELEANOR: You know my name.

RONALD: Eleanor, I can see suffering in your eyes. Let me kiss them. (*He kisses her eyes lightly.*) You're a fine, noble woman, Eleanor. God doesn't mean for you to suffer.

ELEANOR: He doesn't?

RONALD: No. He wants you to accept His will and be happy. (*His hand lightly caresses the top of her head.*)

ELEANOR: I do accept His will. (*Rather suddenly.*) Oh, please, please take me away from here. Far, far away.

RONALD: Yes, Eleanor. I will take you away. I will come for you next week.

ELEANOR: Oh, please. I must leave here.

RONALD: Eleanor, do not give up hope. I will take you away. Next week. (*He kisses her forehead, exits.*)

ELEANOR: Oh, thank you, God. Please let me be happy. I'll promise never to complain again.

(*Enter* GARY *and a female impersonator.*)

GARY: Hello, Eleanor. I'm home.

ELEANOR: Oh, Gary. Gary. I'm so happy. You've brought home a young girl for me to meet. You don't know how happy this makes me. What's your name, dear?

FRIEND: Ralph.

ELEANOR: Oh, Gary. Gary, Gary.

GARY: Can it, Eleanor. Ralph and I are going to be up in your bedroom, so don't bother us.

ELEANOR: Please don't use my room. Gary, please!

GARY: Shut up!

RALPH (*politely*): It was nice to meet you, Mrs. Mann.

(*Exit* GARY *and* RALPH. *Enter* DONALD.)

DONALD: There you are, you slut! I'll have you know Mrs. Ackerman's never heard of you or our television set, and I told her it figured 'cause you're a filthy liar anyway.

ELEANOR: Oh, Donald, please don't hit me. I'll ask your father to buy us all a new television.

DONALD: You'll pay for this, Mom. (*Kicks her a little.*) I'm kind of tired. Where's Crystal?

ELEANOR: I don't know. She must have left.

DONALD: Did she give you the money?

ELEANOR: No. There wasn't any money.

DONALD: What do you mean there wasn't any money? (*He hurls her to the ground.*)

ELEANOR: Don't hit me, Donald! That man thought I was Crystal and he raped me!

DONALD: Well, give me the money!

ELEANOR: He didn't give me any. He made me do awful things.

DONALD: PAY ME!

ELEANOR: Have mercy! Donald!

DONALD: Pay me, you slut!

(*Enter* ANDY, *dressed in a pink dress. He jumps rope.*)

ELEANOR: Donald, please! Andy, help me. Run for help!

(ANDY *keeps jumping rope.*)

DONALD: You pay me the money. Crystal gets thirty dollars, so cough up thirty.

ELEANOR: Donald, the bank is closed.

DONALD: I want it now. (DONALD *is perched over his mother, more or less straddling her. He slaps her face lightly but continually.*)

ELEANOR: Stop! Help me! Help! Help!

DONALD (*slapping*): You slut! Trollop! Tramp!

(STEVE *enters.*)

STEVE: I'm home, Eleanor. Is dinner ready?

(*Slapping stops.*)

ELEANOR (*still under* DONALD): What, dear? I couldn't hear you.

STEVE: I said is dinner ready yet? Have you done your duty as a wife and cooked me and my sons dinner?

ELEANOR: Oh, Steve, I'm sorry. I haven't had time . . .

STEVE: What do you mean, you haven't had time? Great God almighty! (STEVE *pushes* DONALD *away and gets on top of* ELEANOR, *slapping her.*)

ELEANOR: But Steve, I was raped!

STEVE: What kind of wife are you? You give my children a bad example, you don't make supper, you don't make beds, you're incompetent, you're a failure as a woman.

ELEANOR: Oh, God, help me.

(*Enter* RONALD—*though "outside" of the set.*)

RONALD: Do not fear, Eleanor, I will save you in a week.

ELEANOR: Oh, God.

(*A couple of lines before now,* ELAINE *has entered, in her evening gown of the first scene, and she stands by* RONALD's *side. When* ELEANOR *says "Oh, God,"* ELAINE *picks up the phrase and sings it, thereby giving the entire company the starting note for the song they are about to sing.*)

ELAINE (*sings*): Oh God.

(RONALD *and* ELAINE *now sing the hymn* "O God, Our Help in Ages Past." *The whole company joins in, not so much in response to* RONALD *and* ELAINE *singing, but as if they were all overcome with an urge to sing a hymn at this time.* ELEANOR *joins in the hymn also, on the last three lines, though still in much despair.*)

RONALD *and* ELAINE (*And eventually everyone else*) (*sing*):

> O God, our help in ages past,
> Our hope for years to come,

> Our shelter from the stormy blast,
> And our eternal home.
>
> O God, our light against the dark,
> We bow down to thy might,
> Please help us understand thy bark,
> Is far worse than thy bite.
> (*An elaborate, pretty ending.*) Alleluia!

RONALD: The Nature and Purpose of the Universe. End of Part One.

(*All exit except* RONALD)

> The Nature and Purpose of the Universe. Chapter Seven. It was Tuesday of the following week. It was an ordinary Tuesday, much like any other Tuesday. Truth was still beauty, and trudy booth . . . and yet still Eleanor woke with some hope; for today was the day that the Fuller Brush Man was supposed to save her.

(*Enter actors:* STEVE, ANDY, *and* DONALD *are eating breakfast.* ANDY *has a bow in his hair. Enter* ELEANOR, *followed by* GARY *and* RALPH.)

GARY: God damn it, Eleanor. Where is Ralph's bra?

ELEANOR: Gary, I said I just don't know.

DONALD (*throws a spoon*): You're making too much noise.

GARY: Ralph says you've been trying on all his clothes.

ELEANOR: But, Gary, I have my own clothes.

RALPH: Oh. She doesn't like my clothes, she says.

GARY: Why do you insult my guests?

ELEANOR: I don't mean to, dear. Please believe me. I think Ralph's clothes are fine.

GARY: Well, where's his bra?

ELEANOR: I don't know, maybe Andy took it.

DONALD: Shut up!

GARY (*to* ANDY): Did you take Ralph's bra? Did you?

ANDY: I put it back!

GARY: You little bastard!

RALPH (*grabbing the bow from* ANDY's *hair*): And that's my bow!

ANDY: It is not. Miss Mansfield gave it to me.

RALPH: He's taking my clothes!

GARY (*to* ANDY): I'll kill you!

ELEANOR (*pulling* GARY *back*): Don't hit him, he hasn't any genitals!

DONALD: SHUT UP! (*He kicks over the table.*) Why is there never any quiet in this house? Woman, it's your fault. You don't know how to run a house. Now pick up this table and clean up this mess.

(*He stalks out. After a stunned silence,* ANDY *starts to leave.*)

RALPH (*to* GARY): Let's get him!

ANDY: I don't have your stupid bra!

(*Runs out;* GARY *and* RALPH *tear off after him.*)

ELEANOR: Gary! Wait! Don't touch his bandage!

STEVE: Eleanor, will you stay out of the boys' fights for God's sake? No wonder Andy's wearing dresses, you take on so. And pick up the table. Really, you are the worst wife and mother I've ever seen. You deserve an amateur hysterectomy.

ELEANOR (*truly horrified*): Oh, Steven. Can't you please be nice to me?

STEVE: Don't snivel, Eleanor.

(*Phone rings.*)

Hello? Why, hello, Sister Annie De Maupassant. I'm delighted to hear from you. Yes, I'm quite ready. Today's the day then. Alright. I'll be by for you shortly. Will we have any additional help? Oh, fine. I like a good Jesuit on a job. See you later, Sister Annie De Maupassant. Glory be to God. (*Hangs up.*)

ELEANOR: Is this some more Catholic Action work, Steve?

STEVE: Mind your business, woman. And clean this house. We're having ecclesiastic guests tonight, and I don't want them to know that I'm married to a pig.

ELEANOR: Oh, Steve, please be kind to me.

STEVE: Kneel down. (*She kneels.*) Leniency is not kindness, Eleanor. Overlooking faults is not a kindness. It is a sin.

(*He kicks her, exits.* ELEANOR *picks up the table, sets things straight. She brings the vacuum cleaner over toward table, tries to turn it on; it won't function. She starts to cry.*)

ELEANOR: Why doesn't the vacuum cleaner work? Oh, God. Oh, please God, let the Fuller Brush Man come tonight. Please. I know You don't mean for me to be this unhappy.

(*Phone rings.*)

Hello?

(RONALD *stands downstage, not holding a phone.* ELEANOR *does not see him. The following scene is played most sincerely.*)

RONALD (*facing out*): Hello, Eleanor. This is the Fuller Brush Man speaking.

ELEANOR: Oh, God, is it really you? Oh, help me. You will take me away tonight, won't you?

RONALD: Yes, Eleanor. I will. Are you sure you want to leave your family and home?

ELEANOR: Oh, please. I can't stand any more. I'm bruised all over, but it is my heart that is truly wounded.

RONALD: Eleanor, Eleanor. I will come for you tonight at midnight. Have your bags packed.

ELEANOR: Oh I will! I will! But . . . please don't fail me. Hello? Hello? (*She hangs up.* ELEANOR *exits.*)

RONALD: The Nature and Purpose of the Universe. Chapter Eight. No one breathes much in Weehawken, New Jersey. The air drips with a veritable venereal disease of industrial waste. The atmosphere is slowly turning to sludge. It is very romantic. Pope Paul the Sixth was due to arrive in Weehawken that ordinary Tuesday morning, to bless the air. Meanwhile, Sister Annie De Maupassant and her Jesuit friend, Father Anthony Hemmer, meet with Steve to discuss their plans. God has assigned Elaine once more to the role of Sister Annie De Maupassant. Father Hemmer plays himself.

(*Enter* ELAINE, *dressed as a nun.*)

Hello, Elaine. How are you finding the role of the radical nun of Bernardsville?

ELAINE: All right. I was surprised to see you getting in on things with that Fuller Brush Man routine.

RONALD: God works in strange and mysterious ways, Elaine.

(RONALD *exits. Enter* STEVE *and* FATHER ANTHONY HEMMER.)

ELAINE: Ah, there you are. Hurry. The pretender is about to enter. Father Anthony, I presume you've met Mr. Mann, the brilliant Catholic layman Father Obediah told you about.

FATHER ANTHONY: Yes I did. You certainly are a brilliant Catholic layman, sir.

STEVE: Why thank you, Father. I try.

ELAINE: Mr. Mann has some fascinating thoughts on the connection between the guitar folk Mass and the Albigensian heresy, but we have no time to discuss them now. I see the Papal Pretender fast approaching.

FATHER ANTHONY: We seem to be in luck. We seem to be the only ones here.

ELAINE: I'm not surprised. The Lord is thy shepherd. Ssssh.

(*Enter* POPE PAUL, *dressed in a gold outfit with gold slippers and a diamond tiara and droop earrings.*

*He is accompanied by several monks [the other ac-
tors in monk robes, with cowls over their heads,
covering their faces]. The monks enter in procession,
singing in a Gregorian chant fashion.)*

MONKS (*singing*):

> Amo, amas, amat,
> Amamus, amatis, amant.

(Over and over as needed. The POPE *follows behind
them. When he nears downstage, he smiles graciously at the audience and then sings in a piercing,
too high ecclesiastic voice; he has a small scrap of
paper that he checks for the words.)*

POPE:

> Agricola,
> Agricolae,
> Agricolae,
> Agricolam
> Agricola, Ah-men.
> Agricolae,
> Agricolarum,
> Agricolis,
> Agricolas,
> Agricolis, Ah-men.

> Sum, es, est,
> Sumus, estis, sunt.

(One of the monks leads the POPE *away from the
audience, and to the place where he is to speak.)*

My brothers and sisters in Christ, we are gathered here
in Weehawken in the face of this smog, which is a
symbol of evil in the world, to stand up once again for

all that is just and right and proper for salvation. God created man, and the word was made flesh, as it was in the beginning and in the middle and I feel faint. Help me. I feel faint. I am going to faint. Someone help me. I am faint. Where is the Curia? I shall faint.

(*Two monks clutch the* POPE *on either side.*)

MONK: Take deep breaths, Your Holiness.

(*The* POPE *breathes in deeply, giving out terrible gasps at the bad air.* ELAINE *and* STEVE *creep up behind the two monks and strangle them to death. The* POPE *is oblivious to this and shortly passes out due to all his deep breaths.* STEVE *and* FATHER ANTHONY *pick the* POPE *up.*)

ELAINE (*crosses herself*): All that I do I do for God! Forward march for the New Church!

(*Enter* RONALD. *Action freezes, then actors exit.*)

RONALD: The Nature and Purpose of the Universe. Chapter Nine. It was an ordinary day no longer. Eleanor looked at herself in the mirror and felt an inner joy. At least it was joy compared to what she usually felt. For tonight would be her redemption, her escape. For a few moments, she harbored the fear that something would go wrong, that the Fuller Brush Man would not come, that her life would continue as a hell. Her packing is interrupted as God sends Elaine to impersonate the census lady.

(*Enter* ELEANOR *with a suitcase. Enter* ELAINE.)

ELEANOR: Oh! You startled me.

ELAINE: CENSUS!

ELEANOR: What?

ELAINE: I am the census lady come to get you.

ELEANOR: What do you mean?

ELAINE: How many children do you have?

ELEANOR: Three.

ELAINE: Are you married?

ELEANOR: Yes.

ELAINE: Don't get uppity with me. This is a with-it world. You can never tell who's married nowadays. (*Shouts:*) WHAT DOES YOUR HUSBAND DO?

ELEANOR: Please don't shout.

ELAINE: I'm sorry. (*Shouts:*) WHAT DOES YOUR HUS-BAND DO?

ELEANOR: He's a salesman.

ELAINE: I see. A salesman. Attention must be paid, my ass!

ELEANOR: What do you mean?

ELAINE: Does he have sex with you?

ELEANOR: Is this necessary for the census?

ELAINE: The census itself is not necessary, so your question is irrelevant. Do you have sex with your husband?

ELEANOR: I don't think that . . .

ELAINE: Answer the question.

ELEANOR: Yes, when he demands his rights by marriage.

ELAINE: What do you do?

ELEANOR: I don't see how this affects . . .

ELAINE: Do you have oral sex? Do you have anal sex? Do either of you use chains?

ELEANOR: I will not answer any of these . . .

ELAINE: Have you ever had nasal intercourse?

ELEANOR: I . . . don't think I know what it is.

ELAINE: Look at these. (*She takes some photos from her purse.*)

ELEANOR (*pushing photos away*): I don't want to see any more.

ELAINE: Well, have you?

ELEANOR: Certainly not.

ELAINE: Does your husband do anything to your nose at all?

ELEANOR: No.

ELAINE: What do your sons do?

ELEANOR: My two oldest are presently unemployed, waiting to return to college, and my youngest is in the eighth grade.
ELAINE: Oh, is that so?

ELEANOR: Yes.

ELAINE: Really?

ELEANOR: Yes.

ELAINE: It is not!

ELEANOR: Yes, it is!

ELAINE: It is not. (*Shouting:*) You phony liar. Your oldest son pushes dope and is a pimp. I have here a signed affidavit from three hundred badly used women. (*She takes out the paper.*) And your second son is a homosexual. I have super-8 film of him. (*She takes out a roll of film.*) And your youngest son lost his penis in a reaping accident and I have here a signed statement attesting to that fact from the entire eighth-grade girls' gym class. So don't try to fool me with your pathetic lies. Admit that you lead a lousy life. Do you know on a national scale of 1 to 800, you rank 92; and on a local scale you are 33, and on an international scale 106, and on an all-white scale 23, and on an all-black scale 640, and on a pink scale 16, and that your capability ranking places you in the lowest percentile in the entire universe. It's a sad life I see before me, Mrs. Mann. You haven't any friends. None. Do you realize that you never call anybody up and that nobody ever calls you up? And that you're universally snubbed and pitied at PTA cocktail parties? And that your husband married you only because he had to, and your housekeeping is among the most slovenly on the eastern seaboard, and your physical appeal is in the lower quadrangle of the pentanglical scale—and that's not very high, Mrs. Mann—and that your children rank as among the foremost failed children in the nation and are well below the national level in areas of achievement, maturity, and ethical thinking. WHY DO YOU CONTINUE LIVING, MRS. MANN? WHY DON'T YOU DO YOURSELF A FAVOR?

ELEANOR: Please leave now.

ELAINE: One more thing, Mrs. Mann. Even though you and your family are going to have to leave tonight before the Fuller Brush Man is scheduled to arrive, he isn't going to come for you anyway. But you'll never know

for sure, 'cause you'll be gone. So long, Mrs. Mann!
Enjoy Iceland!

ELEANOR: Wait! How do you know about the Fuller Brush
Man? Who are you? He will come! I know it. God has
promised that he will come.

ELAINE: So long, you slob!

(ELAINE *exits.*)

ELEANOR: The Fuller Brush Man will come. I know it. He
will come!\

(*Enter* RONALD. *Freeze. Exit* ELEANOR.)

RONALD: The Nature and Purpose of the Universe. Chapter
Ten. This particular Tuesday Andy sat in the last row in
health class and watched the other boys play with
themselves. Andy realized that he would never be able
to masturbate. Egged on by the other boys, Andy tried
rubbing his sensitive skin, but the stitches popped and
he started to bleed. The school nurse gave him a sani-
tary napkin and took his temperature rectally, in order
to humiliate him. Life is going to be difficult for Andy.
And all throughout the city of Weehawken, a great
search was begun for His Holiness, Pope Paul, and for
the assailants of His Holiness's two bodyguards.

(*Exit* RONALD. *Enter* STEVE *and* FATHER ANTHONY,
carrying the limp body of POPE PAUL. ELAINE, *as*
SISTER ANNIE, *follows, carrying a pistol, and shooting behind her.*)

ELAINE (*firing*): Take that, you anti-Christ copper!

(*Enter* ELEANOR.)

ELEANOR: Steve, what's the matter?

ELAINE: Everybody duck down!

(*Everyone drops to the floor except* ELEANOR.)

ELEANOR: Steve, who are these people?

ELAINE: I'm the new Pope, and that's the old Pope, and this is Father Anthony. (*She fires her gun.*) Pow pow.

ELEANOR: Who is the Pope?

STEVE: Shut up, Eleanor, and make some coffee.

(*Enter* ANDY, *bleeding.*)

ANDY: Mommy, Mommy, I've been shot!

ELEANOR: Oh, my God! Steve! Call an ambulance.

ELAINE: What is it? The dirty anti-Christ copper get you, little boy? Huh?

ANDY: I think it came from the house. I got shot in the stomach.

ELEANOR: Oh, Steve! I'll call the hospital.

STEVE: Don't you dare go to that phone!

ELEANOR: But, Steve, we don't know how seriously Andy's been hurt.

STEVE: Look, Eleanor, Sister and I are on a dangerous mission together. If you go to that phone, I'll be forced to kill you.

ELEANOR: Steven. Steven, what's happening?

STEVE: Shut up.

ELAINE (*firing*): Pow pow pow. Pow. Hey, I seem to have run out.

FATHER ANTHONY: Are you sure?

ELAINE: I think so. (*She aims her gun at the* POPE. *The gun goes off, the* POPE's *body jumps.*) Pow. Oh, my God.

FATHER ANTHONY: You've shot the Pope!

ELAINE: The Pretender Pope, you fool. Well, it was meant to happen. Give me his tiara. (*She puts tiara on her head. Shooting out window.*) Pow pow pow.

ELEANOR: Steven, I think Andy's passed out.

STEVE: Would you shut up? Where's the coffee?

ELAINE: Well, now that the old Pope's dead, we won't have to take him with us tonight.

FATHER ANTHONY: Just as well.

ELEANOR: Who are you? Where are you going?

ELAINE (*to* STEVE): You didn't tell her.

STEVE: She can't be trusted.

ELAINE: She can be trusted under gunpoint. Look here, Mrs. Mann. At exactly midnight tonight the Mystical Body of Christ Kaffe-Klatch Club of Bernardsville is lowering a helicopter into your backyard, and you and your family will have the honor of accompanying me, Sister Annie De Maupassant, the radical nun of Bernardsville and the once and future Pope, as I leave for my exile in Iceland.

ELEANOR: Iceland. Why Iceland?

STEVE: Eleanor, don't ask the Pope questions.

ELAINE: Go ahead. Ask me. I just won't answer.

ELEANOR: She's not the one I'm asking. I'm asking you.

ELAINE: "She" is the cat's mother. I am the Pope.

ELEANOR: Steven, as your wife, I ask you why we have to go to Iceland.

STEVE: You're not my wife. You're a piece of dirt. Now make the coffee.

ELEANOR: I won't go to Iceland!

(FATHER ANTHONY *looks at her kindly.*)

FATHER ANTHONY: It would be better for you, Mrs. Mann, if you did go. If you stay here, your husband will go to jail for killing one of the Pope's guards.

STEVE: The hell I will. I'll say my wife did it.

ELAINE: This talk is boring. Tell the tiresome woman to go make coffee before I shoot another one of her children.

STEVE: Eleanor, make coffee before the Pope shoots another one of our children. Then pack our bags and tell Donald and Gary to get ready. We've got to sit tight until midnight.

(*Exit* ELEANOR, *dragging* ANDY *behind her. Enter* RONALD. *Actors freeze but do not exit.*)

RONALD: The Nature and Purpose of the Universe. Chapter Eleven. That Tuesday night Eleanor's mind was a shambles of thoughts. She worried that Andy would die, she worried that the police outside the house would kill them all or that maybe the Sister Pope inside the house would kill them all. But most of all she worried that she would not be able to get away at midnight with the Fuller Brush Man. And the strange prophecy of the census lady about going to Iceland came back to haunt her with an uncomfortable persistence.

(*Exit* RONALD. *Enter* DONALD, GARY. *End freeze, action resumes.*)

GARY (*seeing the* POPE): Oh my God. (*Bends down.*) Look at those earrings.

DONALD: God damn. I'll have to start all over again in Iceland. I have my clientele all settled out here in Maplewood and everything. I'm a familiar face. No one wants to have to start up all over again. Especially in Iceland.

STEVE: Donald, we've got to keep the family together at all costs. Isn't that so, Your Holiness?

ELAINE: The family is the essential unit of man. When the family crumbles, society crumbles. When society crumbles, man crumbles. But God never crumbles. (*Starts to shriek in her "speaking in tongues" manner.*)

FATHER ANTHONY: Your Holiness, calm yourself. We have a long helicopter flight in front of us.

(*Enter* ELEANOR, *weeping into a dish towel.*)

ELEANOR: Andy's dead.

ELAINE: Let me see if I can raise him up.

ELEANOR (*very angry*): You stay away from him.

STEVE: Eleanor, don't talk to the Pope that way.

ELEANOR (*crying*): Andy was the only one of my sons who was even remotely kind and gentle.

DONALD: Shut up. Every mother wants an emasculated son. You got your wish, so shut up.

FATHER ANTHONY: Perhaps His Holiness should speak on death.

ELAINE: Yes. Yes. I should. (*She stands on a table.*) Death comes to us all, my brothers and sisters in Christ. It comes to the richest of us and to the poorest of us. Our days on this earth are rounded by a little sleep. On the one hand, pre-birth. On the other hand, post-death. It's six of one, half a dozen of another. The world about us is but a valley of tears, full of sorrows for the just and blessings for the unjust. But yet even in the appalling spectacle of death we can see God's face looking down on us. We can see His Great Plan. Like some great spider, God weaves an immense web in which to trap us all and then in a fit of righteous rage He *eats* us. The Eucharist at last finds its just and fitting revenge. But we must not despair that we do not understand God. Rather must we rejoice in our confusion, for in our ignorance is reflected God's wisdom, in our ugliness His beauty, in our imperfections His perfections. For we are the little people of the earth, and His is the power and the glory, and never the twain shall meet. Hubb-ba, hubb-ba, hubb-ba.

STEVE: Thank you, Your Holiness.

(ELAINE *steps off table.*)

FATHER ANTHONY: Hark. I hear the helicopter now.

STEVE: Are the bags packed, Eleanor?

ELEANOR: Yes.

ELAINE: All right. Get ready to board. Father Anthony, I've

decided that you must stay behind in the living room and cover us as we fly away.

FATHER ANTHONY: But, Your Holiness, I shall be arrested.

ELAINE: Casuistry is not my forte, Father Anthony. If you die I shall proclaim you a martyr and wear a red gown. Alright, I'm ready to board.

(*They start to exit.*)

STEVE: Eleanor, why aren't you moving?

ELEANOR: Steven, I'm not going. I've packed my bags but not to go to Iceland. At midnight I shall be carried away by a kind man who has seen my pain and who in his pity and love has vowed to take me away from this hell.

STEVE: Eleanor, get into the helicopter.

ELEANOR: Steven, no! I will not go!

STEVE: You are my legal wife. I will need you in Iceland to cook and to sew and to clean and to scrub and to get on your back and fulfill your wifely duty.

ELEANOR: Steven, I will not go. I am going to be rescued! I know it!

(RONALD, *downstage, not visible to the actors, not in the room.*)

RONALD: Eleanor, I'm on my way. Don't fear. I'll save you.

ELEANOR: I hear him now! He's coming!

STEVE: Get into the helicopter!

RONALD: Eleanor, Eleanor!

ELEANOR: I hear him. Come quickly. Save me!

ELAINE (*slaps her*): You stupid woman. You hear nothing. Do you think anyone in the entire world would run off with you? You are worth nothing. This man is entirely a sick invention of your sick and pathetic mind. You are going to go to Iceland with your husband, as is your duty, and you will suffer through a long succession of tedious days and tedious nights, and you will have no rest because you are not meant to have any rest, and you will not complain because you are doing the will of God. (*Slaps her.*) You are supposed to suffer, you stupid, stupid woman!

ELEANOR (*hysterical*): No!! Help me!

RONALD: Eleanor!

ELAINE: Sons, take your mother forcibly to the helicopter. Knock her unconscious if she gives you any trouble.

ELEANOR: Help me!

DONALD: Shut up, slut!

(DONALD *and* GARY *carry* ELEANOR *offstage.*)

ELAINE: What a thoroughly trivial woman.

FATHER ANTHONY: Perhaps you should have shown more charity, Your Holiness.

ELAINE: Charity schmarity. Come on, Mr. Mann. To the helicopter. So long, lackey!

(ELAINE *and* STEVE *exit. Sound of helicopter. Action freezes.* FATHER ANTHONY *and the dead* POPE *exit.* RONALD *comes forward.*)

RONALD: The Nature and Purpose of the Universe. Chapter Twelve. That Tuesday night the police finally got Father Anthony Hemmer, and he was tried for the murder of Pope Paul and of little Andy. Father Hemmer was sentenced to death, but then the sentence was mitigated to life imprisonment and no rest room facilities. And on that Tuesday night on the helicopter ride to Iceland, Sister Annie De Maupassant, the once and future Pope, mysteriously disappeared midflight, Elaine having more important things to do. The Mann family settled in Iceland, much the same as always except that Eleanor was in a deep depression. Steve, having lost his interest in the new Catholicism, now nurtured an infatuation with the First Lady of the Icelandic Stage, the distinguished Olga Rheinholtenbarkerburkerburr. God assigns Elaine to impersonate Olga in a last effort to finish off Eleanor.

(RONALD *exits. Enter* ELEANOR *and* STEVE. *They sit in two chairs.* ELEANOR *hardly moves, just stares off in complete distraction. She appears to hear very little.*)

STEVE: Stop looking like a zombie, for God's sake, Eleanor. My God, you should be counting your blessings. The igloo takes care of itself, our son Gary is engaged to the son of the Prime Minister, and our son Donald has the Prime Minister's daughter pulling in nine hundred dollars a week. With those sorts of connections, I expect I'll be a big shot in Icelandic politics in a few months. Are you listening, Eleanor? Eleanor? Talking to you is like talking to a mop. So, you see, you should cheer up. Your husband's gonna be quite a big shot.

(*We hear the voice of an announcer.*)

ANNOUNCER: Good evening, lady and gentleman. Tonight the Baked Alaska is proud to present that First Lady of

the Icelandic Stage, Dame Olga Rheinholtenbarkerburkerburr!

(*Enter* ELAINE.)

ELAINE (*bowing graciously*): Thank you. Thank you. I
should like to do a dramatic reading for you. (*She
dimples.*)
How do I love thee?
Let me count the ways.
One. Two. Three. Four, five, six . . . Seven. Eight.

STEVE: Hey! Don't forget nasal intercourse!

ELAINE: Oh, yes. Thank you. Nine. Ten, eleven, twelve,
thirteen, fourteen, fifteen, sixteen, seventeen . . . and
. . . eighteen! And now I should like to give you another reading. It is from *Macbeth* by William Shakespeare.

Tomorrow and tomorrow,
And tomorrow . . . (*Goes blank*)
And tomorrow, and tomorrow, and tomorrow,
and tomorrow,
and tomorrow, and tomorrow, and tomorrow . . .

STEVE: A song! Sing us a song! Would you look at her,
Eleanor. What a piece she is.

ELAINE: I would like to sing a little song for you that was
written for me by a little man in a little black hat with
beady little eyes and greedy little thighs. (*Sings, tune is
"Tiptoe Through the Tulips."*)

Tiptoe through the tundra,
It's a wundra,
We don't catch a chill,
We tiptoe as we use our free will.

Iceskate round the igloo,
If we dig through,
All the tundra here,
We'll find we will be happy next year.
We'll freeze our knees and our toes,
A sneeze will freeze on our nose,
And we will . . .
Tiptoe through the tundra,
And we'll wundra,
When the world will end,
And Jesus is our very best friend!
Dum-dee-dee-dum-dee-dee-dum, dee-dum!

(STEVE *applauds.*)

STEVE: Olga. Come join my table.

ELAINE (*crossing to him*): Oh, Mr. Mann, what a faithful fan you are. What's the matter with your wife?

STEVE: She hasn't made the transition from New Jersey yet.

ELAINE: Oh, I see.

STEVE: Give me a kiss.

ELAINE: Oh, Mr. Mann. Do you think I should? What about your wife?

STEVE: She won't notice. (*They kiss.*) Hey, when am I going to get into your pants?

ELAINE: Oh, Mr. Mann, the things you say! Sometimes I'm surprised out of my little biddle empty-headed mind. But I'll tell you. You aren't ever going to get into my pants because I love my husband. (*Louder, directed at* ELEANOR.) Yes, my sweet husband used to be a Fuller Brush Man from New Jersey. But now he's found the love of his life in little iddle me. The Fuller Brush Man loves me.

ELEANOR (*stirring*): What?

ELAINE: Oh, Mrs. Mann. I was just telling your husband how I'm married to an ex–Fuller Brush Man from New Jersey, and how happy I am. Why, here he comes now. You can meet him.

(*Enter* RONALD. *He kisses* ELAINE.)

RONALD: Hello, darling. How are you? I caught your act from the back. It was magnificent as usual.

ELAINE: Thank you, dear. I'd like you to meet . . .

ELEANOR: It's you. (*Hysterical:*) Oh, please save me, please save me!

STEVE (*shakes her*): STOP THAT. What sort of display are you making? You're embarrassing me!

ELEANOR: Save me, please. It's not too late!

STEVE: Eleanor!

ELAINE: Mr. Mann, let's leave them alone. My husband is very good at dealing with hysterical women.

(ELAINE *and* STEVE *step aside. In the next section* RONALD *acts nonchalant and charming and not outwardly mean.*)

ELEANOR: Please, let me explain why I wasn't there that night. The helicopter had come and . . .

RONALD: There, there, Eleanor, don't be so sentimental . . .

ELEANOR: But if you understood why I wasn't there . . .

RONALD: You weren't there?

ELEANOR: No . . . I . . . but didn't you know?

RONALD: No, silly. I never intended to go back to your house. I just wanted you to buy a brush.

ELEANOR: But you said you saw my suffering, and that you'd take me away.

RONALD: My goodness, you're a silly woman. I say that to all my customers. You're not supposed to believe me.

ELEANOR: Save me!

RONALD: Perhaps you'd like a brush now.

ELEANOR: Save me. Take me away from here!

(STEVE *and* ELAINE *cross back to the two.*)

RONALD: There's nothing I can do with her. She's just a silly little goose.

(*Exit* RONALD *and* ELAINE.)

STEVE: Stop that. (*He throws her to the ground.*) Stop making a spectacle of yourself.

(*Enter* GARY, DONALD, *and* RALPH.)

GARY: Hello there, Eleanor. On the ground again? Making a scene?

RALPH: Hello, Mrs. Mann, how are you? Gary and I share the Prime Minister's son now, isn't that nice?

DONALD: Stop whimpering, slut. The Prime Minister says he's willing to give me five dollars if he can urinate in your face, so he's coming over right after dinner.

STEVE: Get up, Eleanor. Time to make dinner. (*The four of them kick her lightly on the ground.*) Come on, Eleanor. Get up. Get up. Get up now.

(*Phone rings.* STEVE *answers it.*)

Hello? Oh. Alright. Why, it's for you, Eleanor. Someone is actually on the telephone for you.

(*Enter* ELAINE, *way downstage. She stares out.*)

ELEANOR (*in tears*): Hello? Hello? Hello?

ELAINE (*not holding a phone, very serious*): Hello, Eleanor, this is Elaine speaking. I want you to come over to the slaughterhouse right away. Do you understand, Eleanor?

(*The men exit automatically.* ELAINE *crosses over to* ELEANOR, *helps her to lie on the table.* ELAINE *takes out a knife. Enter* RONALD.)

RONALD: The Nature and Purpose of the Universe. Chapter Thirteen. And God said to Elaine, take now thy charge Eleanor, whom thou lovest, and get thee into the land of Moriah; and offer her there for a burnt offering upon one of the mountains which I will tell thee of.
And Elaine came to the place which God had told her of; and she built an altar there, and laid the wood in order, and bound Eleanor her charge, and laid her upon the altar.
And Elaine stretched forth her hand, and took the knife to slay Eleanor.

(ELAINE *raises the knife very high and then lowers it quickly toward* ELEANOR.)

BUT WAIT! And God said to Elaine, spare this woman's life, for I am merciful. And sing forth my glories and my praise, for I am God of Gods, the Father of his children.

ELAINE *and* RONALD (*sing together, Handel*):

Alleluia! Alleluia! Alleluia!

ELEANOR: Kill me! Please kill me! Kill me!

ELAINE *and* RONALD:

Alleluia! Alleluia! Alleluia!

ELEANOR: I don't want to live. Please kill me. Kill me!

(*Lights dim to black.*)

ADDENDUM

Tone and Violence in the Play:

There is a difficult balance needed in the performance of this play: Eleanor's plight must be presented sympathetically so we care about her, and yet her suffering must be sufficiently distanced/or theatricalized (particularly in the first two thirds of the play) so that we can find it funny.

In line with this, I have never seen Eleanor played by an actress who was the proper age to have grown sons; I'm sure it could be done, with the proper actress; but having a younger woman (20 to 30) play the role also works as a distancing device that may be helpful in presenting the play and, perhaps more important, also frees us from worry about the physical demands that the actress playing Eleanor must meet. Common sense and individual taste will have to dictate, but I at least offer that you may be safer casting someone young for Eleanor, and someone the audience can recognize as physically spry so they don't have to worry during the violence.

The violence against Eleanor in the play is a tricky problem; and again common sense and personal taste will have to find what works for each production and group of actors. On the one hand, the violence can't be totally fake or simply too mild, or else we'll never find the humor (particularly in the early scenes) of how *preposterously* awful Eleanor's life is.

And on the other hand, if the violence is too convincing or too "specific," the play will turn too ugly. To give an example of the latter problem, there was a production in which Donald punched Eleanor in the stomach, the actress realistically acted loss of breath, etc., and the scene turned too ugly. It may have been all the fault of a too realistic reaction, or it may have been that a man punching a woman in the stomach may be too "specific" an image ever to be funny in this play.

I have found that the violence that seems to work best in the productions I've seen is what I might call (vaguely, I realize) "generalized" violence. For instance, it always seems to work when Donald throws Eleanor to the ground: It's a large, sudden action, Eleanor gets to react in fear and terror, but she doesn't have to act a specific, localized pain. Things like the throwings to the ground, kicks, arm twists, hair pullings, anything that an audience knows can be easily faked and that also don't have particular "pain resonance" for us seem the safest things to try.

With the violence in particular and with the playing tone in general, the problem is somehow to balance letting the audience feel liking and sympathy for Eleanor at the same time that they find the humor in seeing her "get it." Each production has to find its own solutions, so I can offer no sweeping suggestions. But being aware of the problem may be helpful.

'dentity Crisis

'dentity Crisis was presented by the Yale Repertory Theatre, New Haven, Connecticut, on a double bill with *Guess Work*, by Robert Auletta, on October 13, 1978. The direction of *'dentity Crisis* was by Frank Torok, scenery by Michael H. Yeargan, costumes by Marjorie Graf, lighting by Robert Jared. The cast was as follows:

JANE	Caitlin Clarke
EDITH	Darcy Pulliam
ROBERT	Mark Linn-Baker
MR. SUMMERS	David K. Miller
WOMAN	Nancy Mayans

A previous production of the play was presented at the Yale Cabaret in March 1975, directed by the author. The cast was as follows:

JANE	Catherine Schreiber
EDITH	Kate McGregor-Stewart
ROBERT	James Zitlow
MR. SUMMERS	Alan Mokler
WOMAN	Alma Cuervo

SETTING

The setting of this play could be any living room with a couch, table, chair, etc. Because the living room has been presumably chosen and decorated by Edith, who is fairly insane, there should be some odd things about the decor.

The production at the Yale Repertory Theatre chose (partly due to its wide stage) to have a bizarrely symmetrical set: identical couches, chair, and table stage left and stage right; there was a piano and piano bench upstage center. There were doors, identical, left and right.

On the wall there were five large, framed photographs: four utterly identical ones of Robert, two on either side; and one of Jane, in the center above the piano.

Due to the extreme number of personalities that "Robert" turns out to possess, the four photos of him strike me as an excellent idea.

The symmetrical, mirror-like image of the two couches, two chairs, etc., strikes me as successfully odd and worked well in the Yale Rep production. It doesn't have the thematic resonance of the four photos of Robert, however; and so if your stage is not all that wide, or if you want to experiment with either a more realistic living room, or with a differently odd one (one that mixes styles of furniture radically, for instance), you should feel free to experiment.

SCENE 1

Living room. JANE, *the daughter, in disheveled bathrobe, lies on the couch. She is extremely depressed and sits paging steadily through a* Time *magazine, not looking at it at all.*

VOICE (*offstage*): Cuckoo. Cuckoo.

> (*Enter* EDITH, *carrying a bag of groceries and a dress in a dry cleaner's bag. Dress is very badly stained with blood.*)

EDITH: Hello, dear, I'm back. Did you miss me? Say yes. (*Pause.*) Of course you missed me. A daughter always misses her mother. You're less depressed today, aren't you? I can tell. (*Puts bag down.*) I got your dress back. I'm afraid the stains didn't come out. You should have heard the lady at the cleaners. What did she do, slash her thighs with a razor blade? she said. I had to admit you had. Really, dear, I've never heard of anyone doing that. It was so awful when your father and I went into the bathroom together to brush our teeth and saw you perched up on the toilet, your pretty white dress over your head, slashing away at your thighs. I don't think your father had ever seen your thighs before, and I hope he never will again, at least not under those unpleasant conditions. I mean, what could have possessed you? No one in our family has ever attempted suicide before now, and no one since either. It's a sign of defeat, and no one should do it. You know what I think? Jane? Jane?

JANE: What?

57

EDITH: I don't think you ever attempted suicide at all. That's what I think.

JANE: How do you explain the stains then?

EDITH: I don't. (*Laughs merrily.*) I always say stains will explain themselves, and if they don't then there's nothing can be done about it.

(EDITH *empties the grocery bag on the table. It is filled with loose potato chips, which* EDITH *playfully arranges as if it is some sort of food sculpture.*)

JANE: I did attempt suicide.

EDITH: No, dear, you didn't. A daughter doesn't contradict her mother.

VOICE: Cuckoo, cuckoo.

JANE: Did you hear the voice of my therapist just then?

EDITH: No dear. (*Listens.*) Ah, now I hear it. He's saying what a fine daughter I have.

(*Enter* ROBERT.)

ROBERT: Mother! I'm home.

EDITH: Oh, Jane, it's your brother.

(EDITH *and* ROBERT *kiss passionately and long.* JANE *is very upset and rips up the plastic covering on her dress.*)

ROBERT: Darling, darling.

EDITH: Oh, Dwayne, this is mad. We've got to stop meeting like this. Your father will find out.

JANE: I'll tell him!

EDITH: Jane, you'd never do anything like that.

ROBERT: I'm mad for you. I find you . . . exciting. (*They kiss.*)

EDITH (*looking off*): Quick, there's the postman. Act busy.

(ROBERT *and* EDITH *smash the potato chips on the table with their fists, then they brush the crushed chips into a wastebasket with a little broom.*)

EDITH: There, he's gone.

ROBERT (*holding her*): Oh, why must you taunt me? Let's get married.

EDITH: We have different blood types.

ROBERT: Oh, Mother, I love you. (*They embrace.*)

EDITH: Oh, my God. Here comes your father.

(ROBERT, *with no change of costume—and without exiting or reentering—becomes the father.*)

ROBERT: Edith, what are you doing?

EDITH: Oh, Arthur, I was just finishing off my morning shopping.

ROBERT: And how is our daughter?

JANE: You're not my father.

EDITH: Don't contradict your father. You love your father, Jane.

JANE: He's my brother.

EDITH: Dwayne is your brother, dear.

ROBERT: Has she been seeing that psychologist of hers?

EDITH: Well, not socially.

ROBERT: Good. (*Shouting at Jane:*) I don't ever want to hear of you dating a psychologist again.

JANE: I never have!

EDITH: Of course not, dear. You obey your father. You're a good daughter.

ROBERT: Not like some I could mention.

EDITH: No.

ROBERT: I could mention some.

EDITH: You could.

ROBERT: I could. I will.

EDITH: Now?

ROBERT: Now. Frances, Lucia, Henrietta, Charmant, Dolores, Loretta, and Peggy.

EDITH: Listen to your father, Jane.

ROBERT: No more of this slashing your thighs, young lady. I don't think that psychologist would ever go out with you again if he knew you were slashing your thighs.

JANE: I don't go out with my psychologist.

EDITH: Of course you don't. He has a wife and sixteen children. You're a good girl. You listen to your father.

JANE (*to* ROBERT): You're not my father.

EDITH: Jane, you know he's your father.

JANE: If you're my father, you must be close to fifty.

ROBERT: I am close to fifty.

JANE: Let me see your driver's license.

ROBERT: Here. (*Hands it to her.*)

JANE (*reads it*): This says you're fifty. How did you get them to put that down?

EDITH: The truth is the truth no matter how you look at it, Jane.

JANE: How come you don't look fifty?

EDITH: Your father never looked his age. Most girls would be pleased that their father looked young.

ROBERT: Most girls are pleased.

EDITH: Jane's pleased you look young, aren't you, Jane? Don't you think Arthur looks young for his age, Grandad?

ROBERT: Eh? What?

EDITH (*shouting*): Don't you think Arthur looks young, Grandad!

ROBERT (*smiling senilely*): Yes, yes. Breakfast.

EDITH: Poor Grandad can't hear a thing.

JANE: Where's Father?

EDITH: Isn't he here? That's funny. I didn't hear the door close.

JANE: Grandad, Mother is having an affair with Dwayne!

ROBERT (*not hearing*): What?

EDITH: He can't hear you. Besides you mustn't make up stories. I don't. Oh, listen to the doorbell.

(*Bell rings. Enter* MR. SUMMERS, *the psychologist and the previous offstage voice.*)

Why, Jane, it's your psychologist. (*To* SUMMERS:) I recognized you from your photos. Jane has plastered her walls with your pictures. I don't know why.

SUMMERS: How do you do? You must be Jane's mother.

EDITH: Yes. I'm Edith Fromage. You probably saw my photo in the papers when you were a little boy. I invented cheese in France in the early portion of the century.

SUMMERS: In what way did you invent cheese?

EDITH: In every way. And this is my son, Dwayne Fromage.

ROBERT: How do you do, sir?

SUMMERS: How do you do? I didn't realize Jane's last name was Fromage.

EDITH: It isn't. I had Jane by another husband. A Mr. Carrot.

JANE: My name isn't Carrot.

EDITH: That's right, dear. It's *Jane* Carrot. (*Whispers:*) Jane's very overwrought today. The stains wouldn't come out of her dress.

SUMMERS: Oh, I'm sorry.

EDITH: You think you're sorry. You should have seen the woman at the cleaners. I thought we'd have to chain her to the floor.

ROBERT: Perhaps Mr. Summers is hungry.

EDITH: Oh, forgive me. (*Offers him wastebasket of crushed chips.*)

SUMMERS: No thank you.

EDITH: Then how about some entertainment? Jane, play the piano for Mr. Summers.

JANE: I don't play the piano.

EDITH: Of course you do. I've heard you many times. You play very well.

JANE: I've never played the piano.

EDITH: Jane, Mr. Summers would enjoy your playing. Please play.

JANE: I don't know how!

EDITH (*angry*): How do you know? Have you ever tried?

JANE: No.

EDITH: There. You see then. (*To* SUMMERS:) Cello is her real instrument, but we never talk about it.

ROBERT: Please play, Jane.

(JANE *walks hesitatingly to the piano, sits. Pause. Makes some noise on keyboard, obviously can't play, starts to cry.*)

JANE: I don't know how to play piano!

EDITH: But you do! Why else would we have one? No one else in the house plays.

JANE: I don't remember taking lessons.

EDITH: You probably forgot due to all this strain. (*To* SUMMERS:) You talk to her. She seems in a state. (*To* ROB-

ERT:) Come on, dear. Call me if you want me, Mr. Summers.

(ROBERT *and* EDITH *kiss, then exit.*)

JANE (*at piano*): I don't *remember* taking piano lessons.

SUMMERS: Maybe you've repressed it. (*Sits.*) My wife gave me the message about your attempting suicide. Why did you do it, Jane?

JANE: I can't stand it. My mother says she's invented cheese and I start to think maybe she has. There's a man living in the house and I'm not sure whether he's my brother or my father or my grandfather. I can't be sure of anything anymore.

SUMMERS: You're talking quite rationally now. And your self-doubts are a sign of health. The truly crazy person never thinks he's crazy. Now explain to me what led up to your attempted suicide.

JANE: Well, a few days ago I woke up and I heard this voice saying, "It wasn't enough."

SUMMERS: Did you recognize the voice?

JANE: Not at first. But then it started to come back to me. When I was eight years old, someone brought me to a theatre with lots of other children. We had come to see a production of *Peter Pan*. And I remember something seemed wrong with the whole production, odd things kept happening. Like when the children would fly, the ropes would keep breaking and the actors would come thumping to the ground and they'd have to be carried off by the stagehands. There seemed to be an unlimited supply of understudies to take the children's places, and then *they'd* fall to the ground. And then the crocodile that chases Captain Hook seemed to be a real crocodile, it wasn't an actor, and at one point it fell off the stage, crushing several children in the front row.

SUMMERS: What happened to the children?

JANE: Several understudies came and took their places in the audience. And from scene to scene Wendy seemed to get fatter and fatter until finally by the second act she was immobile and had to be moved with a cart.

SUMMERS: Where does the voice fit in?

JANE: The voice belonged to the actress playing Peter Pan. You remember how in the second act Tinkerbell drinks some poison that Peter's about to drink, in order to save him? And then Peter turns to the audience and he says that Tinkerbell's going to die because not enough people believe in fairies, but that if everybody in the audience claps real hard to show that they *do* believe in fairies, then maybe Tinkerbell won't die. And so then all the children started to clap. We clapped very hard and very long. My palms hurt and even started to bleed I clapped so hard. Then suddenly the actress playing Peter Pan turned to the audience and she said, "That wasn't enough. You didn't clap hard enough. Tinkerbell's dead." Uh . . . well, and . . . and then everyone started to cry. The actress stalked offstage and refused to continue with the play, and they finally had to bring down the curtain. No one could see anything through all the tears, and the ushers had to come help the children up the aisles and out into the street. I don't think any of us were ever the same after that experience.

SUMMERS: How do you think this affected you?

JANE: Well it certainly turned me against theatre; but more

damagingly, I think it's warped my sense of life. You know—nothing seems worth trying if Tinkerbell's just going to die.

SUMMERS: And so you wanted to die like Tinkerbell.

JANE: Yes.

SUMMERS (*with importance*): Jane. I have to bring my wife to the hospital briefly this afternoon, so I have to go now. But I want you to hold on, and I'll check back later today. I think you're going to be all right, but I think you need a complete rest; so when I come back we'll talk about putting you somewhere for a while.

JANE: You mean committing me.

SUMMERS: No. This would just be a rest home, a completely temporary thing. Tinkerbell just needs her batteries recharged, that's all. Now you just make your mind a blank, and I'll be back as soon as I can.

JANE: Thank you. I'll try to stay quiet 'til you return.

(*Enter* EDITH.)

EDITH: Oh, you're leaving. Won't you have some of my cheese first?

SUMMERS: Thank you, Mrs. Fromage, but I have to go now. Please see to it that your daughter stays quiet.

EDITH: Oh, you can rely on me.

SUMMERS (*to* JANE): Chin up.

(*Exits.*)

EDITH: Jane, dear, I've brought you some sheet music. I

thought maybe if you got settled on where middle C was, it might all come back to you.

JANE: Please leave me alone.

EDITH: I don't know why you've turned against the piano.

JANE (*suddenly sharp*): Well, you know my one love was always the cello.

EDITH (*realizing* JANE *is being devious; icy*): A good daughter does not speak to her mother in that tone. I'm sure you didn't mean that. When you are ready to play the piano, let me know. Oh, there's the doorbell.

(*Bell rings. Enter* ROBERT.)

ROBERT (*French accent*): Ah, Madame Fromage.

EDITH: Oh, Count. How nice. I don't think you've met my daughter. Jane, dear, this is the Count de Rochelay, my new benefactor.

ROBERT: How do you do, Mademoiselle? My people and I are most anxious for your mother to make a comeback. All the time, the people of France say, whatever happened to Edith Fromage who gave us cheese? It is time she left her solitude and returned to the spotlight and invented something new. And so I come to your charming mama and I convince her to answer the call of the people of France.

EDITH: Jane, say hello to the Count.

JANE: Hello.

EDITH (*whispers*): You have to forgive her. She's sulking because she's forgotten how to play the piano.

(*He embraces her.*)

ROBERT: Madame Fromage, I love you!

EDITH: Please! I don't want my son or husband to hear you!

ROBERT (*whispers*): Madame Fromage, I love you. (*Kisses her.*)

EDITH: Not now. First I must invent something new. Have you the ingredients?

(ROBERT *has a paper bag.* EDITH *takes out a family-size loaf of Wonder Bread and makes a stack of six slices. Then she takes a banana from the bag and rams it into the center of the stack of bread.*)

ROBERT: Bravo, Madame!

EDITH: Voilà! I have invented banana bread.

ROBERT: Bravo! Let us make love to celebrate!

EDITH: Please, my son or husband might hear.

ROBERT (*deaf*): Eh?

EDITH: Shush, Grandad. Go down to the cellar.

ROBERT: Madame Fromage, France will thank you for this.

EDITH: And I will thank France. It is moments like these when I feel most alive.

(ROBERT *carries* EDITH *off.*)

ROBERT: Vive Madame Fromage!

(JANE *at piano hits middle C several times. Lights dim, slowly to black. As they do, the light of a flash-light flashes about the stage as Tinkerbell.*)

EDITH'S VOICE (*offstage, as Peter Pan*): Tink, are you all right, Tink? Tinkerbell?

(*Light of Tinkerbell starts to blink on and off.*)

JANE: Don't die!

(JANE's *solitary clapping is heard in darkness. Tinkerbell's light goes off.*)

EDITH'S VOICE (*off, in darkness*): That wasn't enough. She's dead. Tinkerbell's dead.

SCENE 2

Lights up on JANE *seated at piano with a paper bag over her head.*

VOICE (*offstage,* SUMMERS): Cuckoo, cuckoo.

(*Enter* ROBERT.)

ROBERT: Have you seen your mother?

JANE (*under bag*): To whom am I speaking?

ROBERT: Take off the bag and see.

(*She takes off the bag.*)

JANE: To whom am I speaking?

ROBERT: Don't act odd, Jane. Tell your father you'll be normal.

JANE: I'll be normal.

ROBERT: I'll be normal, comma, Father.

JANE: I'll be normal, comma, Father.

(*Enter* EDITH.)

EDITH: Oh, there you are, children.

ROBERT: Mother, don't leave me for that Count. Edith, what is Dwayne talking about?

EDITH: I'm sure I don't know, Arthur. (*Whispers to* ROBERT:) Don't let your father hear about the Count.

ROBERT: Mother, I love you. Edith, what did you just whisper to Dwayne?

EDITH: Oh, nothing, dear. Just that Grandad's hearing is getting worse. Look, I've invented banana bread, aren't you proud of me?

ROBERT: Congratulations, Edith. Gee, Mom. (*Deaf:*) What?

EDITH (*shouting*): Banana bread, Grandad!

ROBERT: It's too early for bed.

JANE: I only see two people.

EDITH: I'm sure you see more than that, dear. Oh, the doorbell.

(*Doorbell. Enter a* WOMAN.)

WOMAN: Hello, Mrs. Fromage. How's Jane?

EDITH: Much better. Jane, a visitor.

JANE: Who are you?

WOMAN: I'm your psychologist, Mr. Summers.

JANE: I don't . . . understand.

WOMAN: I guess it's confusing, but I didn't want to tell you earlier. I got a sex change this afternoon.

JANE: I don't believe you.

WOMAN: It's quite true. My wife can substantiate.

(*Calls:*) Harriet.

(*Enter* MR. SUMMERS.)

SUMMERS: Yes, dear.

WOMAN: Explain to Jane that I am Mr. Summers.

SUMMERS: How do you do, Jane? My husband has told me so much about you and your neuroses. You're one of my favorite cases.

JANE: I don't understand.

WOMAN: It simply seemed that the magic had gone out of our marriage, and that we both needed a change.

JANE: You should have told me. You should have prepared me.

WOMAN: I didn't want to spring it on you too quickly.

EDITH: I think it's very courageous of you both.

SUMMERS: Thank you.

WOMAN (*to* SUMMERS): Harriet, is that a banana in your trousers, or are you just happy to see me?

SUMMERS: It's a banana. (*Takes a banana out of his trousers. To* JANE:) They haven't fitted me with any male appendages yet, so I've been trying everything to get the hang of it. I think a banana's too large.

EDITH: Might I have the banana?

SUMMERS: Surely.

(EDITH *makes another thing of banana bread, quickly.*)

WOMAN: I've been wondering how my patients would react to the change.

ROBERT: Mother, I love you.

EDITH: Hush, dear, they'll hear you.

WOMAN (*to* JANE): Now tell me about the dream about the *Peter Pan* play again.

JANE: It wasn't a dream. It was a memory from my childhood.

WOMAN: Oh, I thought you told me it was a dream.

JANE: No, I didn't.

EDITH: I was listening at the door and feel sure you said it was a dream. Didn't you, dear?

JANE: It wasn't a dream, and I didn't say it was. (*To* WOMAN:) And I didn't tell you about it anyway. (*Pointing to* SUMMERS.) I told him.

WOMAN: But you've never met Harriet until this very minute.

JANE: You're pulling a trick on me.

(SUMMERS *whispers to* WOMAN.)

WOMAN: Oh, my God. Mrs. Fromage, have you any glue?

EDITH: Yes. I invented some this morning.

ROBERT: Ah, Madame Fromage, bravo for you.

EDITH (*handing* WOMAN *bottle*): I call it mucilage.

WOMAN (*squeezing some on her breast*): You must excuse me. My wife just noticed that one of my breasts was slipping off.

EDITH: Could I get you a melon?

WOMAN: No thank you. This should do it. Modern surgery is a wonder these days, but it can be sloppily done sometimes.

JANE: I don't think you can help me.

WOMAN: Oh dear. You see, Harriet.

SUMMERS: I see.

WOMAN: A hostile reaction to my change. Jane, dear, I'm just as capable as I was before.

JANE: I think you're crazy.

ROBERT: What? Eh?

JANE: Shut up! You're not my father.

EDITH: Of course not. He's your grandfather.

JANE: Let me see his driver's license.

EDITH: He doesn't drive. It wouldn't be wise.

SUMMERS: Oh my God! (*Scratches all over.*)

WOMAN: Harriet, what's the matter?

SUMMERS: I feel so unused to these clothes. The pants rub my legs and the shoes are too heavy and I miss my breasts.

WOMAN: Harriet. Please. We can talk about this after my session with Jane.

SUMMERS: Walter, we can't. I feel very nervous all of a sudden. May I see you in the other room for a second?

WOMAN: Very well. Mrs. Fromage, might my wife and I talk in your bedroom for a second?

EDITH: Surely. Don't step on the potato chips.

WOMAN: I'll be right back, Jane.

SUMMERS: Do excuse me. I guess I'm making the transition poorly.

(WOMAN *and* SUMMERS *exit.*)

ROBERT: Madame Fromage, now that your husband and son and father have gone down to the cellar for a minute, let me ask you to become my wife. We could live in France, your true home, where the people love you for the great gift you have given them.

(JANE *puts her hands over her ears.*)

EDITH: What about my husband and the rest of my family?

ROBERT: Bring them all along. I have a big heart.

EDITH: That's most generous, but I must consult my daughter. Jane, did you hear the Count's offer? (*She takes* JANE's *hands off her ears.*)

JANE: No.

EDITH: Yes you did. Do you approve?

JANE: No.

EDITH: Yes you do. Do you want to come with us to France?

JANE: No.

EDITH: Yes you do. Oh, Count, Jane's agreed to everything.

ROBERT: Darling!

EDITH: My Count! (*They embrace.*)

ROBERT (*suddenly*): Mother, what is the meaning of this? Edith!

EDITH: Now, Dwayne, Arthur.

ROBERT: Edith, I'm shocked. (*As* COUNT:) Don't jump to any hasty presumptions, Monsieur Fromage.

EDITH: Arthur, the Count and I were discussing my going back to the stage.

ROBERT: You've used that story before.

EDITH: Never.

ROBERT: Yes you have.

EDITH: Albert, you're belligerent.

ROBERT: Arthur.

EDITH: Arthur, you're belligerent.

ROBERT: Father, don't use that tone with my mother.

EDITH: Dwayne, don't speak crossly to your father.

ROBERT (*as* COUNT): I think it is terrible any of you speak rudely to Madame Fromage. (*He coughs violently.*)

EDITH: Oh, dear, Grandad's having a coughing fit. Dwayne, run and get your grandfather some water.

ROBERT (*stops coughing*): You're just trying to distract from the issue. (*Coughs.*)

EDITH: Your grandfather's choking. How can you be so cruel?

ROBERT (*stern*): Listen to your mother. (*Coughs.*) Mother, we've got to get this settled first. Who do you love more—me, Father, or the Count?

EDITH: Do you mean more frequently, or in greater degree?

ROBERT: Degree. (*Coughs, drops to the floor.*)

EDITH: Oh my God, he's fainted.

ROBERT: Good God, Edith, is he dead? (*As* COUNT, *stooping down:*) No. He is just sleeping.

EDITH: Oh, good.

ROBERT: Well, who do you love?

EDITH: Dwayne, when you ask a woman that you ask her to explain her existence. And so I will. Dwayne, I love you as a mother loves a son, as a wife loves a husband, and as a woman loves a lover. Arthur, I love you as a wife loves a son, a husband loves a lover, and a mother loves a woman. Count, I love you as a son loves a husband, as a lover loves a mother, as a wife loves a brother. It's one for all, and all for one. There, are you satisfied?

ROBERT: Mother, you're wonderful. (*Kisses her.*) Edith, I'm touched. (*Kisses her.*) Madame, you are charmante. (*Kisses her.*)

(*Enter* WOMAN *and* SUMMERS. *They have switched clothes:* WOMAN *wears* SUMMERS's *clothes, he wears hers. That is,* SUMMERS *is dressed like a woman; the* WOMAN *is dressed like a man.*)

JANE: Oh God, help me.

WOMAN: Now Jane, there's no need to overreact. Harriet just felt uncomfortable.

SUMMERS (*looking at his flat chest*): I don't look like I used to. Not at all. (*Places a stray banana in his bosom.*)

EDITH: I don't think I've introduced you properly. This is my husband Arthur.

ROBERT: How do you do?

WOMAN: How do you do? I'm Mr. Summers and this is my husband Harriet.

SUMMERS: How do you do?

ROBERT: I do very well, thank you.

EDITH: And this is my son Dwayne.

SUMMERS: How do you do? I'm Mr. Summers and this is my wife Walter.

ROBERT: How do you do?

EDITH: And this is the Count de Rochelay.

ROBERT: Comment ça va?

WOMAN: Très bien, merci. Je m'appelle Jacqueline, et voici mon fromage Claude.

SUMMERS: Bonjour, bonjour.

EDITH: And this is my new invention, banana bread. I dedicate it to Jane, my wonderful daughter. I call the recipe Banana Bread Jane.

ROBERT: Did you hear that, Jane?

JANE: I don't know who you are.

EDITH: Come. Let us taste of the banana bread. Jane, it's your birthday, you cut the first piece.

JANE: It isn't my birthday.

EDITH: It is. We've been wishing you happy birthday all day.

ROBERT: Happy birthday, Jane. We're going to get the piano tuned for you.

JANE: Who are you?

ROBERT: What? Eh?

SUMMERS: Joyeux Noël, Jane.

WOMAN: Allez-vous à la bibliothèque?

EDITH: Jane, cut the banana bread.

> (*The* WOMAN *and* SUMMERS *sing the* "Marseillaise." JANE *takes a knife and goes to cut the bread.*)

> That's right, dear.

> (JANE *suddenly takes the knife and whacks off the top of the banana sticking out of the bread.*)

WOMAN (*screams in agony, holds between her legs*): That's a very inconsiderate thing for you to do. I'm going to have nightmares now.

SUMMERS: Jane, you've upset my wife.

JANE: I thought she was your husband!

EDITH: Jane, I'd like you to meet my daughter Jane.

SUMMERS: How do you do, Jane?

ROBERT: How do you do?

WOMAN: How do you do?

JANE: I don't understand. Which one is Jane?

EDITH: Don't play games with me. You know which one.

JANE: No I don't!

(EDITH, ROBERT, WOMAN, *and* SUMMERS *keep shaking hands, introducing themselves to each other over and over. However, now instead of saying their names, they each are singing different French songs to one another.* ROBERT *and* SUMMERS *sing* "Frères Jacques"; WOMAN *sings the* "Marseillaise"; EDITH *sings* "Sur le pont d'Avignon" *or some other song in French. The whole thing, rather cheerful sounding, sounds like a music box gone berserk.* JANE *runs to the side and screams.*)

Help! HELP! HELP!

(*Lights go out. The French singing continues in the blackout. The singing fades after a bit, and the lights come up again, with only* JANE *and* EDITH *on stage.* JANE *is on the couch. Her hands are tied together, or else she's in a straitjacket; and tape is across her mouth.* EDITH *sits watching her.*)

VOICES (*that of* SUMMERS *and* WOMAN *alternatively*): Cuckoo, cuckoo. Cuckoo, cuckoo.

EDITH: Oh, time for the bandage to come off. (*Takes tape off* JANE'S *mouth.*) How are you, Jane?

(JANE *smiles.*)

Jane? How are you?

JANE: Jane isn't here.

EDITH: Oh. Then who are you?

JANE: I'm Jane's mother.

EDITH: How do you do? I'm Edith Fromage. I invented cheese and banana bread.

JANE: I'm Emily Carrot. I discovered radium in carrots.

EDITH: Really? That's the last time I ever put them in a salad.

JANE: Untie me.

EDITH: Certainly, Emily. (*Does so.*) I was about to make something good to eat for my husband, son, father, and lover. They're tired of cheese and banana bread. Would you help me cook something?

JANE: Yes, Edith.

EDITH: What should we make?

JANE: Let's make a child.

EDITH: I don't know if I have a big enough bowl.

JANE: That's all right. We don't have to put the yeast in. We'll make a small child.

EDITH: Oh fine. What ingredients do we need?

JANE: Cheese and banana bread.

EDITH: I have that.

(*They begin to put ingredients into a vat.*)

JANE: Lots of eggs.

EDITH: Lots of eggs.

JANE: Olives for the eyes.

EDITH: Olives.

JANE: Wheat germ for the hair.

EDITH: Oh really? I didn't know that.

JANE: Oh yes. When I was in Germany, we made the most beautiful children with wheat germ hair.

EDITH: Emily, dear?

JANE: Yes?

EDITH: Welcome home.

(*They embrace. Enter* WOMAN *and* SUMMERS *holding hands.*)

WOMAN *and* SUMMERS (*in unison*): At this point it seems in order to offer the psychological key to this evening's performance.

SUMMERS: Jane's repressed fear of carrots, indicated by her refusal to acknowledge her proper surname, mirrored a disorder in her libidinous regions . . .

WOMAN: . . . which in turn made her unable to distinguish between her father and her brother and her grandfather; as long as she could not recognize to whom she was speaking . . .

SUMMERS: . . . she would not have to react to them sexually. When Jane finally released the forces of her libido by whacking off the banana bread . . .

WOMAN: . . . she freed her imprisoned personality . . .

SUMMERS: . . . and enabled herself to face . . .

WOMAN: . . . her festering . . .

SUMMERS: . . . competition . . .

WOMAN: . . . with her mother.

(WOMAN *and* SUMMERS *kiss.*)

SUMMERS: The moral of the play is that through the miracle of modern psychology . . .

WOMAN: . . . man is able . . .

SUMMERS: . . . to solve his problems . . .

WOMAN: . . . and be happy.

BOTH: Thank you and good night.

(*They kiss and keep kissing.* JANE *and* EDITH *continue baking. Enter* ROBERT.)

ROBERT: Identity. I dentity, you dentity, he, she, or it dentities. We dentity, you dentity, they dentity. Cuckoo. Cuckoo. Cuckoo. (*As* COUNT:) I dentity, (*as* DWAYNE:) you dentity, (*as* GRANDFATHER:) he, she, or it dentities . . .

(*Lights dim to black.*)

Titanic

Titanic was first presented at the Yale Experimental Theatre in May 1974, directed by Peter Mark Schifter. The cast was as follows:

VICTORIA TAMMURAI	Kate McGregor-Stewart
RICHARD TAMMURAI	Kenneth Ryan
TEDDY TAMMURAI, their son	Joel Polis
LIDIA	Christine Estabrook
THE CAPTAIN	Robert Nersesian
HIGGINS, the sailor	Richard Bey

Titanic was presented by the Direct Theatre, 455 West 43rd Street, New York, in February 1976. The production was directed by Peter Mark Schifter, settings and costumes by Ernie Smith, lighting by Richard Winkler. The cast was as follows:

VICTORIA TAMMURAI	Kate McGregor-Stewart
RICHARD TAMMURAI	Stefan Hartman
TEDDY TAMMURAI, their son	Richard Peterson
LIDIA	Sigourney Weaver
THE CAPTAIN	Jeff Brooks
HIGGINS, the sailor	Ralph Redpath

This production was subsequently moved off-Broadway to the Van Dam Theatre in New York in May 1976, and was presented with a curtain raiser, *Das Lusitania Songspiel*, coauthored by and featuring Christopher Durang and Sigourney Weaver.

SCENE 1

The dining room aboard the Titanic. VICTORIA *and* RICHARD TAMMURAI, *expensively dressed, sit at table with their son,* TEDDY, *age twenty, but dressed as a little boy in short pants. The orchestra can be heard playing* "Nearer My God to Thee."

VICTORIA: Richard, listen, they're playing our song. (*They listen. She sings a little.*)

> Nearer my God to thee,
> Floating across the sea . . .

RICHARD: We've had many a happy time listening to that tune.

VICTORIA: The merry-go-round was playing that tune when I first conceived Teddy. Did you know that, Teddy?

TEDDY: No.

VICTORIA: Of course you didn't. You were too young. Yes, your father was quite a devil on the merry-go-round.

RICHARD: I still am.

VICTORIA: I imagine so, although you developed a bad case of vertigo the last time we rode the Wild Mouse.

RICHARD: I've never ridden the Wild Mouse.

VICTORIA: Memories fade as one gets older. Teddy, sit up. People will think you're fourteen years old.

RICHARD: A slouch is bad for shuffleboard, son. I've entered us in the ship's match tomorrow.

VICTORIA: I love shuffleboard. And badminton. And that amusement where one bangs cars together. What is that called, Teddy?

TEDDY: Auto roulette.

VICTORIA: I don't think that's right. Oh, look. The Captain is looking our way. No, I don't think he is. He's getting something out of his eye. A speck.

RICHARD: A distinguished-looking man.

VICTORIA: It's the uniform that does it. Why weren't we placed at the Captain's table?

RICHARD: I don't know. I consider it a snub actually.

VICTORIA: Granted the *Titanic's* passenger list is impressive, but I think we are still among the crème de la crème. We're certainly rich enough.

RICHARD: We may be rich enough, but perhaps the Captain looked into your family background. Your family is not precisely upper class. It's rather dreadful really. A sort of lower form of plant life out in Indiana.

VICTORIA: Richard, is this yet another insult to me? I would not have set one foot upon this boat if I had thought you were going to persist in these endless cruelties to me.

TEDDY (*uncomfortable, changing subject*): Where's Annabella?

VICTORIA (*looks at him blankly; then to Richard*): Teddy has very hairy legs for a fourteen-year-old. Do you think that's right, Richard?

RICHARD: Teddy hasn't been fourteen for years.

VICTORIA: I know, but even so. You're very nice-looking, Teddy. Richard, I want a divorce. As soon as the *Titanic* docks. I am going straight to my solicitor.

TEDDY: Mommy.

VICTORIA: Shush, dear. Act your age.

RICHARD: It's high time we bought you long pants, son.

VICTORIA: Richard, you're changing the subject.

RICHARD: Then I'll return to it. Victoria, as far as I am concerned you can go right back to the pig farms of Indiana. There is no point in continuing this domestic purgatory.

VICTORIA: Not purgatory, Richard. Hell.

TEDDY: Mommy, everyone is staring at us.

VICTORIA: Nonsense, dear. They're admiring me. And don't whimper. It isn't manly.

RICHARD: Teddy, don't listen to what I'm about to say to your mother. Victoria, I have the greatest contempt for you, but perhaps we should stay together for the sake of the children.

VICTORIA: Richard, Teddy is not your son.

RICHARD: Victoria, what do you mean?

VICTORIA: Richard, when you married me you looked down on my American ways. You made fun of the pig farm. You made rude suggestions about my mother. And one night, after you had hurt me deeply in front of our dinner guests—you had ridiculed my boeuf de bordelaise—I went out to our beach and I wept. And on the beach I met a derelict who saw my pain, and he reached out to me as a human being. It was a mad moment, Richard, but although İ never saw him again, it is he who is Teddy's father.

RICHARD: Victoria, what are you saying?

VICTORIA: The meaning is clear enough. Teddy's father was some beachcomber. He is not your son.

RICHARD: I have been sorely deceived.

(TEDDY *starts to cry.*)

VICTORIA: Your son is crying.

RICHARD: I have no son. (*To* TEDDY:) I hope you realize that from this moment I want nothing more to do with you.

TEDDY: Daddy! (*Cries.*)

VICTORIA: Teddy, please act your age. I've never seen a fourteen-year-old with such hairy legs.

RICHARD: Is my daughter of my seed?

VICTORIA (*smiling at another table*): What?

RICHARD: I said, am I the father of my daughter?

VICTORIA: Who? Annabella? Let me think. (*Thinks for a while. Reminisces about a sexy encounter, then shakes head no. Thinks about a few other encounters, still no. Then recalls something unpleasant, and shakes her head affirmatively.*) Yes.

RICHARD: Then I have a daughter. (*To* TEDDY:) I have no son, but I have a daughter.

TEDDY: What of the twenty years you've acted as my father?

RICHARD: This knowledge cancels them out.

VICTORIA: Smile, the Captain's looking at us.

(RICHARD *and* VICTORIA *smile.*)

RICHARD: Most distinguished-looking.

VICTORIA: Don't repeat yourself, Richard.

RICHARD: Victoria, I have something to tell you.

VICTORIA: What?

RICHARD: Annabella is not your daughter.

VICTORIA: What do you mean?

RICHARD: After one of your numerous cruelties to me, I turned for comfort to Harriet Lindsay. She is Annabella's mother.

VICTORIA: Nonsense. I remember the placenta quite distinctly.

RICHARD: No. It was all a trick. You only thought you gave birth. Harriet and I did it with mirrors.

VICTORIA: You mean I went through all that labor for nothing?

RICHARD: Absolutely nothing.

VICTORIA: Well, I certainly never intend to speak to Harriet or Annabella ever again. First thing in the morning I shall have her deck chair moved away from mine.

RICHARD: And I shall withdraw Teddy's and my name from the father-son shuffleboard match.

VICTORIA: You're both embarrassing at shuffleboard anyway.

TEDDY: Please don't argue.

VICTORIA: Don't be tiresome, Teddy.

RICHARD: I'm only surprised to hear that Teddy's father was a derelict you met on the beach rather than one of your mother's prize hogs.

TEDDY: Daddy!

VICTORIA: Richard, you are pushing me to my limit. I shall now make one thing clear. (*She stands.*) THERE NEVER WAS AN ANNABELLA. (*She sits back down again.*) Harriet Lindsay and I have been having an affair since that summer we bought the beach house, and she just invented a pregnancy to keep you from getting suspicious. You never even slept with her. We did it all with mirrors and slices of white bread. You made love to pieces of white bread, you stupid man, and not only that, but I made your toast out of it in the morning. HAH! I trust you'll be more careful next time I say something is just marmalade.

RICHARD (*stands*): Victoria, I shall make arrangements for private accommodations. What you have just told me is monstrous, and it is I who shall sue you for a divorce. Good evening.

(*Exits in rage.*)

VICTORIA: You should have thrown your glass of water at your father when he said that, Teddy. He insulted your mother.

TEDDY (*looks in his glass*): There's a guppy in my glass.

VICTORIA: I don't care what's in your glass. Manners are manners. (*Rises.*) I'm going to the cabin to rest. (*Suddenly exhausted, sad.*) Somehow I wish we had never come on the *Titanic*. Finish your dinner, Teddy. Mother still loves you.

(*She exits.* TEDDY *bends a spoon glumly in half.*
Enter LIDIA, *dressed in a pink party dress with a*
pink bow. She stands on a table and curtsies.)

LIDIA: Ladies and gentlemen, my father says it's all right if I
want to sing a little song, and so I do and I will. (*Sings*
to the tune of "Frères Jacques.")

> Pudding, pudding,
> I'd eat pudding,
> For dessert, 'til it hurt.
> When it pours vanella,
> I get my umbrella,
> Sit and watch, butterscotch.
>
> I take walks right
> In the pudding,
> Such a treat for my feet,
> Then I lose my footing,
> Fall down in the pudding,
> What a mess, on my dress.
>
> Mommy says we
> Won't have pudding
> Anymore 'cause I'm four,
> Who'd have ever thunk it,
> I'd get stuck with junket,
> No more pudding, no more pudding.

(LIDIA *comes and sits at the table with* TEDDY.
Pause.)

TEDDY: Are you sitting at the right table?

LIDIA: That was my favorite song in the whole world. I'm
the Captain's daughter Lidia. It is my task to make the
guests feel at ease. Your fly is open. (*Giggles; he goes to*

fix it.) No, leave it open. Better for circulation if you know what I mean. (*Pause.*) May I sit down? (*She is already seated.*)

TEDDY (*pause*): Yes.

LIDIA: My father thinks I'm very promiscuous for my age. What do you think?

TEDDY: I don't know your age.

LIDIA: We were all listening to your parents arguing. Do you think your father really slept with white bread?

TEDDY: I don't know. It might be a metaphor.

LIDIA: I used to keep a hedgehog up my vagina. (*Pause.*) But my parents made me stop because I kept feeding it in public. I think that's being fussy. (*Pause.*) I got a funny disease from the hedgehog. They thought it was Dutch elm disease, but it wasn't. After a while, I got a reputation, and then none of the boys would sleep with me. (*Pause.*) I used to bring lesbians on for a while, and they all had to get rabies shots. Am I boring you?

TEDDY: No. I'm just upset because of my parents.

LIDIA: I don't blame you. Things that wouldn't bother you normally often bother you just because it's your parents who are doing it. I once saw my parents "doing it." It was on educational television. But that's not my idea of education, do you agree? I mean, certain things should be a mystery. To me, sex is a mystery. Is it a mystery to you?

TEDDY: Yes.

LIDIA (*laughs*): I bet it is! I'd love to see your father on television with all that bread. But I wonder who they'd get to sponsor it? I mean, I don't know if the bread companies would think that that was good publicity or not. Of course, I'm not an advertising expert, but I don't think that's one of the twelve ways to build a strong body that Wonder Bread had in mind. (*Laughs.*) I made a joke. Could I borrow some of your lettuce?

TEDDY: Yes.

LIDIA: Thank you. (*She puts it up her dress.*) I have a couple of hamsters in here now, and do they make a mess! (*Keeps feeding the hamsters. Fairly long pause.*) My gynecologist runs the other way when he sees me coming. (*She smiles.*)

(TEDDY *gulps his water, a little afraid.*)

TEDDY (*clutching his throat*): Does anything happen to you if you swallow a guppy?

LIDIA: Did you know that guppy mothers eat their babies? (*Smiles, puts her hand over his. Lights dim. Orchestra starts playing* "Nearer My God to Thee" *again. Lights dim to black.*)

SCENE 2

CAPTAIN's *quarters. The* CAPTAIN *and* VICTORIA.

CAPTAIN: Well, here we are, Mrs. Tammurai.

VICTORIA: What a lovely cabin, Captain. Why all this pet food?

CAPTAIN: My daughter has a fondness for animals.

VICTORIA: You know, Captain, my husband finds you most distinguished-looking.

CAPTAIN: And what about you?

VICTORIA: He finds me moderately attractive.

CAPTAIN: No, I mean, how do *you* find me?

VICTORIA: I find you a deeply sensitive, considerate seafarer.

CAPTAIN: I'm touched. Do you have any tinfoil with you?

VICTORIA: Why should I have any tinfoil?

CAPTAIN: You're a very attractive woman.

VICTORIA: And you mean attractive women carry tinfoil?

CAPTAIN: No, I meant it as a non sequitur. Tinfoil is a secret passion of mine. And you are very attractive, you know.

VICTORIA: The mother of my nonexistent daughter always thought so. Oh, Harriet, where are you?

CAPTAIN: Pardon me?

VICTORIA: Nothing, I was remembering other voices, other wombs.

CAPTAIN: Wombs?

VICTORIA (*sings sadly*): A woom without windows, a woom without doors.

CAPTAIN: I want to show you something. (*Ducks behind couch, comes out with a dildo strapped to his forehead.*)

VICTORIA: Are you a doctor?

CAPTAIN: I find you exciting.

VICTORIA: Is this a unicorn fetish?

CAPTAIN: Do you deliver?

VICTORIA: I feel our lives becoming quickly trivial.

CAPTAIN (*nuzzling her with his forehead*): Do you deliver?

VICTORIA: If the mood is right, Captain.

CAPTAIN: How can we make the mood right?

VICTORIA (*sadly*): The usual ways. Soft music. (*Music starts.*) Dim lights. (*Lights dim.*) Bread.

CAPTAIN: Did you say bed?

VICTORIA: No. Bread. (*From beneath her dress she brings forth a family-size loaf of Wonder Bread.*)

CAPTAIN: You're an unusual woman, Mrs. Tammurai.

VICTORIA: I've seen too much of the world.

(*Lights dim to black; in darkness.*)

Oh, you men are fools.

SCENE 3

A cabin. LIDIA *pulling* TEDDY *in.*

LIDIA: Come on, Teddy. You can't stay a virgin forever.

TEDDY: It's been such a trying day.

LIDIA: Come on, relax. Take your clothes off, and I'll get the rope.

TEDDY: Rope?

LIDIA: Boy, you are a novice.

(*Quick fade to black.*)

SCENE 4

The deck. SAILOR *is on watch. Enter* RICHARD.

RICHARD: Hello there, Sailor. What do you see?

SAILOR: Nothing much, sir. Lot of mist and haze.

RICHARD: You look rather familiar.

SAILOR: Do I, sir? Some people say I look like Leif Ericson.

RICHARD: The Nordic chap? Yes, you look rather Nordic. Actually, the person you most remind me of was—no, I doubt it could be the same one.

SAILOR: Who did you have in mind, sir?

RICHARD: Well, this is going to sound silly—but do you go around in drag much? You know, women's clothing?

SAILOR: I beg your pardon?

RICHARD: You're not the same one then? You're not Dicky Miller from Portsmouth?

SAILOR: I've never dressed as a woman in my entire life.

RICHARD: Not even as a child? Didn't you like to go rummaging through your mummy's lingerie drawer?

SAILOR: I find this conversation offensive, sir.

RICHARD: Well, very well, I guess you're not Dicky Miller. I could never tell, of course, unless you dressed up as Queen Victoria. That was Dicky's most frequent guise. We'd all be sitting around the bar in this club I belong to, and in would waltz Dicky with three tiaras on his head and a tiny poodle stuffed in his bosom. "I am Queen Victoria," he'd say. We'd all play along, all the guys. "Sorry, Your Majesty, no women allowed in this club," we'd say. "I am not a woman," Dicky would say. "I am the Queen." Strange fellow, Dicky.

SAILOR: I'm finding it difficult to concentrate on my task, sir.

RICHARD: What? Watching the sea? I can tell you if we see any icebergs. Just you relax.

SAILOR: That friend of yours doesn't sound like a regular guy to me.

RICHARD: He was. The friendliest, nicest guy you'd ever want to meet. Give you the blouse off his back, he would. We used to take him in the back room and play along with him, kind of, you know, give him a pinch in the rear, or tweak his cheek; we stopped after a while though when one of the poodles smothered to death in Dicky's bodice. It kind of put an edge on things.

SAILOR: Are you a member of Parliament, sir?

RICHARD: No. I'm just a poor soul looking for friendship on this bitch of an earth out in the middle of this bitch of a sea.

SAILOR: I think I see an iceberg!

RICHARD: Really? Where?

SAILOR: Good God! We're heading right for it!

RICHARD: Then we're done for. Sailor, before we go down, I wonder if you'd do me one small favor . . .

SAILOR: No time for that! I've got to find the Captain.

(*He exits.*)

RICHARD: Oh, very well.

(*He follows the* SAILOR *out.*)

(*Quick fade to black.*)

SCENE 5

LIDIA's *cabin.* TEDDY *bound in bed.* LIDIA *is smoking a cigarette.*

TEDDY: I had no idea it would be so awful.

LIDIA: The first is always awful.

TEDDY: Why is it necessary that the man be tied?

LIDIA: So the woman can be safe, dopey, in case you try something funny.

TEDDY: The hamsters bit me.

LIDIA: That's your own fault. You did it all wrong. Those quick pokes always send 'em into hysterics.

TEDDY: Was your first as bad?

LIDIA: Course. My first was a gang-bang with twenty-two Portuguese sailors. They didn't know a word of English and it lasted for two days.

TEDDY: Did they tie you up?

LIDIA: No, they punched me.

TEDDY: I guess I prefer being tied to being punched.

LIDIA: Next time we can try it with punching if you like.

TEDDY: I bet I'm going to get an infection from the hamsters.

LIDIA: You men are always complaining. Just be glad I got rid of the hedgehog.

(*Enter the* CAPTAIN *in his underwear with a slice of bread stuck on the dildo on his forehead.*)

CAPTAIN: Lidia, did you see a woman pass through here?

LIDIA: No I didn't. What *are* you up to?

CAPTAIN: I was entertaining in my cabin, but the woman seems to have slipped away.

LIDIA: You look like you've been engendering biscuits.

CAPTAIN: Biscuits? What about biscuits?

LIDIA: You have a piece of bread on your dildo.

CAPTAIN: Watch your tongue, young lady! You're incessantly vulgar. Your mother and I shall ask for a refund from your finishing school in Hampshire.

(*Enter* SAILOR *and* RICHARD.)

SAILOR: Begging pardon, sir, but we've sighted an iceberg.

CAPTAIN: I've told you not to bother me in my quarters, Higgins. Put your complaint in the log and I'll consider it later. (*Calling.*) Mrs. Tammurai!

(*He exits.*)

SAILOR: I'm afraid we're going to sink. Why will no one listen?

(*He exits.*)

RICHARD: Poor chap.

TEDDY: Daddy!

RICHARD: Teddy! What are you . . . I don't even know who you are.

TEDDY: You didn't tell me about the hamsters.

RICHARD: Don't bother me with your tales of petulance. (*Sees* LIDIA.) Oh, my God. Is it you?

LIDIA: Certainly not. I'm the Captain's daughter Lidia. Your son's not much of a ladies' man, I might suggest.

RICHARD: I have no son, *Harriet.*

LIDIA: Why did you call me Harriet?

RICHARD: You can't fool me. White bread or no white bread, I remember Harriet Lindsay of Wallington Park.

TEDDY: Then this is the mother of my sister Annabella?

RICHARD: Shut up, Teddy. There is no Annabella.

(*Enter* VICTORIA, *pursued by the* CAPTAIN.)

CAPTAIN: Mrs. Tammurai, don't tease.

RICHARD: Victoria!

VICTORIA: Good evening, Richard. I believe you should speak harshly to the Captain. He is attempting to violate my bread box.

RICHARD: Your doings are no longer a concern of mine. You can run a whole-wheat brothel, as far as I'm concerned.

TEDDY: I'm all tied up.

LIDIA: Hello, Victoria.

VICTORIA: Oh, my God. That voice.

LIDIA (*sings seductively*): A womb without windows, a womb without doors.

VICTORIA: Harriet, Harriet. You've come back.

CAPTAIN: I don't understand. Who is Harriet?

VICTORIA: She is.

CAPTAIN: But this is my daughter Lidia.

VICTORIA: Certainly I can be expected to recognize my own sister Harriet!

RICHARD: I didn't realize Harriet Lindsay was your sister!

VICTORIA: There are many things you don't realize, Richard.

CAPTAIN: But I don't understand. What is the meaning of this, Lidia?

VICTORIA: This is not Lidia. This is my sister Harriet.

TEDDY: I'm all tied up.

VICTORIA: Teddy. Why are you here?

TEDDY: I don't know.

CAPTAIN: I don't understand. Who is Harriet?

LIDIA (*triumphant*): I am Harriet Lindsay, sister of Victoria Tammurai. I am Eternal Youth!

CAPTAIN: My daughter Lidia was blond. You're not blond—now that I look. Where is my daughter?

LIDIA: Your daughter Lidia is in locker 2838 in Port Authority Bus Terminal in New York and has been for three years. (*She suddenly feels pangs within her, reaches up in her skirt, and pulls out two dead hamsters.*) My hamsters are dead! Too much marmalade. Here's a souvenir of your first night with your mother's sister, Teddy! (*She whirls the hamsters around her head and then throws them at* TEDDY.)

VICTORIA (*somewhat concerned*): Oh dear. Teddy really shouldn't be witnessing all this.

RICHARD: Victoria, I am appalled. When we reach London, I am going to *my* solicitor. I intend to take custody of the boy regardless of his parentage.

TEDDY: Daddy, untie me!

VICTORIA: No court would separate a mother and her son.

RICHARD: When the mother's moral life is at the level yours is, Victoria, the court will jump at the chance.

VICTORIA: Don't speak to me of morals, Richard. I know all about your secret life in that so-called club in London. Masquerading as royalty, suffocating poodles. What court would let a child enter that sort of life?

RICHARD: You are an incestuous snail.

(*Enter* SAILOR.)

Hello there, young man.

SAILOR: Captain, please sir! We're going to ram the iceberg!

CAPTAIN: Very well, Higgins. I heard you the first time. (*To* LIDIA:) Don't think I'll forget this, Lidia. I shall resent you to my last living day.

(*Exits.*)

VICTORIA: Come, Harriet, let's pack. You and I must prepare to shoulder the burden of being new parents to Teddy.

RICHARD: You'll hear from me, Victoria. No incestuous slattern is going to turn my boy into a degenerate.

VICTORIA: He's not your son!

(VICTORIA *and* LIDIA *exit.*)

SAILOR: I'm afraid we're done for. That berg's going to rip right through us.

(*Exits.*)

RICHARD: Don't worry, Teddy. Daddy still loves you.

(*Exits after the* SAILOR.)

TEDDY: It's chilly. I wish they'd have pulled blankets up over me. (*Calls plaintively.*) Blankets! Blankets!

(*A loud* crash. *Sounds of enormous ripping, water gushing, alarms, sirens, etc.* TEDDY, *still tied, rushes off, screaming. Various entrances of shipwreck chaos: the* CAPTAIN *and* SAILOR *are hysterical;* LIDIA *fairly calm;* RICHARD *has trouble with his life jacket;* VICTORIA *is hysterical. The* SAILOR, *from en-*

trance to entrance, inexplicably is losing his uni-form. The final crossover is TEDDY, *tied and hop-ping, calling* "Daddy! Mommy!" *etc.*)

SCENE 6

The noise stops. TEDDY *reenters, unbound, and hav-ing found the* SAILOR's *uniform, which he begins to put on in audience view. The* CAPTAIN's *voice comes over the loudspeaker.*

CAPTAIN: This is your Captain speaking. Do not panic. We have not hit an iceberg. What you have just heard is a sound effects record. My wife put it on. It is her idea of a little joke. Please return to your cabins. There is no cause for alarm.

(*Enter* SAILOR, *who sees* TEDDY *with his clothes.*)

SAILOR: I beg your pardon? Are those my clothes?

(TEDDY *rushes off. Before* SAILOR *has a chance to pursue him, enter* RICHARD, *who sees* SAILOR.)

RICHARD: Hello there, young man. Forget something?

SAILOR: Where's the Captain?

RICHARD: He's . . . on the loudspeaker.

SAILOR: Forget it.

(*Runs off after where* TEDDY *went.*)

RICHARD: Do you play bridge? Ah well . . .

(*Enter* TEDDY, *now completely dressed as* SAILOR, *from other side.*)

Hello there, Sailor.

TEDDY: I couldn't find my other clothes.

RICHARD: What other clothes? These suit you remarkably well, young man.

TEDDY: I think I have an infection.

RICHARD: Oh, piffle. You can't scare me off with that. Say, I know this is going to sound like a line, but you look awfully familiar.

TEDDY: What do you mean, I *look* familiar?

RICHARD: I suppose it's just that you're wearing the same kind of uniform the other fellow was wearing.

TEDDY: This *is* his uniform.

RICHARD: You share it? That's oddly titillating.

TEDDY: I've lost my shoes.

RICHARD: So you have. Have you ever read Nietzsche's *Genealogy of Morals*?

TEDDY: I don't remember.

RICHARD: I want you to come to my cabin and reevaluate your concepts of good and bad.

TEDDY: I don't know if I have any concepts of good and bad.

RICHARD: Well, we must in any case evaluate what you *do* have.

(*They exit. Quick fade to black.*)

SCENE 7

The cabin. VICTORIA, *nervous.*

VICTORIA: Oh my God, my God. Harriet, where are you?

(*Knock on door. Enter* SAILOR.)

SAILOR: Captain requests your presence on deck, ma'am. Oh, I'm sorry. I was looking for his wife. Have you seen her?

VICTORIA: No, I haven't. Where's Harriet?

SAILOR: Lidia?

VICTORIA: Harriet.

SAILOR: I don't know.

(*Exits.*)

VICTORIA: Oh, Harriet, so many illusions shattered, so many dreams trodden in the dust.

(*Enter* RICHARD *in his bathrobe from the bedroom.*)

RICHARD: Oh, Victoria. I didn't know you were here. Are you about to leave?

(*Enter* TEDDY *in underwear, also from the bedroom.*)

VICTORIA: Richard, where *is* Harriet?

TEDDY: Harriet has my clothes somewhere.

VICTORIA: Teddy, why are you here?

RICHARD: My God! Are you Teddy?

VICTORIA: Of course he's Teddy. Who did you think he was?

RICHARD: I thought he was a sailor.

VICTORIA: Teddy doesn't look anything like a sailor. Where are your clothes, Teddy?

RICHARD: Give me back the money I gave you at once!

VICTORIA: What money?

RICHARD: I am hardly going to pay my own son!

VICTORIA: Pay him for what? Richard, what did you pay him for?

TEDDY: I don't feel well.

RICHARD: You should have told me who you were. Give me back the money.

TEDDY: No, I earned it.

VICTORIA: Teddy, did you solicit your father?

TEDDY: I don't have a father.

VICTORIA: That's no excuse to solicit him, Teddy. I'm surprised at you. That's *two* bad things you've done today. And you, Richard. What sort of example is this for you to give your son? Picking up male riffraff on the deck.

RICHARD: I would hardly call my son riffraff.

VICTORIA: Well, I should hope not. Really, Richard, what could you have been thinking of?

RICHARD: Victoria, mistakes happen.

VICTORIA: Well, I suppose they do.

RICHARD: I forgive you with the derelict on the beach, if you forgive me with Teddy.

VICTORIA: That's a generous offer, Richard. (*They kiss.*) Now Teddy, give your father the money back.

(*Enter* LIDIA, *who watches from the back.*)

TEDDY: I don't want to.

VICTORIA: Teddy, is this any way for a ten-year-old to behave?

RICHARD: He needs to see a psychologist.

VICTORIA (*horrified*): Oh, Richard—no!

LIDIA (*very harsh*): That's no way to speak to your parents, Teddy. (*Slaps him.*) APOLOGIZE!

TEDDY (*stunned*): I don't want to.

LIDIA: APOLOGIZE! (*Slaps him again.*)

TEDDY: I'm sorry. (*Gives money to* RICHARD.)

VICTORIA: After all, Teddy, you really shouldn't charge your father. We can't be proud of you if you're rude, Teddy.

RICHARD: I'm sure Teddy didn't mean it. All's forgiven. (RICHARD *kisses* TEDDY; VICTORIA *and* LIDIA *kiss.*)

LIDIA (*clutches her stomach*): I caught a sea gull up on deck. It's not sitting well. (*Feathers fall from beneath her dress.*) Look. I'm molting. I am a sea gull. I am a sea gull.

(*Sudden crash. Everyone is thrown to ground.*)

CAPTAIN (*on loudspeaker*): This is your Captain. Please do not be alarmed. Would anyone seeing a woman carrying a sound effects record please advise the Captain of this fact as soon as possible? Thank you.

LIDIA (*hating life*): Oh, why won't we sink, why?

(*Lights dim to black.*)

SCENE 8

The Titanic *lounge. At table:* VICTORIA, RICHARD, TEDDY, LIDIA.

VICTORIA (*distressed*): Richard, why will the Captain never eat with us?

RICHARD: There, there, get a hold on.

(*Enter the* SAILOR *with dish of mints.*)

SAILOR: The Captain sends his regrets and promises to join you for coffee momentarily. He offers you these delicious after-dinner mints. (*Offers them.*)

VICTORIA: How nice. I love mints.

(LIDIA *takes dish. Puts a mint up her dress. Pause.*)

Harriet, don't do that.

LIDIA: What? (*Puts another mint up her dress.*)

RICHARD: Harriet, please. This is a public lounge.

LIDIA (*pretending not to understand*): What's the matter?

VICTORIA: Harriet, people are staring at us. They won't know what you're doing.

LIDIA (*loudly, to supposed onlookers*): I'VE GOT A SEA GULL IN HERE.

VICTORIA: Harriet!

RICHARD: Victoria, let's just ignore her.

(*Pause.*)

LIDIA: You wanna try, Teddy?

(TEDDY *feeds* LIDIA's *sea gull.*)

RICHARD: Teddy, behave!

VICTORIA: Harriet, I hardly think after-dinner mints are suitable eating for sea gulls. No wonder you're molting.

LIDIA: My gynecologist says my molting disease is catching.

VICTORIA: I don't believe you *have* a gynecologist. Really, Harriet, a douche is one thing but a vaginal zoo is quite another!

RICHARD: I couldn't agree more. Next thing we know she's going to install trapeze artists.

VICTORIA: We can do without your contributions, Richard.

RICHARD: I was agreeing with you.

VICTORIA: I don't want you to agree with me.

TEDDY: I agree with Mother *and* with Father. (*Feeds* LIDIA *again.*)

RICHARD: Teddy, Mother and I do not wish you to feed Annabella's sea gull.

VICTORIA: Richard, you called Harriet Annabella.

RICHARD: Did I? I get so confused.

VICTORIA: Ah, "Confusion," that famous poem by A. E. Housman. (*Begins to recite:*)

> Ah, Confusion, with rue my heart is laden;
> For golden friends I had,
> For many a rose-lipped maiden,
> And many a lightfoot lad.

(*During above,* LIDIA *whispers to* TEDDY. *Then suddenly they get up, attacking the* SAILOR *and removing his clothes.* LIDIA *is the driving force behind this.*)

VICTORIA: Children, children!

RICHARD: No, let them be, Victoria. I want to see what they come up with.

(TEDDY *puts on the* SAILOR's *clothes.*)

SAILOR: I shall have to report this to the Captain.

LIDIA: Teddy is a passenger on this boat, and he needs to have clothes.

(*Enter the* CAPTAIN. *He hulks sorrowfully.*)

CAPTAIN: I'm sorry I'm late.

SAILOR: Captain, they've taken my clothes.

CAPTAIN (*sadly*): Ah, Higgins. (*To all:*) I fear I've just been through a rather harrowing experience. We've had to execute my wife. It's nautical law. You're not allowed to incite to sinking. We hanged her from the mast.

VICTORIA: Oh, Captain, how difficult for you.

CAPTAIN: Well, the others did it actually. I just blew the whistle. (*Blows whistle.*) So you'll excuse me. We're holding the burial tomorrow at dawn. I'd appreciate it if you could make it. Good evening.

(*Exits with* SAILOR.)

RICHARD: How unfortunate for the man.

VICTORIA: He's taking it well, I think.

LIDIA (*taking last mint*): Here goes the last one.

VICTORIA: Wait. Let's make a wish on it.

RICHARD: Victoria, one doesn't make wishes on after-dinner mints.

VICTORIA: One can if one wants to.

RICHARD: Very well, have it your own way.

VICTORIA (*wishing on mint*): I wish for happiness and good fortune and love and faithfulness. Harriet?

LIDIA: I wish that the ship would sink.

VICTORIA: Harriet, don't say that! (*Knocks the table three times.*)

LIDIA: We keep almost sinking. I'm tired of not sinking.

VICTORIA: Let's just close the subject.

LIDIA: What do you wish for, Teddy?

VICTORIA: I don't even want to know. Here, feed your damn sea gull. (*Feeds* LIDIA.) It's time for bed.

RICHARD: Ah, bed, a good suggestion. Come along, Teddy. (*Takes* TEDDY'*s arm.*)

TEDDY: I wish for . . .

VICTORIA: That's enough, Teddy. We *don't* want to hear. Harriet, when you feel more civil, we'll be in the cabin. Richard, take *my* arm.

TEDDY: Good night, Aunt Harriet.

(*Exit* RICHARD, VICTORIA, TEDDY.)

LIDIA: I still hope the boat sinks. (LIDIA *takes out large hand drill, tries to make holes in the floor. Singing while drilling:*)

> Death by drowning.
> Death by water,
>> Father, mother, son and daughter . . .

(SAILOR *enters and takes drill away from her.*)

SAILOR: I'm sorry, I can't allow you to do that.

LIDIA: I don't know what you're talking about.

SAILOR: It wouldn't do any good. We're several floors above the water anyway.

LIDIA (*seductively*): That's a nice uniform you've got there, Sailor.

SAILOR: You've taken my uniform.

LIDIA: Don't be a stranger, Sailor.

(*Lights dim to black.*)

SCENE 9

The cabin. TEDDY, *in his sailor suit, sits on* RICH-
ARD's *knee.*

RICHARD: Come on. Sing!

TEDDY: I don't want to.

RICHARD: Please. (*Puts money in* TEDDY's *pocket.*)

TEDDY (*sings*):

On the good ship lollipop,
It's a short trip into bed you hop
And dream away, something something something
Butterneck bay. . . .

(RICHARD *bounces* TEDDY *up and down.*)

TEDDY: Don't do that. You'll make me seasick.

RICHARD: You know, Dorothy, you could make an effort to
be a little more pleasant.

TEDDY: Don't call me Dorothy, I don't feel right. I don't
have my own clothes.

RICHARD: You look very charming in these.

TEDDY: Where's Mommy and Aunt Harriet?

RICHARD: They're in the bedroom.

TEDDY: Is Aunt Harriet a man?

RICHARD: Your Aunt Harriet is an enigma.

(*Scream offstage. Enter* VICTORIA, *hysterical.*)

VICTORIA: She did it again! Something bit me!

TEDDY: Of course, it was a sea gull.

(*Enter* LIDIA.)

VICTORIA: You said you took the sea gull out.

LIDIA: I was mistaken.

RICHARD: Annabella, why do you treat your mother this way?

VICTORIA (*looking at her hand*): Oh God, it might be rabid.

RICHARD (*looks at her hand*): Dorothy, get your mother's hypodermic, love.

(TEDDY *does.*)

He's very handsome today.

VICTORIA: It's this sea air that does it.

RICHARD: You know, Harriet, these constant booster shots for Victoria are pushing us straight to the poorhouse. Lie down, Victoria.

VICTORIA: Oh God, the pain! I want Harriet to do it.

LIDIA: Very well. Lie down, Victoria.

(VICTORIA *lies down, bares her stomach.*)

Is it nine times or six?

RICHARD: I'm not a doctor.

LIDIA: Alright. Ready, on your mark, get set, go! (LIDIA *jabs* VICTORIA's *stomach nine times with hypodermic, very fast. Awful screams.*)

VICTORIA: Oh it's so sordid. Richard, take me away. Help me to the bathroom.

(RICHARD *helps* VICTORIA *off.*)

LIDIA: Hello, Teddy.

TEDDY: Aren't you my sister Annabella?

LIDIA: What if I am?

TEDDY: Then there really *is* an Annabella?

LIDIA: Yes.

TEDDY: And there isn't a Harriet?

LIDIA: I suppose not.

TEDDY: Why haven't Mommy and Daddy recognized you?

LIDIA: Because they're very bad parents.

TEDDY (*a true realization*): Yes they are. They're very bad. Do you think the boat will ever dock and we can get away from them?

LIDIA: The ship isn't going to dock. It's going to sink.

TEDDY: Soon?

LIDIA: I hope so.

TEDDY: Do you think we should tell our parents you're their daughter and not Harriet?

LIDIA: Not until I'm good and ready.

TEDDY (*disappointed*): Oh.

LIDIA: Poor Teddy.

(*Enter* HIGGINS.)

SAILOR: Is the Captain here?

LIDIA: Oh, good, I have nothing in here now. Come on, Teddy.

(*Exit* LIDIA, TEDDY, SAILOR. *Enter the* CAPTAIN.)

CAPTAIN: Hallo? Anyone home?

(*Enter* RICHARD.)

Is Mrs. Tammurai at home?

RICHARD: Well, it is rather late.

(*Enter* VICTORIA *quickly, all cheered up.*)

VICTORIA: That's all right, Richard. I'm feeling better. Oh, Captain. How nice of you to visit us. Won't you have tea, Captain?

CAPTAIN: If it's no bother.

VICTORIA: No bother.

(*No one gets tea. All sit.*)

CAPTAIN: Now that my wife is dead, I would like to propose to you.

RICHARD: Perhaps I should leave.

VICTORIA: Richard's such a gentleman. (*Kisses him.*) I have always loved men. (*Kisses the* CAPTAIN.) How did your wife die?

CAPTAIN: I had her executed.

VICTORIA: Oh yes, of course.

CAPTAIN: Nautical law.

VICTORIA: Well that happens at sea. How sad to view death. Someday I shall face my death, and I shall look back and see the overview of my life. And what shall I see? Rabies shots. Deceit. Mirrors. White bread. More white bread. Ah, Captain, you remember the bread.

CAPTAIN: Fondly, madam.

VICTORIA (*takes bread from his vest pocket*): Here's some here. (*Offers it to* RICHARD.) Richard?

RICHARD: No thank you.

VICTORIA: For a while I was the toast of this city. What days they were, Richard. Muffins in the winter, popovers in the fall; strawberry tarts during the Mardi Gras. But then one realizes how empty and sterile it has all been. And what do we see, when we bread awaken? We see that we have not really been alive, that a crust of bread has mattered more than we. (*To* RICHARD:) Oh, Richard, if only we could have made one another happy; (*looks at* CAPTAIN) or if all *three* of us could have made one another happy. If only I was not cursed with loving Harriet . . . Harriet . . . WHERE IS HARRIET?

RICHARD: WHERE IS TEDDY?

VICTORIA: OH MY GOD!

RICHARD: DOROTHY!

(VICTORIA *and* RICHARD *exit, hysterical. They bring back* LIDIA, TEDDY, *and* SAILOR, *the last two of whom are in their underwear.*)

VICTORIA: Dirty! That's dirty! (*Hits* TEDDY's *hand.*)

RICHARD: Little girls don't play with other little girls that way, Teddy. (*Slaps him.*)

CAPTAIN: Good God, Higgins, you're not on deck. Who's on watch?

SAILOR: I can't do everything.

VICTORIA: Big boys don't sleep with their aunts, Teddy.

RICHARD: How could my son behave this way?

CAPTAIN: Higgins, report to deck at once. And put on your uniform.

(*Exit* SAILOR.)

VICTORIA: Harriet, Teddy is too young to be treated in a carnal manner.

LIDIA: You're right. But I see a solution.

RICHARD: You do?

VICTORIA (*sits; speaks with a true and deep yearning*): I have always *longed* for a solution.

LIDIA: The Captain can marry us all. Ship captains can do that, can't they?

CAPTAIN: But only on board ship. (*All look deeply disappointed; then* LIDIA *with irritation snaps them out of it.*)

LIDIA: Well, then, that's perfect!

VICTORIA: Oh Harriet, what a wonderful idea.

TEDDY: Do I have to, Daddy?

RICHARD: Shush, Dorothy. Act your age.

CAPTAIN: I do have to bury my wife at dawn.

LIDIA: What better time. A burial, that's death; and a marriage, that's life.

VICTORIA: At dawn.

TEDDY: Who's steering the ship now?

CAPTAIN: I could check.

VICTORIA: Don't bother. First, let's have that tea.

(*They sit and wait. Foghorn. Lights dim to black.*)

SCENE 10

Deck of ship at dawn. Ship whistle. Rooster crows. Wedding march. Enter the CAPTAIN. *He is followed by the* SAILOR *who is still in his underwear and is wheeling in a wrapped dead body on a handcart. Enter* RICHARD, TEDDY, LIDIA, VICTORIA, *all wearing bridal veils. They stand in front of* CAPTAIN.

CAPTAIN: Dearly beloved and dearly bereaved, we are gathered here to bury my wife and we are gathered here today in the face of God to join these men and these women in the holy sacrament of marriage, which is an honorable estate. Bring my wife closer, Higgins, I shall use her for inspiration.

(SAILOR *brings body closer.*)

Some people might consider this ceremony sick. Who among you think it is sick?

(LIDIA *and* TEDDY *raise their hands. After a while, so does the* SAILOR.)

Well, I think that is wrong. Because you see, there is no right or wrong. And thus my thinking your rejection is wrong may itself be wrong because nothing is wrong. And nothing is right. We have passed from the rigid law of the Old Testament—how many of you have read the Old Testament?

(RICHARD *and* SAILOR *raise hands.*)

—to the more humane law of love in the New Testament—how many of you believe in love?

(VICTORIA *raises her hand.*)

—onward finally to the new nonexistent law of today, to the deep-think of nothingness. If God is alive, he is a crackpot. If he's dead, he's causing a terrible stink. How many of you know of the death stench of Father Zosima in Dostoevsky?

(SAILOR *raises his hand.*)

You're doing very well today, Higgins. Who can tell about these things? Can you? Can I? I used to go to the movies with my wife, and we wouldn't understand a *single* thing we saw on the screen. (*Pause.*) Let me put it this way. Right or wrong, up or down, dead or alive, I have no opinion on it either way because—who am I to say? I'm nobody. Do what you want then because I have no advice to give you. In the name of the Father, of the Son, and of the Holy Spirit. Amen.

ALL: Amen.

CAPTAIN: Do you, Harriet, take this woman as your . . . (*can't think of a word, moves on*) . . . to amuse and enjoy, to frighten and destroy, 'til whatever time you cease being interested?

LIDIA: Yes.

CAPTAIN: And vice versa?

VICTORIA: Yes, thank you.

CAPTAIN: I pronounce you . . . married. And do you, Richard, take . . . (*Pause.*)

RICHARD: Dorothy, your Reverend.

CAPTAIN: Take Dorothy, to love and correct, to bend and erect, 'til things do you in?

RICHARD: I do.

CAPTAIN: And vice versa?

TEDDY: I do.

CAPTAIN: I pronounce you . . . man'n'wife. You may kiss your son.

RICHARD: I have no son.

CAPTAIN: I can sympathize, having no wife or daughter. Though once I did . . . (*Gets teary.*)

SAILOR: Get a hold on, sir.

CAPTAIN: Before you all embark on your honeymoons below decks, I think I should tell you that Higgins here has graciously offered to marry my wife. However, I have not accepted his offer. It's touching when an enlisted man tries to warm an old man's heart, but we cannot lose our grip on reality. So as planned, I have ordered a full military burial for my wife and ask only to see her face one more time before we hurl her over. Higgins.

(SAILOR *brings body closer.* CAPTAIN *peeks under sheet.*)

This isn't my wife! My wife wasn't Chinese!

RICHARD: Perhaps it's the effects of hanging.

CAPTAIN: Nonsense. My wife never wore a lotus blossom in her entire life. She'd sooner be found dead. Higgins, cancel the funeral. Oh, and take this thing with you. Toss it over first chance you get.

SAILOR: Yes, sir.

(SAILOR *exits with body.*)

CAPTAIN: Well, this has soured my day.

RICHARD: Now, now. Don't let it. Why don't you join us for dinner? We'll make it a fivesome.

CAPTAIN: Very well. I accept your invitation.

RICHARD: Good. Let's just get out of these wet things, and meet in the dining room.

(*All start to exit.* RICHARD *catches* VICTORIA.)

You see, Victoria, we're ending up at the Captain's table after all. Why, Victoria, you're crying.

VICTORIA: It's happiness. Or maybe the absence of it. Leave me by myself for a moment.

(*All exit but* VICTORIA.)

Weddings make me cry. I guess I must be a sentimental goose. Harriet had a goose once, but I don't want to go into that. Isn't love a strange thing? I find it very humiliating. I love the movies, especially Jennifer Jones. *Portrait of Jennie*, and the lighthouse and the hurricane. Teddy loves me. When all else fails, the love of a son for his mother is a sturdy thing. That was a *wonderful* movie. She was Eurasian in that one. Who was Eurasian? What am I talking about? (*Thinks for a while, but can't get a bead on what she was talking about; laughs.*) Sometimes when I don't make connections between statements, I worry. And sometimes I'm like the Captain, and I don't care.

(*Lights dim to black.*)

SCENE 11

The Titanic *dining room. The* CAPTAIN, RICHARD, VICTORIA.

CAPTAIN: Where are your spouses?

VICTORIA: They're changing still, I guess. Richard, this is the second honeymoon we've had together, isn't it? I've always been fond of Richard.

RICHARD: Oh, here comes Higgins. Nice-looking, don't you think, Victoria?

VICTORIA: Richard. You're worse than Dicky Miller.

RICHARD: I've never worn a tiara in my life.

CAPTAIN: What is it, Higgins?

SAILOR: Sir, there's a heavy fog out, and there's been a general warning about . . .

CAPTAIN: Higgins, I've told you to put these comments in the log. Stop worrying about the weather, son.

SAILOR: But . . .

CAPTAIN: Yes, I know. *Icebergs. (Cocks his head at* RICHARD *and* VICTORIA, *makes a little joke.)* But my wife's dead, that's taken care of *one* iceberg. *(Laughs lightly;* RICHARD *and* VICTORIA *don't really like the joke.)* By the way, have you found her body yet?

SAILOR: There are several waiting for your identification, sir.

CAPTAIN: I'm sure she's one of them. Good night, Higgins.

SAILOR: But sir . . .

CAPTAIN: That will be all.

(SAILOR *exits.)*

VICTORIA: He seems a charming young man.

CAPTAIN: Bit of a stickler for the rules.

VICTORIA: Oh here come Harriet and Teddy.

(*Enter* LIDIA *and* TEDDY, *dressed in mourning. They look attractive, very grown-up and somehow dan-*

gerous. LIDIA's *"mourning" in particular is disturbing—shiny black material, low-cut, sexy, but sort of perverse. She might be on her way to a Black Mass.)*

Oh.

TEDDY: Don't stand up.

LIDIA: Good evening.

VICTORIA: Oh, Harriet. You look like you're . . . in mourning.

LIDIA: Yes?

VICTORIA: But this is a celebration.

LIDIA: Well one should always be prepared for everything.

VICTORIA: Richard, she's acting hostile.

CAPTAIN: Here, here, let's keep our tempers. How about a jolly song, Lidia? I mean, Harriet.

VICTORIA: Yes, something festive.

RICHARD: Why are you wearing black, Teddy?

TEDDY: I'm in mourning for my life. (*Grins.*)

LIDIA: Song time. Come on, Teddy.

VICTORIA: Oh, good, this will be a celebration then.

(TEDDY *and* LIDIA *get in place to sing. Enter the* SAILOR.)

SAILOR: Captain, an iceberg's been . . .

CAPTAIN: Hush, Higgins. They're singing.

TEDDY *and* LIDIA (*singing; alternating lines to* "Twinkle, Twinkle"):

> Hedgehog, hedgehog,
> Burning bright,
> In the forests of the night,
> Hedgehog, hedgehog,
> Can't you see?
> You were always meant for me.
> Who knows what I'm waiting for,
> When I sit I feel quite sore,
> Hedgehog, hedgehog, come with me,
> Away, away to Innisfree.

LIDIA: In this next part of the song, Teddy plays the part of the hedgehog.

(TEDDY *gets on his hands and knees.* LIDIA *insinuatingly begins to lift her skirt.* TEDDY *begins to crawl toward her as* LIDIA *sings. The song is turning obscene;* LIDIA *sings.*)

> Teddy, Teddy,
> You're all right,
> In the forests of the night . . .

VICTORIA (*interrupting*): Stop it! It's horrible.

SAILOR: Captain, I've sighted one. It's . . .

CAPTAIN (*in a foul humor from the song too*): Go away, Higgins!

(SAILOR *exits.*)

VICTORIA (*to* LIDIA): That wasn't a particularly winning song. Did you think it would be winning?

LIDIA: You didn't like it?

RICHARD: Now, now. Harriet always knew the off songs, we used to say.

VICTORIA: Well, I'm sure you thought I'd like it. It was a nice gesture, Harriet. (*Having convinced herself.*) I loved it. Oh, I'm all aglow with happiness tonight.

LIDIA: Why, because I'm legally bound to you?

VICTORIA: Harriet, the wedding was your idea. (*Angry.*) And I wish you hadn't worn mourning.

RICHARD: Let's not bicker on our honeymoons. Let's start over. Harriet, you look ravishing.

TEDDY: What about me?

RICHARD: You're a nice-looking boy, Teddy.

VICTORIA: I didn't know you had long pants, did you, Harriet?

LIDIA: Why don't you call me Annabella?

VICTORIA: What?

CAPTAIN (*embarrassed*): I wonder if the orchestra would play something else.

RICHARD: What orchestra?

CAPTAIN: I don't know. I'll go check.

(*Exits.*)

RICHARD: Harriet, I don't know why you're acting this way,

but have the decency to control your tongue in front of the Captain.

TEDDY: You shouldn't talk about tongue at the table.

RICHARD: Teddy, are you trying to give us difficulty?

VICTORIA: Don't be harsh with Teddy, Richard, he's confused. Have you spoken to him about the bad word beginning with "m" yet? He's that age.

RICHARD: What bad word beginning with "m"?

VICTORIA: I'm embarrassed to say it.

RICHARD: What? Menstruation?

VICTORIA: No, silly, that's girls. Masturbation.

TEDDY: Oh, that bad word beginning with "m." I thought you meant "mother."

VICTORIA (*stunned*): That's very unkind. (*Cries.*)

RICHARD: Look what you've done to your mother.

VICTORIA: Give me your leg, Teddy.

TEDDY: You shouldn't talk about leg at the table.

VICTORIA: This pre-pubescent temper tantrum is to stop this instant. GIVE ME YOUR LEG. (*She grabs his leg.*) You are obviously too young for long pants. (*Shrieking,* VICTORIA *tears off the bottom part of* TEDDY'*s pants legs, making his long pants now short pants. This is a sudden and insane motion, and is quite ferocious. Upon completion of her task,* VICTORIA *returns to a calm if strained manner.*) Harriet, you're very silent. As an adult, you should give Richard and me your support.

LIDIA: Why did you call me Harriet?

VICTORIA: What?

(*Enter the* CAPTAIN, *with a dildo strapped to his nose.*)

CAPTAIN: Guess who I am!

LIDIA: I thought you had caught on by now. Teddy caught on. I AM YOUR DAUGHTER ANNABELLA.

VICTORIA: What do you mean? There is no Annabella. It was a trick you and I played on Richard.

CAPTAIN: Guess who I am.

VICTORIA: *Hush*, we haven't time.

(CAPTAIN *is abashed, sulks.*)

LIDIA: I've tricked you, Mother. You never had an affair with your sister Harriet. You had an affair with me. You don't even have a sister. You're an only child.

VICTORIA: I was a lonely child.

LIDIA: Teddy and I have been mistreated.

VICTORIA: This is all petty complaining, meant to distract from the main issue.

LIDIA: We're the main issue, we're the only issue.

VICTORIA (*slaps her*): Don't you ever play with words that way again.
(TEDDY *slaps* VICTORIA.)   Teddy!

(RICHARD *slaps* TEDDY.)

Thank you, Richard.

(LIDIA *slaps* RICHARD. VICTORIA *slaps* LIDIA. TEDDY *slaps* VICTORIA *and* RICHARD. *They all slap one another, grow furious, throw food, etc.*)

RICHARD (*stopping it*): Teddy, you're to go to bed at once, without supper.

CAPTAIN: Guess who I am!

RICHARD: Look, nobody cares.

CAPTAIN: I'm supposed to be Cyrano de Bergerac.

(*Enter the* SAILOR.)

SAILOR: Captain! The iceberg!

CAPTAIN: Not now, Higgins.

SAILOR: Captain, we're done for.

(*Sound of ship scraping the iceberg, water gushing in, sirens, etc.*)

VICTORIA: Richard, we're sinking.

RICHARD: Wait, maybe it's that record again.

CAPTAIN: Let's listen and see if the Captain says anything on the loudspeaker.

(*They all listen. Nothing but the noises of sinking.*)

Oh my God. (*Takes off dildo.*)

RICHARD: Victoria, this is the end.

VICTORIA: Richard, where did we go wrong?

RICHARD: Do you think we could try again?

(*Orchestra plays* "Nearer My God to Thee.")

VICTORIA: Richard, let's try.

(*They sing* "Nearer My God to Thee." CAPTAIN *joins them.* LIDIA *and* TEDDY *keep interrupting them.* SAILOR *keeps trying to get the* CAPTAIN *away from the singing,* CAPTAIN *gets annoyed.*)

TEDDY, RICHARD, CAPTAIN:

> Nearer my God to Thee,
> Nearer to Thee . . .

SAILOR: Captain, please, the lifeboats, sir . . .

CAPTAIN: Keep your pants on, for God's sake! (*Goes back to singing.*)

VICTORIA, RICHARD, CAPTAIN:

> E'en though it be a cross,
> That raiseth me . . .

LIDIA (*shouting over the singing*): Teddy and I have an announcement!

RICHARD: We've all heard quite enough from you, thank you.

VICTORIA: Teddy and you have both become spiteful.

VICTORIA, RICHARD, CAPTAIN:

> Still all my song shall be,
> Nearer my God to Thee,
> Nearer my God to Thee,
> Nearer to . . .

LIDIA (*shouting over the above singing*): This isn't Teddy.

There is no Teddy. This is my hedgehog. GO GET 'EM, HEDGEHOG!

(VICTORIA, RICHARD, *and the* CAPTAIN *continue singing.* TEDDY *takes out a gun and shoots* VICTORIA *and* RICHARD. *The* CAPTAIN *does not notice.*)

RICHARD (*dying*): Victoria.

VICTORIA (*dying*): Richard.

(*Lights dim to black.*)

(*In blackout, the sounds of sinking continue until suddenly we hear the sound of a needle being knocked off a record and then silence.*)

VOICE OF CAPTAIN: This is your Captain speaking. Everything is all right again.

SCENE 12

Same as before. The dead bodies of VICTORIA *and* RICHARD *have been propped up in chairs, side by side for the coming funeral.* TEDDY *and* LIDIA *are apart by themselves.*

LIDIA: We keep almost sinking.

TEDDY: I wonder where I got the gun.

LIDIA: Do you think the Captain noticed who shot them?

TEDDY: No. Do you?

LIDIA: No.

(*Enter the* CAPTAIN *and* SAILOR. CAPTAIN *wears a black arm band.* SAILOR *perhaps has flowers for the two corpses.*)

CAPTAIN: We are gathered here to mourn the passing of Richard and Victoria Tammurai, passengers on the S.S. *Titanic* and fellow seafarers on the voyage of Life. They were fine, worthy people, good manners, good stock, good breeding, generally the sort of people one would want to be passengers on one's boat. I remember the first time I met Mr. and Mrs. Tammurai. It was . . . (*can't remember, becomes disturbed*). Higgins . . . (*He and* SAILOR *whisper for a bit;* SAILOR *can't seem to help him.*)

TEDDY (*during* CAPTAIN's *whispering*): I feel better having killed them, don't you?

LIDIA: I miss my hedgehog. Listen! I think I hear something. Like the ship scraping an iceberg . . .

(*They listen.*)

CAPTAIN (*having remembered; starting again*): I first met Mr. and . . .

LIDIA: SSSSSHH! (*She and* TEDDY *listen;* CAPTAIN *is insulted.*)

TEDDY: I don't hear anything.

LIDIA: Oh why won't we sink, why? (*To* CAPTAIN:) You can go on.

CAPTAIN: You've made me forget again. (*Sour humor.*) Higgins, the funeral's over. Throw them overboard.

SAILOR: Yes sir.

LIDIA: Sssssh. (TEDDY *and she listen.*) No.

SAILOR (*trying to budge them*): I can't move them alone, sir. (*Looks at* CAPTAIN *and* TEDDY.)

TEDDY: I don't want to touch them.

CAPTAIN: Well, I can't lift them, Higgins.

LIDIA: Ssssssh. Listen. No.

SAILOR: But what shall I do?

CAPTAIN (*irritated*): Well, we'll just have to let them sit here and decompose until they're lighter and you can lift them.

SAILOR: Yes sir.

CAPTAIN: This has been a most dissatisfactory . . .

LIDIA: Sssssh! (*Listens.*)

CAPTAIN: I do not wish to be shushed again, young lady.

LIDIA: I'm listening for the bottom to rip.

CAPTAIN: In my day young ladies occupied themselves in more constructive social activities. Higgins, bring me the log.

SAILOR: Yes sir. (*Gives it to him.*)

CAPTAIN (*with great authority, glaring at* LIDIA): I am now going to enter a complaint against you in the log. What longitude and latitude are we, Higgins?

SAILOR: I don't know, sir.

CAPTAIN: No matter. (*Makes them up.*) Longitude 35, latitude 87. I hereby register a complaint against a certain young woman . . . (*Continues writing, moving his lips to himself. SAILOR stands at attention.*)

TEDDY: I'm going to wake up now. (*Closes his eyes, opens them again, hoping to have awakened out of a dream; he hasn't though; patiently he tries again; then again, this time pinching himself; he can't wake up; keeps trying.*)

LIDIA: Listen . . . (*She listens hopefully. LIDIA keeps listening; TEDDY keeps trying to wake up; CAPTAIN keeps writing in his log and moving his lips; SAILOR stands at attention.*)

(*Lights dim to black.*)

The Actor's Nightmare

The Actor's Nightmare was first presented by Playwrights Horizons in New York City on a double bill with *Sister Mary Ignatius Explains It All for You* on October 14, 1981. The production was directed by Jerry Zaks, set design by Karen Schulz, costume design by William Ivey Long, lighting design by Paul Gallo, sound design by Aural Fixation; production stage manager was Esther Cohen. The cast was as follows:

GEORGE SPELVIN	Jeff Brooks
MEG, the stage manager	Polly Draper
SARAH SIDDONS	Elizabeth Franz
DAME ELLEN TERRY	Mary Catherine Wright
HENRY IRVING	Timothy Landfield

During the subsequent run of *The Actor's Nightmare* and *Sister Mary Ignatius*, the following actors also joined the production: as Meg in *Actor's* and Diane in *Sister*, Carolyn Mignini, Brenda Currin; as Sarah and Sister Mary, Nancy Marchand; as Ellen and Philomena, Deborah Rush, Alice Playten, Cynthia Darlow; as Henry and Gary, Jeff Hayenga, Mark Herrier; and as Thomas in *Sister*, Evan Sandman, Guy Paris Thompson.

SCENE: *Basically an empty stage, maybe with a few set pieces on it or around it.*

GEORGE SPELVIN, *a young man (twenty to thirty), wanders in. He looks baffled and uncertain about where he is.*

Enter MEG, *the stage manager. In jeans and sweat shirt, perhaps, pleasant, efficient, age twenty-five to thirty probably.*

GEORGE: Oh, I'm sorry. I don't know how I got in here.

MEG: Oh thank goodness you're here. I've been calling you.

GEORGE: Pardon?

MEG: An awful thing has happened. Eddie's been in a car accident, and you'll have to go on for him.

GEORGE: Good heavens, how awful. Who's Eddie?

MEG: Eddie. (*He looks blank.*) Edwin. You have to go on for him.

GEORGE: On for him.

MEG: Well he can't go on. He's been in a car accident.

GEORGE: Yes I understood that part. But what do you mean "go on for him"?

MEG: You play the part. Now I know you haven't had a chance to rehearse it exactly, but presumably you know your lines, and you've certainly seen it enough.

GEORGE: I don't understand. Do I know you?

MEG: George, we really don't have time for this kind of joshing. Half-hour.

(*Exits.*)

GEORGE: My name isn't George, it's . . . well, I don't know what it is, but it isn't George.

(*Enter* SARAH SIDDONS, *a glamorous actress, perhaps in a sweeping cape.*)

SARAH: My God, did you hear about Eddie?

GEORGE: Yes I did.

SARAH: It's just too, too awful. Now good luck tonight, George darling, we're all counting on you. Of course, you're a little too young for the part, and you are shorter than Edwin so we'll cut all the lines about bumping your head on the ceiling. And don't forget when I cough three times, that's your cue to unzip the back of my dress and then I'll slap you. We changed it from last night. (*She starts to exit.*)

GEORGE: Wait, please. What play are we doing exactly?

SARAH (*stares at him*): What?

GEORGE: What is the play, please.

SARAH: Coward.

GEORGE: Pardon?

SARAH: Coward. (*Looks at him as if he's crazy.*) It's the Coward. Noel Coward. (*Suddenly relaxing.*) George, don't do that. For a second, I thought you were serious. Break a leg, darling.

(*Exits.*)

GEORGE (*to himself*): Coward. I wonder if it's *Private Lives.* At least I've seen that one. I don't remember rehearsing it exactly. And am I an actor? I thought I was an accountant. And why does everyone call me George?

(*Enter* DAME ELLEN TERRY, *younger than* SARAH, *a bit less grand.*)

ELLEN: Hello, Stanley. I heard about Edwin. Good luck tonight. We're counting on you.

GEORGE: Wait. What play are we doing?

ELLEN: Very funny, Stanley.

GEORGE: No really. I've forgotten.

ELLEN: *Checkmate.*

GEORGE: *Checkmate?*

ELLEN: By Samuel Beckett. You know, in the garbage cans. You always play these jokes, Stanley, just don't do it onstage. Well, good luck tonight. I mean, break a leg. Did you hear? Edwin broke both legs.

(*Exits.*)

GEORGE: I've never heard of *Checkmate.*

(*Re-enter* MEG.)

MEG: George, get into costume. We have fifteen minutes.

(*Exits. Enter* HENRY IRVING, *age twenty-eight to thirty-three, also grand, proud of his resonant voice.*)

HENRY: Good God, I'm late. Hi, Eddie. Oh you're not Eddie. Who are you?

GEORGE: You've never seen me before?

HENRY: Who the devil are you?

GEORGE: I don't really know. George, I think. Maybe Stanley, but probably George. I think I'm an accountant.

HENRY: Look, no one's allowed backstage before a performance. So you'll have to leave, or I'll be forced to report you to the stage manager.

GEORGE: Oh she knows I'm here already.

HENRY: Oh. Well, if Meg knows you're here it must be alright. I suppose. It's not my affair. I'm late enough already.

(*Exits.*)

MEG (*offstage*): Ten minutes, the call is ten minutes, everybody.

GEORGE: I better just go home. (*Takes off his pants.*) Oh dear, I didn't mean to do that.

(*Enter* MEG.)

MEG: George, stop that. Go into the dressing room to change. Really, you keep this up and we'll bring you up on charges.

GEORGE: But where is the dressing room?

MEG: George, you're not amusing. It's that way. And give me those. (*Takes his pants.*) I'll go soak them for you.

GEORGE: Please don't soak my pants.

MEG: Don't tell me my job. Now go get changed. The call is five minutes. (*Pushes him off to dressing room; crosses back the other way, calling out.*) Five minutes, everyone. Five minutes. Places.

(*Exits. A curtain closes on the stage. Darkness. Lights come up on the curtain.* MEG's *voice is heard.*)

VOICE: Ladies and gentlemen, may I have your attention please? At this evening's performance, the role of Elyot, normally played by Edwin Booth, will be played by George Spelvin. The role of Amanda, normally played by Sarah Bernhardt, will be played by Sarah Siddons. The role of Kitty the barmaid will be played by Mrs. Patrick Campbell. Dr. Crippin will play himself. The management wishes to remind the audience that the taking of photographs is strictly forbidden by law, and is dangerous as it may disorient the actor. Thank you.

(*The curtain opens. There is very little set, but probably a small set piece to indicate the railing of a terrace balcony. Some other set piece [a chair, a table, a cocktail bar] might be used to indicate wealth, elegance, French Riviera.*

SARAH SIDDONS *is present when the curtain opens. She is in a glamorous evening gown, and is holding a cocktail glass and standing behind the terrace railing, staring out above the audience's head. There is the sound of applause.*

After a moment GEORGE *arrives onstage, fairly pushed on. He is dressed as Hamlet—black leotard and large gold medallion around his neck. As soon as he enters, several flash photos are taken, which disorient him greatly. When he can, he looks out and sees the audience and is very taken aback.*

We hear music.)

SARAH: Extraordinary how potent cheap music is.

GEORGE: What?

SARAH: Extraordinary how potent cheap music is.

GEORGE: Yes, that's true. Am I supposed to be Hamlet?

SARAH (*alarmed; then going on*): Whose yacht do you think that is?

GEORGE: Where?

SARAH: The duke of Westminster, I expect. It always is.

GEORGE: Ah, well, perhaps. To be or not to be. I don't know any more of it.

(*She looks irritated at him; then she coughs three times. He unzips her dress; she slaps him.*)

SARAH: Elyot, please. We are on our honeymoons.

GEORGE: Are we?

SARAH: Yes. (*Irritated, being over-explicit.*) Me with Victor, and you with Sibyl.

GEORGE: Ah.

SARAH: Tell me about Sibyl.

GEORGE: I've never met her.

SARAH: Ah, Elyot, you're so amusing. You're married to Sibyl. Tell me about her.

GEORGE: Nothing much to tell really. She's sort of nondescript, I'd say.

SARAH: I bet you were going to say that she's just like Lady Bundle, and that she has several chins, and one blue eye and one brown eye, and a third eye in the center of her forehead. Weren't you?

GEORGE: Yes. I think so.

SARAH: Victor's like that, too. (*Long pause.*) I bet you were just about to tell me that you traveled around the world.

GEORGE: Yes I was. I traveled around the world.

SARAH: How was it?

GEORGE: The world?

SARAH: Yes.

GEORGE: Oh, very nice.

SARAH: I always feared the Taj Mahal would look like a biscuit box. Did it?

GEORGE: Not really.

SARAH (*she's going to give him the cue again*): I always feared the Taj Mahal would look like a biscuit box. Did it?

GEORGE: I guess it did.

SARAH (*again*): I always feared the Taj Mahal would look like a biscuit box. Did it?

GEORGE: Hard to say. What brand biscuit box?

SARAH: I always feared the Taj Mahal would look like a biscuit box. Did it? (*Pause.*) Did it? Did it?

GEORGE: I wonder whose yacht that is out there.

SARAH: Did it? Did it? Did it? Did it?

(*Enter* MEG. *She's put on an apron and maid's hat*

and carries a duster, but is otherwise still in her stage manager's garb.)

MEG: My, this balcony looks dusty. I think I'll just clean it up a little. (*Dusts and goes to* GEORGE *and whispers in his ear; exits.*)

GEORGE: Not only did the Taj Mahal look like a biscuit box, but women should be struck regularly, like gongs.

(*Applause.*)

SARAH: Extraordinary how potent cheap music is.

GEORGE: Yes. Quite extraordinary.

SARAH: How was China?

GEORGE: China?

SARAH: You traveled around the world. How was China?

GEORGE: I liked it, but I felt homesick.

SARAH (*again this is happening; gives him cue again*): How was China?

GEORGE: Lots of rice. The women bind their feet.

SARAH: How was China?

GEORGE: I hated it. I missed you.

SARAH: How was China?

GEORGE: I hated it. I missed . . . Sibyl.

SARAH: *How was China?*

GEORGE: I . . . miss the maid. Oh, maid!

SARAH: HOW WAS CHINA?

GEORGE: Just wait a moment please. Oh, maid!

(*Enter* MEG.)

Ah, there you are. I think you missed a spot here.

(*She crosses, dusts, and whispers in his ear; exits.*)

SARAH: How was China?

GEORGE (*with authority*): Very large, China.

SARAH: And Japan?

GEORGE (*doesn't know, but makes a guess*): Very . . . small, Japan.

SARAH: And Ireland?

GEORGE: Very . . . green.

SARAH: And Iceland?

GEORGE: Very white.

SARAH: And Italy?

GEORGE: Very . . . Neapolitan.

SARAH: And Copenhagen?

GEORGE: Very . . . cosmopolitan.

SARAH: And Florida?

GEORGE: Very . . . condominium.

SARAH: And Perth Amboy?

GEORGE: Very . . . mobile home, I don't know.

SARAH: And Sibyl?

GEORGE: What?

SARAH: Do you love Sibyl?

GEORGE: Who's Sibyl?

SARAH: Your new wife, who you married after you and I got our divorce.

GEORGE: Oh, were we married? Oh, yes, I forgot that part.

SARAH: Elyot, you're so amusing. You make me laugh all the time. (*Laughs.*) So, do you love Sibyl?

GEORGE: Probably. I married her.

(*Pause. She coughs three times, he unzips her dress, she slaps him.*)

SARAH: Oh, Elyot, darling, I'm sorry. We were mad to have left each other. Kiss me.

(*They kiss. Enter* DAME ELLEN TERRY *as Sibyl, in an evening gown.*)

ELLEN: Oh, how ghastly.

SARAH: Oh dear. And this must be Sibyl.

ELLEN: Oh, how ghastly. What shall we do?

SARAH: We must all speak in very low voices and attempt to be civilized.

ELLEN: Is this Amanda? Oh, Elyot, I think she's simply obnoxious.

SARAH: How very rude.

ELLEN: Oh, Elyot, how can you treat me like this?

GEORGE: Hello, Sibyl.

ELLEN: Well, since you ask, I'm very upset. I was inside writing a letter to your mother and wanted to know how to spell apothecary.

SARAH: A-P-O-T-H-E-C-A-R-Y.

ELLEN (*icy*): Thank you. (*She writes it down;* SARAH *looks over her shoulder.*)

SARAH: Don't scribble, Sibyl.

ELLEN: Did my eyes deceive me, or were you kissing my husband a moment ago?

SARAH: We must all speak in very low voices and attempt to be civilized.

ELLEN: I was speaking in a low voice.

SARAH: Yes, but I could still hear you.

ELLEN: Oh. Sorry. (*Speaks too low to be heard.*)

SARAH: (*Speaks inaudibly also.*)

ELLEN: (*Speaks inaudibly.*)

SARAH: (*Speaks inaudibly.*)

ELLEN: (*Speaks inaudibly.*)

SARAH: I can't hear a bloody word she's saying. The woman's a nincompoop. Say something, Elyot.

GEORGE: I couldn't hear her either.

ELLEN: Elyot, you have to choose between us immediately—do you love this creature, or do you love me?

GEORGE: I wonder where the maid is.

ELLEN and SARAH (*together, furious*): Forget about the maid, Elyot! (*They look embarrassed.*)

ELLEN: You could never have a lasting relationship with a maid. Choose between the two of us.

GEORGE: I choose . . . Oh God, I don't know my lines. I don't know how I got here. I wish I *weren't* here. I wish I had joined the monastery like I almost did right after high school. I almost joined, but then I didn't.

SARAH (*trying to cover*): Oh, Elyot, your malaria is acting up again and you're ranting. Come, come, who do you choose, me or that baggage over there.

ELLEN: You're the baggage, not I. Yes, Elyot, who do you choose?

GEORGE: I choose . . . (*To* SARAH:) I'm sorry, what is your name?

SARAH: Amanda.

GEORGE: I choose Amanda. I think that's what he does in the play.

ELLEN: Very well. I can accept defeat gracefully. I don't think I'll send this letter to your mother. She has a loud voice and an overbearing manner and I don't like her taste in tea china. I hope, Elyot, that when you find me hanging from the hotel lobby chandelier with my eyes all bulged out and my tongue hanging out, that you'll be very, very sorry. Goodbye.

(*Exits.*)

SARAH: What a dreadful sport she is.

GEORGE (*doing his best to say something his character might*): Poor Sibyl. She's going to hang herself.

SARAH: Some women should be hung regularly, like tapestries. Oh who cares? Whose yacht do you think that is?

GEORGE (*remembering*): The duke of Westminster, I exp . . .

SARAH (*furious*): How dare you mention that time in Mozambique? (*Slaps him.*) Oh, darling, I'm sorry. (*Moving her cigarette grandly.*) I love you madly!

GEORGE (*gasps*): I've inhaled your cigarette ash. (*He coughs three times.* SARAH *looks confused, then unzips the front of his Hamlet doublet. He looks confused, then slaps her. She slaps him back with a vengeance. They both look confused.*)

SARAH: There, we're not angry anymore, are we? Oh, Elyot, wait for me here and I'll pack my things and we'll run away together before Victor gets back. Oh, darling, isn't it extraordinary how potent cheap music can be?

(*She exits; recorded applause on her exit.* GEORGE *sort of follows a bit, but then turns back to face the audience. Flash photos are taken again;* GEORGE *blinks and is disoriented. Lights change, the sound of trumpets is heard, and* HENRY IRVING, *dressed in Shakespearean garb, enters and bows grandly to* GEORGE.)

HENRY: Hail to your Lordship!

GEORGE: Oh hello. Are you Victor?

HENRY: The same, my Lord, and your poor servant ever.

GEORGE: This doesn't sound like Noel Coward.

HENRY: A truant disposition, good my Lord.

GEORGE: You're not Victor, are you?

HENRY: My Lord, I came to see your father's funeral.

GEORGE: Oh yes? And how was it?

HENRY: Indeed, my Lord, it followed hard upon.

GEORGE: Hard upon? Yes, I see.

(*Enter* MEG.)

Oh, good, the maid. (*He rushes to her. She whispers his line to him, which he dutifully reiterates.*) Thrift, thrift, Horatio. The funeral baked meats did coldly furnish forth the marriage tables.

(MEG *exits.*)

What does that mean??? (*Looks off after the disappearing* MEG.) Ah, she's gone already.

HENRY: My Lord, I think I saw him yesternight.

GEORGE: Did you? Who?

HENRY: My Lord, the king your father.

GEORGE: The king my father?

HENRY: Season your admiration for a while with an attent ear till I may deliver upon the witness of these gentlemen this marvel to you.

GEORGE: I see. I'm Hamlet now, right?

HENRY: Ssssh! (*Rattling this off in a very Shakespearean way.*)

Two nights together had these gentlemen,
Marcellus and Bernardo, on their watch
In the dead waste and middle of the night
Been thus encountered. A figure like your father,
Arméd at point exactly, cap-a-pe,
Appears before them and with solemn march
Goes slow and stately by them. Thrice he walked

By their oppressed and fear-surprised eyes
Within his truncheon's length, whilst they, distilled
Almost to jelly with the act of fear,
Stand dumb and speak not to him. This to me
In dreadful secrecy impart they did,
And I with them the third night kept the watch,
Where, as they had delivered, both in time,
Form of the thing, each word made true and good,
The apparition comes. I knew your father.
These hands are not more like.

GEORGE: Oh, my turn? Most strange and wondrous tale you tell, Horatio. It doth turn my ear into a very . . . (*at a loss*) merry . . . bare bodkin.

HENRY:

As I do live, my honored lord, 'tis true,
And we did think it writ down in our duty
To let you know of it.

GEORGE: Well, thank you very much. (*Pause.*)

HENRY: Oh yes, my Lord. He wore his beaver up.

GEORGE: His beaver up. He wore his beaver up. And does he usually wear it down?

HENRY: A countenance more in sorrow than in anger.

GEORGE: Well I am sorry to hear that. My father was a king of much renown. A favorite . . . (*suddenly finds himself unable to rhyme*) . . . amongst all in London town! (*Delighted with himself, he grins at audience, then realizes there's a problem.*) And in Denmark.

HENRY: I war'nt it will.

GEORGE: I war'nt it will also.

HENRY: Our duty to your honor.

(*Exits.*)

GEORGE: Where are you going? Don't go.

(*He smiles out at audience. Enter* SARAH *dressed as Queen Gertrude.*)

Oh, Amanda, good to see you. Whose yacht do you think that is?

SARAH:

O Hamlet, speak no more.
Thou turn'st mine eyes into my very soul,
And there I see such black and grainéd spots
As will not leave their tinct.

GEORGE: I haven't seen Victor. Someone was here who I thought might have been him, but it wasn't.

SARAH:

O speak to me no more.
These words like daggers enter in mine ears.
No more, sweet Hamlet.

GEORGE: Very well. What do you want to talk about?

SARAH: No more!

(*Exits.*)

GEORGE: Oh don't go. (*Pause; smiles uncomfortably at the audience.*) Maybe someone else will come out in a

minute. (*Pause.*) Of course, sometimes people have
soliloquies in Shakespeare. Let's just wait a moment
more and maybe someone will come.

(*The lights suddenly change to a dim blue background and one bright, white spot center stage.
GEORGE is not standing in the spot.*)

Oh dear.

(*He moves somewhat awkwardly into the spot, de-
cides to do his best to live up to the requirements of
the moment.*)

To be or not to be, that is the question.
Oh maid!

(*No response; remembers that actors call for "line."*)

Line! Line! Ohhh.

O, what a rogue and peasant slave am I.
Whether 'tis nobler in the mind's eye to kill oneself,
or not killing oneself, to sleep a great deal.
We are such stuff as dreams are made on; and
our lives are rounded by a little sleep.

(*The lights change. The spot goes out, and another
one comes onstage right. GEORGE moves into it.*)

Uh, thrift, thrift, Horatio. Neither a borrower
nor a lender be. But to thine own self be true.
There is a special providence in the fall of a sparrow.
Extraordinary how potent cheap music can be.
Out, out, damn spot! I come to wive it wealthily in
Padua; if wealthily, then happily in Padua.

(*Sings:*) Brush up your Shakespeare; start quoting him now; da da . . .

(*Lights change again. That spot goes off; another one comes on, center stage, though closer to audience.* GEORGE *moves into that.*)

I wonder whose yacht that is. How was China? Very large, China. How was Japan? Very small, Japan.

I pledge allegiance to the flag of the United States of America and to the republic for which it stands, one nation, under God, indivisible with liberty and justice for all.

Line! Line! Oh my God. (*Gets idea.*)

O my God, I am heartily sorry for having offended thee, and I detest all my sins because I dread the loss of heaven and the pains of hell. But most of all because they offend thee, my God, who art all good and deserving of all my love. And I resolve to confess my sins, to do penance, and to amend my life, Amen. (*Friendly.*) That's the act of contrition that Catholic schoolchildren say in confession in order to be forgiven their sins. Catholic adults say it too, I imagine. I don't know any Catholic adults.

Line! (*Explaining:*) When you call for a line, the stage manager normally gives you your next line, to refresh your memory.

Line!

The quality of mercy is not strained. It droppeth as the gentle rain upon the place below, when we have shuffled off this mortal coil.

Alas, poor Yorick. I knew him well. Get thee to a nunnery.

Line. Nunnery. As a child, I was taught by nuns, and then in high school I was taught by Benedictine priests. I really rather liked the nuns, they were sort of warm, though they were fairly crazy too.

Line.

I liked the priests also. The school was on the grounds of the monastery, and my junior and senior years I spent a few weekends joining in the daily routine of the monastery—prayers, then breakfast, then prayers, then lunch, then prayers, then dinner, then prayers, then sleep. I found the predictability quite attractive. And the food was good. I was going to join the monastery after high school, but they said I was too young and should wait. And then I just stopped believing in all those things, so I never did join the monastery. I became an accountant. I've studied logarithms, and cosine and tangent . . .

(*Furious and despairing:*) Line! (*Totally defeated, apologetic:*) I'm sorry. This is supposed to be *Hamlet* or *Private Lives* or something, and I keep rattling on like a maniac. I really do apologize. I just can't recall attending a *single* rehearsal. I can't imagine what I was doing.

And also you come expecting to see Edwin Booth and you get me. I really am very embarrassed. (*Weakly:*) Sorry. (*Pleading, looks up to heaven:*) Line. (*No response from heaven.*) I have always depended upon the kindness of strangers. (*Yells in the same tone of voice he has yelled for "line":*) STELLA! (*Laughs weakly.*) 'Tis a far, far better thing I do now than I have ever done before, 'tis a far, far better place I go to than I have ever been before. (*Sings the alphabet song.*) A, B, C, D, E, F, G; H, I, J, K, L, M, N, O, P; Q, R, S, T . . .

(*As he starts to sing, enter* ELLEN TERRY, *dragging two large garbage cans. She puts them side by side, gets in one.*)

Oh, good. Are you Ophelia? Get thee to a nunnery.

(*She points to the other garbage can, indicating he should get in it.*)

Get in? Okay. (*He does.*) This must be one of those modern *Hamlets*.

(*Lights change abruptly to "Beckett lighting."*)

ELLEN: Nothing to be done. Pause. Pause. Wrinkle nose. (*Wrinkles nose.*) Nothing to be done.

GEORGE: I guess you're not Ophelia.

ELLEN: We'll just wait. Pause. Either he'll come, pause pause pause, or he won't.

GEORGE: That's a reasonable attitude. Are we, on a guess, waiting for Godot?

ELLEN: No, Willie. He came already and was an awful bore. Yesterday he came. Garlic on his breath, telling a lot of unpleasant jokes about Jews and Polacks and stewardesses. He was just dreadful, pause, rolls her eyes upward. (*She rolls her eyes upward.*)

GEORGE: Well I am sorry to hear that. Pause. So who are we waiting for?

ELLEN: We're waiting for Lefty.

GEORGE: Ah. And is he a political organizer or something, I seem to recall?

ELLEN: Yes, dear, he is a political organizer. He's always coming around saying get involved, get off your behind and organize, fight the system, do this, do that, uh, he's exhausting, he's worse than Jane Fonda. And he has garlic breath just like Godot, I don't know which of them is worse, and I hope neither of them ever comes here again. Blinks left eye, blinks right eye, closes eyes, opens them. (*Does this.*)

GEORGE: So we're really not waiting for anyone, are we?

ELLEN: No, dear, we're not. It's just another happy day, pause, smile, pause, picks nit from head. (*Picks nit from head.*)

GEORGE: Do you smell something?

ELLEN: That's not your line. Willie doesn't have that many lines. (*Louder.*) Oh, Willie, how talkative you are this morning!

GEORGE: There seems to be some sort of muck at the bottom of this garbage can.

ELLEN: Mustn't complain, Willie. There's muck at the bottom of everyone's garbage can. Count your blessings, Willie. I do. (*Counts to herself, eyes closed.*) One. Two. Three. Are you counting, Willie?

GEORGE: I guess so.

ELLEN: I'm up to three. Three is my eyesight. (*Opens her eyes.*) Oh my God, I've gone blind. I can't see, Willie. Oh my God. Oh what a terrible day. Oh dear. Oh my. (*Suddenly very cheerful again.*) Oh well. Not so bad really. I only used my eyes occasionally. When I wanted to see something. But no more!

GEORGE: I really don't know *this* play at all.

ELLEN: Count your blessings, Willie. Let me hear you count them.

GEORGE: Alright. One. Two. Three. That's my eyesight. Four. That's my hearing. Five, that's my . . . Master Charge. Six, that's . . .

ELLEN: Did you say God, Willie?

GEORGE: No.

ELLEN: Why did you leave the monastery, Willie? Was it the same reason I left the opera?

GEORGE: I have no idea.

ELLEN: I left the opera because I couldn't sing. They were mad to have hired me. Certifiable. And they *were* certified shortly afterward, the entire staff. They reside now at the Rigoletto Home for the Mentally Incapacitated. In Turin. Pause. Tries to touch her nose with her tongue. (*Does this. Meg's voice is heard.*)

VOICE: Ladies and gentlemen, may I have your attention please?

ELLEN: Oh, Willie, listen. A voice. Perhaps there is a God.

VOICE: At this evening's performance, the role of Sir Thomas More, the man for all seasons, normally played by Edwin Booth, will be played by George Spelvin. The role of Lady Alice, normally played by Sarah Bernhardt, will be played by Sarah Siddons. The role of Lady Margaret, normally played by Eleonora Duse, will be read by the stage manager. And at this evening's performance the executioner will play himself.

GEORGE: What did she say?

ELLEN: The executioner will play himself.

GEORGE: What does she mean, the executioner will play himself?

(*Enter* SARAH *as Lady Alice* [*Sir Thomas More's wife*] *and* MEG *with a few costume touches but otherwise in her stage manager's garb and carrying a script as Lady Margaret* [*Sir Thomas More's daughter*].)

MEG: Oh Father, why have they locked you up in this dreadful dungeon, it's more than I can bear.

SARAH: I've brought you a custard, Thomas.

MEG: Mother's brought you a custard, Father.

GEORGE: Yes, thank you.

MEG: Oh Father, if you don't give in to King Henry, they're going to cut your head off.

SARAH: Aren't you going to eat the custard I brought you, Thomas?

GEORGE: I'm not hungry, thank you.

(*Sudden alarming crash of cymbals, or something similarly startling musically occurs. The* EXECU-TIONER *appears upstage. He is dressed as the traditional headsman—the black mask, bare chest and arms, the large ax.*)

GEORGE: Oh my God, I've got to get out of here.

MEG: He's over here. And he'll never give in to the King.

GEORGE: No, no, I might. Quick, is this all about Anne Boleyn and everything?

MEG: Yes, and you won't give in because you believe in the Catholic Church and the infallibility of the Pope and the everlasting life of the soul.

GEORGE: I don't necessarily believe in any of that. (*To* EXE-CUTIONER:) Oh, sir, there's been an error. I think it's fine if the King marries Anne Boleyn. I just want to wake up.

MEG: Oh don't deny God, Father, just to spare our feelings.

Mother and I are willing to have you dead if it's a question of principle.

SARAH: The first batch of custard didn't come out all that well, Thomas. This is the second batch. But it has a piece of hair in it, I think.

GEORGE: Oh shut up about your custard, would you? I don't think the Pope is infallible at all. I think he's a normal man with normal capabilities who wears gold slippers. I thought about joining the monastery when I was younger, but I didn't do it.

ELLEN (*waking up from a brief doze*): Oh I was having such a pleasant dream, Willie. Go ahead, let him cut your head off, it'll be a nice change of pace.

(*The* EXECUTIONER, *who has been motionless, now moves. In a sudden gesture, he kicks one of the* Private Lives *set pieces—a balustrade, or perhaps an Art Deco cube with cocktail glasses on it; this set piece suddenly breaks apart, revealing within it the bloodied cutting block that waits for* GEORGE's *head.*)

GEORGE: That blade looks very real to me. I want to wake up now. Or change plays. I wonder whose yacht that is out there.

(SARAH *offers him the custard again.*)

No, thank you! A horse, a horse! My kingdom for a horse!

EXECUTIONER: Sir Thomas More, you have been found guilty of the charge of High Treason. The sentence of the court is that you be taken to the Tower of London, thence to the place of execution, and there your head shall be stricken from your body, and may God have mercy on your soul.

(MEG *helps* GEORGE *out of the garbage can.*)

GEORGE: All this talk about God. Alright, I'm sorry I didn't join the monastery, maybe I should have, and I'm sorry I giggled during Mass in third grade, but I see no reason to be killed for it.

ELLEN: Nothing to be done. That's what I find so wonderful.

(MEG *puts* GEORGE's *head on the block.*)

GEORGE: No!

EXECUTIONER: Do I understand you right? You wish to reverse your previous stand on King Henry's marriage to Anne and to deny the Bishop of Rome?

GEORGE: Yes, yes, God, yes. I could care less. Let him marry eight wives.

EXECUTIONER: That's a terrible legacy of cowardice for Sir Thomas More to leave behind.

GEORGE: I don't care.

EXECUTIONER: I'm going to ignore what you've said and cut your head off anyway, and then we'll all pretend you went to your death nobly. The Church needs its saints, and schoolchildren have got to have heroes to look up to, don't you all agree?

ELLEN: I agree. I know I need someone to look up to. Pause smile picks her nose. (*Does this.*)

GEORGE: Yes, yes, I can feel myself waking up now. The covers have fallen off the bed, and I'm cold, and I'm going to wake up so that I can reach down and pull them up again.

EXECUTIONER: Sir Thomas, prepare to meet your death.

GEORGE: Be quiet, I'm about to wake up.

EXECUTIONER: Sir Thomas, prepare to meet your death.

GEORGE: I'm awake! (*Looks around him;* SARAH *offers him custard again.*) No, I'm not.

SARAH: He doesn't know his lines.

EXECUTIONER: Sir Thomas, prepare to meet your death.

GEORGE (*frantic*): Line! Line!

MEG: You turn to the executioner and say, "Friend, be not afraid of your office. You send me to God."

GEORGE: I don't like that line. Give me another.

MEG: That's the line in the script, George. Say it.

GEORGE: I don't want to.

MEG: Say it.

ELLEN: Say it, Willie. It'll mean a lot to me and to generations of schoolchildren to come.

SARAH: O Hamlet, speak the speech, I pray you, trippingly on the tongue.

EXECUTIONER: Say it!

GEORGE: Friend, be not afraid of your office. You send me . . . Extraordinary how potent cheap music is.

MEG: That's not the line.

GEORGE: Women should be struck regularly, like gongs.

MEG: George, say the line right.

GEORGE: They say you can never dream your own death, so I expect I'll wake up just as soon as he starts to bring the blade down. So perhaps I should get it over with.

MEG: Say the proper line, George.

GEORGE: Friend, be not afraid of your office.

ELLEN: Goodbye, Willie.

SARAH: Goodbye, Hamlet.

MEG: Goodbye, George.

EXECUTIONER: Goodbye, Sir Thomas.

GEORGE: You send me to God.

(EXECUTIONER *raises the ax to bring it down. Black-out. Sound of the ax coming down.*)

EXECUTIONER (*in darkness*): Behold the head of Sir Thomas More.

ELLEN (*in darkness*): Oh I wish I weren't blind and could see that, Willie. Oh well, no matter. It's still been another happy day. Pause, smile, wrinkles nose, pause, picks nit from head, pause, pause, wiggles ears, all in darkness, utterly useless, no one can see her. She stares ahead. Count two. End of play.

(*Music plays. Maybe canned applause. Lights come up for curtain calls. The four take their bows. [If* HENRY IRVING *does not play the* EXECUTIONER, *he comes out for his bow as well.*] SARAH *and* ELLEN *have fairly elaborate bows, perhaps receiving flowers from the* EXECUTIONER. *They gesture for* GEORGE *to take his bow, but he seems to be dead. They applaud him, and then bow again, and lights out.*)

Sister Mary Ignatius
Explains It All
for You

Sister Mary Ignatius Explains It All for You was first presented by the Ensemble Studio Theatre in New York City on a bill with one-act plays by David Mamet, Marsha Norman, and Tennessee Williams on December 14, 1979. The production was directed by Jerry Zaks, set design by Brian Martin, light design by Marie Louise Moreto, costume design by Madeline Cohen. The cast was as follows:

SISTER MARY IGNATIUS	Elizabeth Franz
THOMAS	Mark Stefan
GARY SULLAVAN	Gregory Grove
DIANE SYMONDS	Ann McDonough
PHILOMENA ROSTOVITCH	Prudence Wright Holmes
ALOYSIUS BUSICCIO	Don Marino

Sister Mary Ignatius Explains It All for You was then presented off-Broadway by Playwrights Horizons in New York City on a double bill with *The Actor's Nightmare* on October 14, 1981. The production was directed by Jerry Zaks, set design by Karen Schulz, costume design by William Ivey Long, lighting design by Paul Gallo, sound design by Aural Fixation; production stage manager was Esther Cohen. The cast was as follows:

SISTER MARY IGNATIUS	Elizabeth Franz
THOMAS	Mark Stefan
GARY SULLAVAN	Timothy Landfield
DIANE SYMONDS	Polly Draper
PHILOMENA ROSTOVITCH	Mary Catherine Wright
ALOYSIUS BENHEIM	Jeff Brooks

SCENE: *The stage is fairly simple. There should be a lectern, a potted palm, a few chairs. There is also an easel, or some sort of stand, on which are several drawings made on cardboard; the only one we can see at the top of the play is either blank or is a simple cross.*

Enter SISTER MARY IGNATIUS, *dressed in an old-fashioned nun's habit.* SISTER *looks at the audience until she has their attention, then smiles, albeit somewhat wearily. She then begins her lecture, addressing the audience directly.*

SISTER (*crossing herself*): In the name of the Father, and of the Son, and of the Holy Ghost, Amen. (*Shows the next drawing on the easel, which is a neat if childlike picture of the planet earth, the sun, and moon.*) First there is the earth. Near the earth is the sun, and also nearby is the moon. (*Goes to next picture which, split in three, shows the gates of heaven amid clouds; some sort of murky area of paths, or some other image that might suggest waiting, wandering; and a third area of people burning up in flames, with little devils with little pitchforks, poking them.*) Outside the universe, where we go after death, is heaven, hell, and purgatory. Heaven is where we live in eternal bliss with our Lord Jesus Christ. (*Bows her head.*) Hell is where we are eternally deprived of the presence of our Lord Jesus Christ (*bows her head*), and are thus miserable. This is the greatest agony of hell, but there are also unspeakable physical torments, which we shall nonetheless speak of later. Purgatory is the middle area where we go after death to suffer if we have not been perfect in

169

our lives and are thus not ready for heaven, or if we have not received the sacraments and made a good confession to a priest right before our death. Purgatory, depending on our sins, can go on for a very, *very* long time and is fairly unpleasant. Though we do not yet know whether there is any physical torment in purgatory, we do know that there is much psychological torment because we are being delayed from being in the presence of our Lord Jesus Christ. (*Bows her head.*) For those non-Catholics present, I bow my head to show respect for our Savior when I say His Name. Our Lord Jesus Christ. (*Bows head.*) Our Lord Jesus Christ. (*Bows head.*) Our Lord Jesus Christ. (*Bows head.*) You can expect to be in purgatory for anywhere from 300 years to 700 billion years. This may sound like forever, but don't forget in terms of eternity 700 billion years *does* come to an end. All things come to an end except our Lord Jesus Christ. (*Bows head. Points to the drawing again, reviewing her point.*) Heaven, hell, purgatory. (*Smiles. Goes to the next drawing which, like that of purgatory, is of a murky area, perhaps with a prison-like fence, and which has unhappy baby-like creatures floating about in it.*) There is also limbo, which is where unbaptized babies were sent for eternity before the Ecumenical Council and Pope John XXIII. The unbaptized babies sent to limbo never leave limbo and so never get to heaven. *Now* unbaptized babies are sent straight to purgatory where, presumably, someone baptizes them and *then* they are sent on to heaven. The unbaptized babies who died before the Ecumenical Council, however, remain in limbo and will never be admitted to heaven. Limbo is not all that unpleasant, it's just that it isn't heaven and you never leave there. I want to be very clear about the Immaculate Conception. It does not mean that the

Blessed Mother gave birth to Christ without the prior unpleasantness of physical intimacy. That is true but is not called the Immaculate Conception; that is called the Virgin Birth. The Immaculate Conception means that the Blessed Mother was herself born without original sin. Everyone makes this error, it makes me lose my patience. That Mary's conception was immaculate is an infallible statement. A lot of fault-finding non-Catholics run around saying that Catholics believe that the Pope is infallible whenever he speaks. This is untrue. The Pope is infallible only on certain occasions, when he speaks "ex cathedra," which is Latin for "out of the cathedral." When he speaks ex cathedra, we must accept what he says at that moment as dogma, or risk hell fire; or, now that things are becoming more liberal, many, many years in purgatory. I would now like a glass of water. Thomas.

(*Enter* THOMAS, *a parochial school boy wearing tie and blazer.*)

This is Thomas, he is seven years old and in the second grade of Our Lady of Perpetual Sorrow School. Seven is the age of reason, so now that Thomas has turned seven he is capable of choosing to commit sin or not to commit sin, and God will hold him accountable for whatever he does. Isn't that so, Thomas?

THOMAS: Yes, Sister.

SISTER: Before we turn seven, God tends to pay no attention to the bad things we do because He knows we can know no better. Once we turn seven, He feels we are capable of knowing. Thomas, who made you?

THOMAS: God made me.

SISTER: Why did God make you?

THOMAS: God made me to show forth His goodness and share with us His happiness.

SISTER: What is the sixth commandment?

THOMAS: The sixth commandment is thou shalt not commit adultery.

SISTER: What is forbidden by the sixth commandment?

THOMAS: The sixth commandment forbids all impurities in thought, word, or deed, whether alone or with others.

SISTER: That's correct, Thomas. (*Gives him a cookie.*) Thomas has a lovely soprano voice which the Church used to preserve by creating castrati. Thomas unfortunately will lose his soprano voice in a few years and will receive facial hair and psychological difficulties in its place. To me, it is not a worthwhile exchange. You may go now, Thomas. What is the fourth commandment?

THOMAS: The fourth commandment is honor thy mother and thy father.

SISTER: Very good. (*Gives him a cookie. He exits.*) Sometimes in the mornings I look at all the children lining up in front of school, and I'm overwhelmed by a sense of sadness and exhaustion thinking of all the pain and suffering and personal unhappiness they're going to face in their lives. (*Looks sad, eats a cookie.*) But can their suffering compare with Christ's on the cross? Let us think of Christ on the cross for a moment. Try to feel the nails ripping through His hands and feet. Some experts say that the nails actually went through His wrists, which was better for keeping Him up on the cross, though of course most of the statues have the nails going right through His palms. Imagine those nails being driven through: pound, pound, pound, rip, rip, rip. Think of the crown of thorns eating into His skull, and the sense of infection that He must have felt in His brain and near His eyes. Imagine blood from His brain spurting forth through His eyes, imagine His vision squinting through a veil of red liquid. Imagine these things, and then just *dare* to feel sorry for the children lining up outside of school. We dare not; His suffering was greater than ours. He died for our sins! Yours and mine. We put Him up there, you did, all you people sitting out there. He loved us so much that He came all the way down to earth just so He could be nailed painfully to a cross and hang there for three hours. Who else has loved us as much as that? I come from a large family. My father was big and ugly, my mother had a nasty disposition and didn't like me. There were twenty-six of us. It took three hours just to wash the dishes, but Christ hung on that cross for three hours and *He* never complained. We lived in a small, ugly house, and I shared a room with all my sisters. My father would bring home drunken bums off the street, and let them stay in the same room as himself and my mother. "Whatever you do to the least of these, you do also to Me," Christ said. Sometimes these bums would make my mother hysterical, and we'd have to throw water on her. Thomas, could I have some more water please? And some chocolates?

(*Enter* THOMAS.)

Who made you?

THOMAS: God made me.

SISTER: What is the ninth commandment?

THOMAS: The ninth commandment is thou shalt not covet thy neighbor's wife.

SISTER: What is forbidden by the ninth commandment?

THOMAS: The ninth commandment forbids all indecency in thought, word, and deed, whether alone or with thy neighbor's wife.

SISTER: Thank you. Go away again.

(*He exits.*)

Bring the little children unto me, our Lord said. I don't remember in reference to what. I have your questions here on some little file cards. (*Reads:*) If God is all powerful, why does He allow evil in the world? (*Goes to next card with no reaction. Reads:*) Tell us some more about your family. (*Smiles.*) We said grace before every meal. My mother was a terrible cook. She used to boil chopped meat. She hated little children, but they couldn't use birth control. Let me explain this one more time. Birth control is wrong because God, whatever you may think about the wisdom involved, created sex for the purpose of procreation, *not* recreation. Everything in this world has a purpose. We eat food to feed our bodies. We don't eat and then make ourselves throw up immediately afterward, do we? So it should be with sex. Either it is done for its proper purpose, or it is just so much throwing up, morally speaking. Next question. (*Reads:*) Do nuns go to the bathroom? Yes. (*Reads:*) Was Jesus effeminate? Yes. (*Reads:*) I have a brain tumor and am afraid of dying. What should I do? Now I thought I had explained what happens after

death to you already. There is heaven, hell, and purgatory. What's the problem? O ye of little faith, Christ
said to someone. All right. As any seven-year-old
knows, there are two kinds of sin: mortal sin and venial
sin. Venial sin is the less serious kind, like if you tell a
small lie to your parents, or when you take the Lord's
name in vain when you break your thumb with a hammer, or when you kick a barking dog. If you die with
any venial sins on your conscience, no matter how
many of them there are, you can eventually work it all
out in purgatory. However—mortal sin, on the other
hand, is the most serious kind of sin you can do—
murder, sex outside of marriage, hijacking a plane,
masturbation—and if you die with any of these sins on
your soul, even just one, you will go straight to hell and
burn for all of eternity. Now to rid yourself of mortal
sin, you must go make a good confession and vow never
to do it again. If, as many of you know, you are on your
way to confession to confess a mortal sin and you are
struck by a car or bus before you get there, God may
forgive you without confession if before you die you
manage to say a good act of contrition. If you die instan-
taneously and are unable to say a good act of contrition,
you will go straight to hell. Thomas, come read this partial list of those who are going to burn in hell.

(*Enter* THOMAS.)

THOMAS (*reads*): Christine Keeler, Roman Polanski, Zsa Zsa
    Gabor, the editors of *After Dark* magazine, Linda
    Lovelace, Georgina Spelvin, Big John Holmes, Brooke
    Shields, David Bowie, Mick Jagger, Patty Hearst,
    Betty Comden, Adolph Green.

SISTER: This is just a partial list. It is added to constantly.
    Thomas, how can we best keep from going to hell?

THOMAS: By not committing a mortal sin, by keeping close to the sacraments, especially going to confession and receiving communion, and by obeying our parents.

(*She gives him a cookie.*)

SISTER: Good boy. Do you love our Lord, Thomas?

THOMAS: Yes, Sister.

SISTER: How much?

THOMAS: This much. (*Holds arms out wide.*)

SISTER: Well, that's very nice, but Christ loves us an infinite amount. How do we know that, Thomas?

THOMAS: Because you tell us.

SISTER: That's right. And by His actions. He died on the cross for us to make up for our sins. Wasn't that nice of Him?

THOMAS: Very nice.

SISTER: And shouldn't we be grateful?

THOMAS: Yes we should.

SISTER: That's right, we should. (*Gives him a cookie.*) How do you spell cookie?

THOMAS: C-O-O-K-I-E.

SISTER: Very good. (*Gives him a cookie.*) Mary has had an argument with her parents and has shot and killed them. Is that a venial sin or a mortal sin?

THOMAS: That's a mortal sin.

SISTER: If she dies with this mortal sin on her soul, will she go to heaven or to hell?

THOMAS: She will go to hell.

SISTER: Very good. How do you spell ecumenical?

THOMAS (*sounding it out*): Eck—E-C-K; you—U; men—M-E-N; ical—I-C-K-L-E.

SISTER: Very good. (*Gives him a cookie.*) What's two plus two?

THOMAS: Four.

SISTER: What's one and one and one and one and one and one and one and one and one?

THOMAS: Nine.

SISTER: Very good. (*Gives him a cookie.*) Because she is afraid to show her parents her bad report card, Susan goes to the top of a tall building and jumps off. Is this a venial sin or a mortal sin?

THOMAS: Mortal sin.

SISTER: And where will she go?

THOMAS: Hell.

SISTER: Sit on my lap.

(*He does.*)

Would you like to keep your pretty soprano voice forever?

THOMAS: Yes, Sister.

SISTER: Well, we'll see what we can do about it. (*Sings:*)

>Cookies in the morning,
>Cookies in the evening,
>Cookies in the summertime,

Be my little cookie,
And love me all the time.

God, I've done so much talking, I've got to rest my voice some. Here, you take care of some of these questions, Thomas, while I rest, all right, dear? (*She hands him the file cards.*)

THOMAS: Yes, Sister. (*Reads:*) How do we know there is a God? We know that there is a God because the Church tells us so. And also because everything has a primary cause. Dinner is put on the table because the primary cause, our mother, has put it in the oven and cooked it. (*Reads:*) If God is all powerful, why does He allow evil? (*Skips that one; next one:*) What does God look like? God looks like an old man, a young man, and a small white dove.

SISTER: I'll take the next one. (*Reads:*) Are you ever sorry you became a nun? (*With deep sincerity and simplicity.*) I am never sorry I became a nun. (*Reads:*) It used to be a mortal sin to eat meat on Fridays, and now it isn't. Does that mean that people who ate meat on Fridays back when it was a sin are in hell? Or what? People who ate meat on Fridays back when it was a mortal sin are indeed in hell if they did not confess the sin before they died. If they confessed it, they are not in hell, unless they did not confess some other mortal sin they committed. People who would eat meat on Fridays back in the fifties tended to be the sort who would commit other mortal sins, so on a guess, I bet many of them *are* in hell for other sins, even if they did confess the eating of meat. (*Reads:*) What exactly went on in Sodom? (*Irritated.*) Who asked me this question? (*Reads:*) I am an Aries. Is it a sin to follow your horoscope? It is a sin to follow your horoscope because only

God knows the future and He won't tell us. Also, we can tell that horoscopes are false because according to astrology Christ would be a Capricorn, and Capricorn people are cold, ambitious, and attracted to Scorpio and Virgo, and we know that Christ was warm, loving, and not attracted to anybody. Give *me* a cookie, Thomas.

(*He does.*)

I'm going to talk about Sodom a bit. (*Kisses the top of* THOMAS's *head.*) Thomas, please leave the stage.

(*He does.*)

To answer your question, Sodom is where they committed acts of homosexuality and bestiality in the Old Testament, and God, infuriated by this, destroyed them all in one fell swoop. Modern-day Sodoms are New York City, San Francisco, Amsterdam, Los Angeles . . . well, basically anywhere where the population is over fifty thousand. The only reason that God has not destroyed these modern-day Sodoms is that Catholic nuns and priests live in these cities, and God does not wish to destroy them. He does, however, give these people body lice and hepatitis. It's so hard to know why God allows wickedness to flourish. I guess it's because God wants man to choose goodness freely of his own free will; sometimes one wonders if free will is worth all the trouble if there's going to be so much evil and unhappiness, but God knows best, presumably. If it were up to me, I might be tempted to wipe out cities and civilizations, but luckily for New York and Amsterdam, I'm not God. (*Reads:*) Why is St. Christopher no longer a saint, and did anyone listen to the prayers I prayed to him before they decided he didn't exist? The name Christopher means Christ-bearer and we used to believe that he carried the Christ child across a river on his shoulders. Then sometime around Pope John XXIII, the Catholic Church decided that this was just a story and didn't really happen. I am not convinced that when we get to heaven we may not find that St. Christopher does indeed exist and that he dislikes Pope John XXIII; however, if he does not exist, then the prayers you prayed to him would have been picked up by St. Jude. St. Jude is the patron saint of hopeless causes. When you have a particularly terrible problem that has little hope of being solved, you pray to St. Jude. When you lose or misplace something, you pray to St. Anthony. (*Reads:*) Tell us some more about your family. (*Smiles, pleased.*) I had twenty-six brothers and sisters. From my family five became priests, seven became nuns, three became brothers, and the rest were institutionalized. My mother was also institutionalized shortly after she started thinking my father was Satan. Some days when we were little, we'd come home and not be able to find our mother so we'd pray to St. Anthony to help us find her. Then when we'd find her with her head in the oven, we would pray to St. Jude to make her sane again. (*Reads:*) Are all our prayers answered? Yes, they are; what people who ask that question often don't realize is that sometimes the answer to our prayer is no. Dear God, please make my mother not be crazy. God's answer: No. Dear God, please let me recover from cancer. God's answer: No. Dear God, please take away this toothache. God's answer: Alright, but you're going to be run over by a car. But every bad thing that happens to us, God has a special reason for. God is the good shepherd, we are His flock. And if God is grouchy or busy with more important matters, His beloved mother

Mary is always there to intercede for us. I shall now sing the Hail Mary in Latin. (SISTER *motions to the lighting booth, and the lights change to an apparently pre-arranged special spotlight for her, atmospheric with blue spill and back lighting; the rest of the stage becomes fairly dim. Sings:*)

> Ave Maria,
> Gratia plena,
> Maria, gratia plena,
> Maria, gratia plena,
> Ave, Ave! . . . (*etc.*)

(*As* SISTER *sings, enter four people, ages twenty-eight to thirty. They are a woman dressed as the* BLESSED MOTHER, *a man dressed as* ST. JOSEPH, *and two people, a man and a woman, dressed as a camel. Because of the dim lighting, we don't see them too clearly at first.* SISTER, *either sensing something happening due to the audience or else just by turning her head, suddenly sees them and is terribly startled and confused.*)

ST. JOSEPH: We're sorry we're late.

SISTER: Oh dear God. (*Kneels.*)

ST. JOSEPH: Sister, what are you doing?

SISTER: You look so real.

ST. JOSEPH: Sister, I'm Gary Sullavan, and (*pointing to the Blessed Mother*) this is Diane Symonds. We were in your fifth-grade class in 1959, and you asked us to come today. Don't you remember?

SISTER: 1959?

GARY: Don't you remember asking us?

SISTER: Not very distinctly. (*Louder, to lighting booth:*) Could I have some lights please? (*Lights come back up to where they were before. To* GARY:) What did I want you to do?

GARY: You wanted us to put on a pageant.

SISTER: That camel looks false to me.

PHILOMENA: Hello, Sister. (*She's the front of the camel.*)

SISTER: I thought so.

PHILOMENA: It's Philomena, Sister. Philomena Rostovitch.

ALOYSIUS: And Aloysius Benheim. (*He's the back of the camel.*)

SISTER: I don't really recognize any of you. Of course, you're not in your school uniforms.

DIANE: 1959.

SISTER: What?

DIANE: You taught us in 1959.

SISTER: I recognize you. Mary Jean Mahoney.

DIANE: I'm not Mary Jean Mahoney. I'm Diane Symonds.

SISTER: This is all so confusing.

GARY: Don't you want to see the pageant?

SISTER: What pageant is it?

GARY: We used to perform it at Christmas in your class; every class did. You said it was written in 1948 by Mary Jean Mahoney, who was your best student, you said.

DIANE: You said she was very elevated, and that when she

was in the seventh grade she didn't have her first period, she had a stigmata.

SISTER: Oh yes. They discovered it in gym class. Mary Jean Mahoney. She entered a cloistered order of nuns upon her graduation from twelfth grade. Sometimes late at night I can hear her praying. Mary Jean Mahoney. Yes, let's see her pageant again. (*To audience:*) She was such a bright student. (*Vague.*) I remember asking them to come now, I think. I wanted to tell you about Mary Jean Mahoney, and the perfect faith of a child. Yes, the pageant, please. Thomas, come watch with me.

(THOMAS *enters and sits on* SISTER'S *lap.*)

GARY (*announcing*): The pageant of the birth and death of Our Beloved Savior Jesus Christ, by Mary Jean Mahoney as told to Mrs. Robert J. Mahoney. The setting: a desert near Bethlehem. St. Joseph and the Virgin Mary and their trusty camel must flee from the wicked King Herod.

DIANE (*sings to tune of "We Gather Together to Ask the Lord's Blessing"*):

> Hello, my name's Mary,
> And his name is Joseph,
> We're parents of Jesus,
> Who's not been born yet.
>
> We're fleeing from Herod,
> And nobody knows if
> We'll make it to the town,
> But we'll try, you can bet.
>
> And I'm still a virgin,
> And he's not the father,

> The father descended
> From heaven above.
>
> And this is our camel,
> He's really not much bother,
> We're off to Bethlehem,
> Because God is love.

GARY: Here's an inn, Mary. But there doesn't look like there's any room.

DIANE: Well ask them, Joseph.

GARY (*knocks on imaginary door*): Excuse me, you don't have room at this inn, do you? (*Listens.*) He said they don't, Mary.

DIANE: Oh dear. Well let's try another inn.

GARY (*knocks*): Excuse me, you don't have room at this inn, do you? (*Listens.*) He says they don't allow camels.

DIANE: Let's try the third inn.

GARY (*knocks*): Excuse me, you don't have room at your inn, do you? (*Listens.*) I thought not . . . what? You would? Oh, Mary, this kind innkeeper says that even though he has no room at the inn, we can sleep in his stable.

DIANE: Oh dear.

GARY: Mary, we really haven't any choice.

DIANE: Yes we do. Sister says we have choice over everything, because God gave us free will to decide between good and evil. And so I *choose* to stay in the stable.

GARY: Well here it is.

DIANE: Pew. It smells just like the zoo Mommy took me and

Cynthia to visit last summer. We liked to look at the animals, but we didn't like to smell them.

GARY: I don't think there are any sheets.

DIANE: I don't need sheets. I'm so tired, I could sleep anywhere.

GARY: Well that's good. Good night, Mary.

DIANE: But I do need pillows.

GARY: Mary, what can I do? We don't have any pillows.

DIANE: I can't sleep without pillows.

GARY: Let's pray to God then. If you just pray, He answers your prayers.

DIANE: Sometimes He says no, Joseph.

GARY: I know, but let's try. Dear God, we beseech Thee, hear our prayer.

DIANE: Pillows! Pillows! Pillows!

GARY: And behold God answered their prayers.

CAMEL (PHILOMENA): We have an idea, Mary and Joseph. We have two humps, and you can use them as pillows.

DIANE: Thank you, God! Come on, Joseph. Let's go to sleep.

CAMEL (*sings a lullaby, as* MARY *and* JOSEPH *start to sleep*):

> Rockabye, and good night,
> May God keep you and watch you,
> Rockabye, and good night, (*etc.*)

(*They sleep.* ALOYSIUS *makes baby-crying noises, tosses out a doll onto the floor.*)

DIANE (*seeing the doll*): Joseph, He's born. Jesus is born.

GARY, DIANE, *and* CAMEL (*sing*):

> Joy to the world, the Savior's come,
> Let earth receive her king,
> La la la la la la la la,
> La la la la la la la la,
> Let heaven and nature sing,
> Let heaven and nature sing,
> Let heaven, and heaven, and nature sing!

GARY (*to doll*): Can you say Poppa, Jesus? Can you say Momma?

DIANE: He's not that kind of child, Joseph. He was born without original sin like me. This is called my Immaculate Conception, which is not to be confused with my Virgin Birth. Everyone makes this error, it makes me lose my patience. We must learn from *Him*, Joseph.

GARY (*to audience*): And so Jesus instructed His parents, and the priests in the Temple. And He performed many miracles.

DIANE: He turned water into wine.

GARY: He made cripples walk.

DIANE: He walked on the water.

GARY: And then came the time for His crucifixion. And His mother said to him:

DIANE (*to doll*): But why, Jesus, why? Why must You be crucified?

GARY: And Jesus explained that because Adam and Eve,

especially Eve, had sinned that mankind was cursed until Jesus could redeem us by dying on the cross.

DIANE: But that sounds silly. Why can't God just forgive us?

GARY: But Jesus laughed at her and He said, "Yours is not to reason why, yours is but to do and die." And then He said, "But seriously, Mother, it is not up to God to justify His ways to man." And then Mary said:

DIANE: I understand. Or rather, I understand that I am not supposed to understand. Come, let us go to Golgotha and watch You be crucified.

GARY: And Mary and the apostles and the faithful camel, whose name was Misty, followed Jesus to the rock of Golgotha and watched Him be nailed to a cross. (GARY *has a hammer and nails, and nails the doll to a little cross; then stands it up that way.*) And then He hung there for three hours in terrible agony.

DIANE: Imagine the agony. Try to feel the nails ripping through His hands and feet. Pound, pound, pound, rip, rip, rip. Washing the dishes for three hours is nothing compared to hanging on a cross.

GARY: And then He died. He's dead now, Mary.

DIANE (*sad, lost*): Oh.

GARY: Let's go for a long walk.

DIANE: Oh, Joseph, I feel so alone.

GARY: So do I, Mary.

DIANE (*truly wondering*): Do you think He was just a nut? Do you think maybe the Holy Ghost isn't His Father at all, that I made it all up? Maybe I'm not a virgin . . . Maybe . . .

GARY: But then Misty said . . .

CAMEL (PHILOMENA): Do not despair, Mary and Joseph. Of course He is God; He'll rise again in three days.

DIANE: If only I could believe you. But why should I listen to a dumb animal?

CAMEL (PHILOMENA): O ye of little faith.

DIANE (*sad*): Oh, Joseph, I'm losing my mind.

GARY: And so Mary and Joseph and the camel hid for three days and three nights, and on Sunday morning they got up and went to the Tomb where Christ was buried. And when they got there, standing by the Tomb was an angel. And the angel spoke.

ALOYSIUS (BACK OF CAMEL): Mary and Joseph, your son has risen from the dead, just like your dumb animal Misty told you He would.

DIANE: Thank you, Misty. You were right. (*Kisses Misty.*)

GARY: And then Mary and Joseph, realizing their lack of faith, thanked Misty and made a good act of contrition. And then Jesus came out from behind the tree where He was hiding, they spent forty days on earth enjoying themselves and setting the groundwork for the Catholic Church, and then Jesus, Mary, Joseph, and Misty ascended into heaven and lived happily ever after.

(DIANE *and* GARY, *holding the doll between them, stand in front of the camel. All sing the final jubilant phrase of "Angels We Have Heard on High" Christmas carol, as* DIANE *and* GARY *mime ascension by waving their arms in a flying motion.*)

ALL (*singing*): Glor-or-or-or-ia! In Excelsis Deo!

(*All four bow.* SISTER *applauds enthusiastically. After their bow, the four quickly get out of their costumes, continuing to do so during some of* SISTER's *next speech if necessary. Their "regular" clothes are indeed regular and not too noteworthy:* DIANE *might wear slacks or jeans but with an attractive sweater or blouse and with a blazer;* GARY *might wear chinos, a nice shirt with even a tie, or a vest— casual but neat, pleasant;* PHILOMENA *might wear a dress;* ALOYSIUS *a shirt and slacks [or, if played as a bit formal, even a suit].*)

SISTER: Oh, thank you, children. That was lovely. Thank you. (*To audience:*) The old stories really are the best, aren't they? Mary Jean Mahoney. What a good child. And what a nice reunion *we're* having. What year did you say you were in my class again?

GARY: 1959.

SISTER: 1959. Oh, those were happy years. Eisenhower, Pope Pius still alive, then the first Catholic president. And so now you've all grown up. Let's do some of the old questions, shall we? (*To* ALOYSIUS:) Who made you?

ALOYSIUS: God made me.

SISTER: Quite correct. What is the seventh commandment?

PHILOMENA: The seventh commandment is thou shalt not steal.

SISTER: Very good. (*To* DIANE:) What is contrition? You.

DIANE: Uh . . . being sorry for sin?

SISTER (*cheerfully chastising*): That's not how we answer questions here, young lady. Thomas?

THOMAS: Contrition is sincere sorrow for having offended God, and hatred for the sins we have committed, with a firm purpose of sinning no more.

DIANE: Oh yes. Right.

SISTER (*still kindly*): For someone who's just played the Virgin, you don't know your catechism responses very well. What grade are you in?

DIANE: I'm not in a grade. I'm in life.

SISTER: Oh yes, right. Well, cookies anyone? Thomas, go bring our nice guests some cookies.

(THOMAS *exits.*)

It's so nice to see you all again. You must all be married by now, I imagine. I hope you all have large families like we encouraged?

PHILOMENA: I have a little girl, age three.

SISTER: That's nice.

ALOYSIUS: I have two boys.

SISTER: I like boys. (*To* GARY:) And you?

GARY: I'm not married.

SISTER: Well, a nice-looking boy like you, it won't be long before some pretty girl snatches you up. (*To* DIANE:) And you?

DIANE: I don't have any children. But I've had two abortions.

(SISTER *is stunned. Enter* THOMAS *with cookies.*)

SISTER: No cookies, Thomas. Take them away.

(THOMAS *exits immediately. To* DIANE:)

You are in a state of mortal sin, young woman. What is the fifth commandment?

DIANE: Thou shalt not kill.

SISTER: You are a murderer.

DIANE (*unemotional*): The first one was when I was raped when I was eighteen.

SISTER: Well I am sorry to hear that. But only God has power over life and death. God might have had very special plans for your baby. Are you sure I taught you?

DIANE: Yes you taught me.

SISTER: Did I give you good grades?

DIANE: Yes. Very good.

SISTER: Have you told these sins in confession?

DIANE: What sins?

SISTER: You know very well what I mean.

DIANE: I don't go to confession.

SISTER: Well, it looks pretty clear to me, we'll just add you to the list of people going to hell. (*Calling:*) Thomas!

(*Enter* THOMAS.)

We'll put her name right after Comden and Green.

THOMAS: All right.

(*Exits.*)

SISTER: Now somebody change the subject. I don't want to hear any more about this.

GARY (*trying to oblige*): Ummmm . . . it certainly is strange being able to chew the communion wafer now, isn't it?

SISTER: What?

GARY: Well, you used to tell us that because the communion wafer was really the body of Christ, if we chewed it, it might bleed.

SISTER: I was speaking metaphorically.

GARY: Oh.

SISTER (*pause*): Well, I still feel shaken by that girl over there. Let's talk about something positive. (*Gestures to* PHILOMENA.) You, with the little girl. Tell me about yourself.

PHILOMENA: Well my little girl is three, and her name is Wendy.

SISTER: There is no St. Wendy.

PHILOMENA: Her middle name is Mary.

SISTER: Wendy Mary. Too many y's. I'd change it. What does your husband do?

PHILOMENA: I don't have a husband. (*Long pause.*)

SISTER: Did he die?

PHILOMENA: I don't think so. I didn't know him for very long.

SISTER: Do you sign your letters Mrs. or Miss?

PHILOMENA: I don't write letters.

SISTER: Did this person you lost track of *marry* you before he left?

PHILOMENA (*quiet*): No.

SISTER: Children, you are making me very sad. (*To* PHILOMENA:) Did you get good grades in my class?

PHILOMENA: No, Sister. You said I was stupid.

SISTER: Are you a prostitute?

PHILOMENA: Sister! Certainly not. I just get lonely.

SISTER: The Mother Superior of my own convent may get lonely, but does she have illegitimate children?

ALOYSIUS: There *was* that nun who stuffed her baby behind her dresser last year.

(SISTER *stares at him.*)

It was in the news.

SISTER: No one was addressing you, Aloysius. Philomena, my point is that loneliness does not excuse sin.

PHILOMENA: But there are worse sins. And I believe Jesus forgives me. After all, He didn't want them to stone the woman taken in adultery.

SISTER: That was merely a *political* gesture. In private Christ stoned *many* women taken in adultery.

DIANE: That's not in the Bible.

SISTER (*suddenly very angry*): Not everything has to be in the Bible! (*To audience, trying to recoup:*) There's oral tradition within the Church. One priest tells another priest something, it gets passed down through the years.

PHILOMENA (*unhappy*): But don't you believe Jesus forgives people who sin?

SISTER: Yes, of course He forgives sin, but He's *tricky*. You have to be *truly* sorry, and you have to *truly* resolve not to sin again, or else He'll send you straight to hell just like the thief He was crucified next to.

PHILOMENA: Well I think Jesus forgives me.

SISTER: Well I think you're going to hell. (*To* ALOYSIUS:) And what about you? Is there anything the matter with you?

ALOYSIUS: Nothing. I'm fine.

SISTER: But are you living properly?

ALOYSIUS: Yes.

SISTER: And you're married?

ALOYSIUS: Yes.

SISTER: And you don't use birth control?

ALOYSIUS: No.

SISTER: But you only have two children. Why is that? You're not spilling your seed like Onan, are you? That's a sin, you know.

ALOYSIUS: No. It's just chance that we haven't had more.

SISTER: And you go to Mass once a week, and communion at least once a year, and confession at least once a year? Right?

ALOYSIUS: Yes.

SISTER: Well I'm very pleased then.

ALOYSIUS (*suddenly guilty, unhappy*): I am an alcoholic, and recently I've started to hit my wife, and I keep thinking about suicide.

SISTER: Within bounds, all those things are venial sins. At least one of my students turned out well. Of course, I don't know how hard you're hitting your wife; but with prayer and God's grace . . .

ALOYSIUS: My wife is very unhappy.

SISTER: Yes, but eventually there's death. And then everlasting happiness in heaven. Some days I long for heaven. (*To* GARY:) And you? Have you turned out all right?

GARY: I'm okay.

SISTER: And you don't use birth control?

GARY: Definitely not.

SISTER: That's good. (*Looks at him.*) What do you mean, "definitely not"?

GARY: I don't use it.

SISTER: And you're not married. Have you not found the right girl?

GARY (*evasively*): In a manner of speaking.

SISTER (*grim, not going to pursue it*): Okay. (*Walks away, but then knows she has to pursue it.*) You do that thing that makes Jesus puke, don't you?

GARY: Pardon?

SISTER: Drop the polite boy manners, buster. When your mother looks at you, she turns into a pillar of salt, right?

GARY: What?

SISTER: Sodom and Gomorrah, stupid. You sleep with men, don't you?

GARY: Well . . . yes.

SISTER: Jesus, Mary, and Joseph! We have a regular cross section in here.

GARY: I got seduced when I was in the seminary. I mean, I guess I'd been denying it up to then.

SISTER: We don't want to hear about it.

GARY: And then when I left the seminary I was very upset, and then I went to New York and I slept with five hundred different people.

SISTER: Jesus is going to throw up.

GARY: But then I decided I was trashing my life, and so I only had sex with guys I had an emotional relationship with.

SISTER: That must have cut it down to about *three* hundred.

GARY: And now I'm living with this one guy who I'd gone to grade school with and only ran into again two years ago, and we're faithful with one another and stuff. He was in your class too. Jeff Hannigan.

SISTER: He was a bad boy. Some of them should be left on the side of a hill to die, and he was one.

GARY: You remember him?

SISTER: Not really. His type.

GARY: Anyway, when I met him again, he was still a practicing Catholic, and so now I am again too.

SISTER: I'd practice a little harder if I were you.

GARY: So I don't think I'm so bad.

SISTER (*vomit sound*): Blah. You make me want to blah. Didn't any of you listen to me when I was teaching you? What were you all doing? (*Mad, trying to set the record straight again.*) There is the universe, created by God. Eve ate the apple, man got original sin, God sent down Jesus to redeem us. Jesus said to St. Peter, "Upon this rock," rock meaning Peter, "I build my Church," by which he meant that Peter was the first Pope and that he and the subsequent Popes would be infallible on matters of doctrine and morals. So your way is very clear: You have this infallible Church that tells you what is right and wrong, and you follow its teaching, and then you get to heaven. Didn't you all *hear* me say that? Did you all have wax in your ears? Did I speak in a foreign language? Or what? And you've all sinned against sex—(*to* ALOYSIUS:) not you, you're just depressed, you probably need vitamins—but the rest of you. Why this obsession with sex? The Church has been very clear setting up the guidelines for you. (*To* PHILOMENA *and* DIANE:) For you two girls, why can't you simply marry one Catholic man and have as many babies as chance and the good Lord allows you to? Simple, easy to follow directions. (*To* GARY:) And for you, you can *force* yourself to marry and procreate with some nice Catholic girl—try it, it's not so hard— or you can be celibate for the rest of your life. Again, simple advice. (*Suddenly furious.*) Those are your options! No others. They are your direct paths to heaven and salvation, to everlasting happiness! Why aren't you following these paths? Are you insane?

DIANE: You're insane.

SISTER: You know, you're my least favorite person here

today. I mean, the great big effeminate one over there (*points to* GARY) makes me want to blah, but I can tell he once was nice, and he might get better with shock treatments and aversion therapy. But I can tell shock treatments wouldn't help you. You're fresh as paint, and you're nasty. I can see it in your face.

DIANE: You shouldn't be teaching children. You should be locked up in a convent where you can't hurt anybody.

SISTER: Me hurt someone. You're the one who runs around killing babies at the drop of a hat.

DIANE: It's a medical procedure. And even the Church admits it can't pinpoint *when* life begins in the womb. Why should you decide that the minute the sperm touches the ovum that . . .

SISTER: Don't talk filth to me, I don't want to hear it. (*Suddenly very suspicious.*) Why did you all come here today? I don't remember asking you.

GARY: It was Diane's idea.

SISTER: What? What was?

PHILOMENA: We wanted to embarrass you.

ALOYSIUS: None of us ever liked you.

SISTER: What do you mean? My students always loved me. I was the favorite.

ALOYSIUS: No. We thought you were a bully.

SISTER: I was the *favorite*.

ALOYSIUS: You never let me go to the bathroom when I needed to.

SISTER: All you had to do was raise your hand.

ALOYSIUS: There were sixty children, and I sat in the back of the room; and I did raise my hand, but you never acknowledged me. Every afternoon my bladder became very full, and I always ended up wetting my pants.

SISTER: Big deal.

ALOYSIUS: I spoke to you about recognizing me sooner, and about my problem, but all you said then was "big deal."

SISTER: I remember you. You used to make a puddle in the last row every day.

ALOYSIUS: I have bladder problems to this day.

SISTER: What a baby. You flunked. I was giving you a lesson in life, and you flunked. It was up to you to solve the problem: don't drink your little carton of milk at lunch; bring a little container with you and urinate behind your desk; or simply hold it in and offer the discomfort up to Christ. He suffered three hours of agony on the cross, surely a full bladder pales by comparison. I talk about the universe and original sin and heaven and hell, and you complain to me about bathroom privileges. You're a ridiculous crybaby. (*Cuffs him on the head.*)

PHILOMENA: You used to hit me too.

SISTER: You probably said stupid things.

PHILOMENA: I did. I told you I was stupid. That was no reason to hit me.

SISTER: It seems a very good reason to hit you. Knock some sense into you.

PHILOMENA: You used to take the point of your pencil and

poke it up and down on my head when I didn't do my homework.

SISTER: You should have done your homework.

PHILOMENA: And when I didn't know how to do long division, you slammed my head against the blackboard.

SISTER: Did I ever break a bone?

PHILOMENA: No.

SISTER: There, you see! (*To* GARY:) And what about you?

GARY: You didn't do anything to me in particular. I just found you scary.

SISTER: Well I am scary.

GARY: But my lover Jeff doesn't like you 'cause you made him wet his pants too.

SISTER: All this obsession with the bladder. (*To* DIANE:) And you, the nasty one, why did you want to embarrass me?

DIANE (*said simply*): Because I believed you. I believed how you said the world worked, and that God loved us, and the story of the Good Shepherd and the lost sheep; and I don't think you should lie to people.

SISTER: But that's how things are. I didn't lie.

DIANE: When I was sixteen, my mother got breast cancer, which spread. I prayed to God to let her suffering be small, but her suffering seemed to me quite extreme. She was in bad pain for half a year, and then terrible pain for much of a full year. The ulcerations on her body were horrifying to her and to me. Her last few weeks she slipped into a semi-conscious state, which allowed her, unfortunately, to wake up for a few minutes at a time and to have a full awareness of her pain and her fear of death. She was able to recognize me, and she would try to cry, but she was unable to; and to speak, but she was unable to. I think she wanted me to get her new doctors; she never really accepted that her disease was going to kill her, and she thought in her panic that her doctors must be incompetent and that new ones could magically cure her. Then, thank goodness, she went into a full coma. A nurse who I knew to be Catholic assured me that everything would be done to keep her alive—a dubious comfort. Happily, the doctor was not Catholic, or if he was, not doctrinaire, and they didn't use extraordinary means to keep her alive; and she finally died after several more weeks in her coma. Now there are, I'm sure, far worse deaths— terrible burnings, tortures, plague, pestilence, famine; Christ on the cross even, as Sister likes to say. But I thought my mother's death was bad enough, and I got confused as to why I had been praying and to whom. I mean, if prayer was really this sort of button you pressed—admit you need the Lord, then He stops your suffering—then why didn't it always work? Or ever work? And when it worked, so-called, and our prayers were supposedly answered, wasn't it as likely to be chance as God? God always answers our prayers, you said, He just sometimes says no. But why would He say no to stopping my mother's suffering? I wasn't even asking that she live, just that He end her suffering. And it can't be that He was letting her suffer because she'd been bad, because she hadn't been bad and besides suffering doesn't seem to work that way, considering the suffering of children who've obviously done nothing wrong. So why was He letting her suffer? Spite? Was the Lord God actually malicious? That seemed possible, but farfetched. Maybe He had no control over it, maybe He wasn't omnipotent as you taught us He was. Maybe He created the world sort of by accident by belching one morning or getting the hiccups, and maybe He had no idea how the whole thing worked. In which case, He wouldn't be malicious, just useless. Or, of course, more likely than that, He didn't exist at all, the universe was hiccupped or belched into existence all on its own, and my mother's suffering just existed like rain or wind or humidity. I became angry at myself, and by extension at you, for ever having expected anything beyond randomness from the world. And while I was thinking these things, the day that my mother died, I was raped. Now I know that's really too much, one really loses all sympathy for me because I sound like I'm making it up or something. But bad things sometimes happen all at once, and this particular day on my return from the hospital I was raped by some maniac who broke into the house. He had a knife and cut me up some. Anyway, I don't really want to go on about the experience, but I got very depressed for about five years. Somehow the utter randomness of things—my mother's suffering, my attack by a lunatic who was either born a lunatic or made one by cruel parents or perhaps by an imbalance of hormones or whatever, etcetera, etcetera—*this randomness seemed intolerable.* I found I grew to hate you, Sister, for making me once expect everything to be ordered and to make sense. My psychiatrist said he thought my hatred of you was obsessive, that I was just looking for someone to blame. Then he seduced me, and he was the father of my second abortion.

SISTER: I think she's making all this up.

DIANE: He said I seduced him. And maybe that's so. But he could be lying just to make himself feel better. (*To* SISTER:) And of course your idea that I should have had this baby, either baby, is preposterous. Have you any idea what a terrible mother I'd be? I'm a nervous wreck.

SISTER: God would have given you the strength.

DIANE: I suppose it is childish to look for blame, part of the randomness of things is that there is no one to blame; but basically I think everything is your fault, Sister.

SISTER: You have obviously never read the Book of Job.

DIANE: I have read it. And I think it's a nasty story.

SISTER: God explains in that story why He lets us suffer, and a very lovely explanation it is too. He likes to test us so that when we choose to love Him no matter what He does to us, that proves how great and deep our love for Him is.

DIANE: That sounds like *The Story of O.*

SISTER: Well there's obviously no talking to you. You don't want help or knowledge or enlightenment, so there's nothing left for you but an unhappy life, sickness, death, and hell.

DIANE: Last evening I killed my psychiatrist and now I'm going to kill you. (*Takes out a gun.*)

GARY: Oh dear. I thought we were just going to embarrass her.

SISTER (*stalling for time*): And you have, very much so. So no need to kill me at all. Goodbye, Diane, Gary, Aloysius . . .

DIANE: You're insane. You shouldn't be allowed to teach children. I see that there's that little boy here today. You're going to make him crazy.

SISTER: Thomas, stay offstage with the cookies, dear.

DIANE: I want you to admit that everything's your fault, and then I'm going to kill you.

PHILOMENA: Maybe we should all wait outside.

SISTER: Stay here. Diane, look at me. I was wrong. I admit it. I'm sorry. I thought everything made sense, but I didn't understand things properly. There's nothing I can say to make it up to you but . . . (*as if seeing something awful behind* DIANE's *head*) LOOK OUT!

(DIANE *looks behind her,* SISTER *whips out her own gun and shoots* DIANE *dead.* SISTER *like a circus artist completing a stunt, hands up.*)

Ta-da! For those non-Catholics present, murder is allowable in self-defense, one doesn't even have to tell it in confession. Thomas, bring me some water.

GARY: We didn't know she was bringing a gun.

(THOMAS *brings water.*)

SISTER: I remember her now from class. (*Looks at her dead body.*) She had no sense of humor.

ALOYSIUS: I have to go to the bathroom.

SISTER (*aims gun at him*): Stay where you are. Raise your hand if you want to go to the bathroom, Aloysius, and wait until I have acknowledged you. (*She ignores him now, though keeps gun aimed at him most of the time.*) Thomas, bring me a cookie.

(*He does.*)

Most of my students turned out beautifully, these are the few exceptions. But we never give up on those who've turned out badly, do we, Thomas? What is the story of the Good Shepherd and the Lost Sheep?

THOMAS: The Good Shepherd was so concerned about his Lost Sheep that he left His flock to go find the Lost Sheep, and then He found it.

SISTER: That's right. And while he was gone, a great big wolf came and killed his entire flock. No, just kidding, I'm feeling lightheaded from all this excitement. No, by the story of the Lost Sheep, Christ tells us that when a sinner strays we mustn't give up on the sinner. (SISTER *indicates for* THOMAS *to exit; he does.*) So I don't totally despair for these people standing here. Gary, I hope that you will leave your friend Jeff, don't even tell him where you're going, just disappear, and then I hope you will live your life as a celibate. Like me. Celibate rhymes with celebrate. Our Lord loves celibate people. And you, Philomena, I hope you will get married to some nice Catholic man, or if you stay unmarried then you too will become a celibate. Rhymes with celebrate.

ALOYSIUS: Sister, I have my hand up.

SISTER: Keep it up. And you, Aloysius, I hope you'll remember not to kill yourself, which is a mortal sin. For if we live by God's laws even though we are having a miserable life, remember heaven and eternal happiness are our reward.

GARY: Should we help you with the body, Sister?

SISTER (*confused for a moment, but then responds*): The janitor will help me later, thank you. You two may go now, so I can finish my lecture.

GARY: Why don't you let him go to the bathroom?

SISTER: Gary?

GARY: Yes, Sister?

SISTER: You still believe what you do with Jeff is wrong, don't you? I mean, you still confess it in confession, don't you?

GARY: Well I don't really think it's wrong, but I'm not sure, so I do still tell it in confession.

SISTER: When did you last go to confession?

GARY: This morning actually. I was going to be playing St. Joseph and all.

SISTER: And you haven't sinned since then, have you?

GARY: No, Sister.

(SISTER *shoots him dead*.)

SISTER (*triumphantly*): I've sent him to Heaven! (*To* PHILOMENA:) Okay, you with the little girl, go home before I decide your little girl would be better off in a Catholic orphanage. (PHILOMENA *exits in terror. To audience:*) I'm not really within the letter of the law shooting Gary like this, but really, if he did make a good confession I have sent him straight to heaven and eternal, blissful happiness. And I'm afraid otherwise he would have ended up in hell. I think Christ will allow me this little dispensation from the letter of the law, but I'll go to confession later today, just to be sure.

ALOYSIUS: Sister, I have to go to the bathroom.

SISTER: Wait until I recognize you, Aloysius.

ALOYSIUS: I'm going to leave now.

SISTER (*angry, emphasizing the gun*): I've used this twice today, don't tempt me to use it again. Thomas!

(*He enters.*)

Who made you?

THOMAS: God made me.

SISTER: Why did God make you?

THOMAS: God made me to show forth His goodness and to share with us His happiness.

ALOYSIUS: If you don't let me go to the bathroom, I'm going to wet my pants.

SISTER: We all have free will, Aloysius. Thomas, explain about the primary cause again.

THOMAS: Everything has a primary cause. Dinner is put on the table because the primary cause . . .

SISTER: Thomas, I'm going to nap some, I'm exhausted. (*Hands him gun.*) You keep that dangerous man over there covered, and if he moves, shoot him; and also recite some nice catechism questions for us all while I rest. All right, dear?

THOMAS: Yes, Sister. (*He aims the gun at* ALOYSIUS. SISTER *sits on a chair, about to nap.*)

SISTER: Sit on my lap.

(THOMAS, *still aiming the gun at* ALOYSIUS, *sits on her lap, and begins to recite from memory.* ALOYSIUS *keeps his hand up.*)

THOMAS: "What must we do to gain the happiness of heaven?"

To gain the happiness of heaven, we must know, love, and serve God in this world.

(*Lights start to dim.*)

"From whom do we learn to know, love, and serve God?"

We learn to know, love, and serve God from Jesus Christ, the Son of God, who teaches us through the Catholic Church.

"What are some of the perfections of God?"

Some of the perfections of God are: God is eternal, all-good, all-knowing, all-present, and almighty.

(*Lights have dimmed to black.*)

ADDENDUM

Since scripts are so open to interpretations, I wanted to suggest some things to avoid, as well as to aim for, in presenting this play; and to make a few clarifications.

The casting of Sister Mary is obviously of the utmost importance. In casting for the Ensemble Studio Theatre production, we saw a great many different types for Sister, and these auditions were helpful in suggesting the various pitfalls of casting and playing the role.

For starters, it's a mistake to have an actress play (or, worse, seem to be) mean. Though a strident, bullying approach may work in an audition and even be funny, it can't really sustain for the whole play; we see Sister kill two people at the end of the play, we shouldn't expect her to do so five minutes after we first see her. (There are places, of course, where Sister *should* be strident and bullying; but it should be underneath and revealed only sometimes.) Also, perhaps more important, the strength and power of figures like Sister Mary (or, say, Jean Brodie) is in their charm; we believe them because they take us in. If Sister were obviously a horror, we'd know not to believe her.

In line with this, the relationship between Sister and Thomas should have warmth and even love. It's true that she presents him as one might present a dog doing tricks; and yet he does all the tricks well, and she rewards him with not only cookies but warmth, approval, bounces on the knee, etc. All this fondness and attention could easily make Thomas adore Sister.

The actress playing Sister should avoid commenting on her role. (All the actors should avoid commenting.) The humor works best when presented straight. That is, it's fine that we as an audience think it outrageous that Sister contemplates Thomas's castration to save his pretty voice; the actress should not indicate her own awareness of this outrageousness (that kind of comic-wink acting that is effective sometimes in a skit, rarely in a play). Sister thinks nothing is wrong with her contemplation, and it's only her feelings we should see.

In terms of age range for Sister, anywhere between forty and sixty seems correct to me. The over-sixty, more grandmotherly-looking actresses we auditioned seemed to throw the play out of whack: They seemed less powerful and more dotty, and also we felt bad for them when the ex-students berated them.

It is possible to consider casting someone younger as Sister, though you will lose the important theatrical fact of having three generations on stage. However, depending on your casting resources, a younger Sister Mary with comic flair and believability is, of course, preferable to an older one with neither attribute.

One other thought in terms of casting: The excellent Sister Mary at E.S.T., Elizabeth Franz, also brought to the role a delicate femininity that was true to a certain kind of real-life nun, very much added to her charm with Thomas and with the audience, and was an extremely effective starting point that nowhere tipped off Sister's potential for murderous rages.

Thomas should be seven or eight, and be smart and polite. There should be no attempt to play up his being a child (like having him not be able to read the list of names going to hell; he should read them easily). An older child could play it, but seven or eight has a genuine innocence that can't be faked—an innocence which is central to the play's meaning.

The tone of the pageant is tricky. It should be childlike, as opposed to childish. It is thirty-year-olds performing it, so they shouldn't pretend to be children, but they can't act like adults precisely either. They should be simple and direct, presenting the story as if we didn't know it and as if it didn't have a child's imprint on the writing. Lots of busy stage business making fun of clunky amateur productions will get in the way.

There is an enormous trap to be avoided in the playing of the four ex-students, and that centers around their apparent plot to come to Sister's lecture to "embarrass" her.

For starters, you mustn't play the plot as a subtext in the pageant or really anywhere before it's mentioned because the audience simply won't know what you're doing. Plus, there's a further trap: If you choose to play that the four have come to embarrass Sister by telling her how much they've strayed from her teaching (Philomena's illegitimate child, Gary's being gay), those revelation scenes won't work comically (as they're intended) because the comedy is based partially on Gary and Philomena not meaning to reveal what Sister drags out of them.

I think to make sense of the "plot" (happily, this is something the audience doesn't really have time to brood about) one would have to imagine Diane calling up the other three with an extremely *vague* plan: Let's put on that old pageant, which is so silly and which will disrupt her lecture; then the "point" of the intrusion will be to eventually tell Sister that she's not fondly remembered (her temper, her not letting people go to the bathroom, etc.). Or maybe the plan is only to put on the pageant, just as a joke to themselves on their past. The vaguer you allow the plan to be in your head, the less saddled with unnecessary subtext you'll be and the more easily (and humorously) the various confrontations with Sister will play. (Diane's sense of the plan has to be different and darker than the others, of course, because she's packing a gun; but even she can be unsure of what she's going to do. Note: I do see the logic of Diane showing some of her bitterness and edge in the pageant, but I warn against it as confusing to the audience and as destructive to the enjoyment of the pageant.)

A final danger in playing the foursome: Avoid kvetching (admittedly tricky since complaining *is* more or less what they're doing in some sections). With Philomena's complaints about being hit and with Aloysius's complaints about the bathroom, it's important to find a balance between the legitimate complaints (Sister was indeed spiteful) and the fact that Philomena and Aloysius are near thirty and that these things are in the past. Apropos of this, real horror and sense memory of what it was like not to go to the bathroom are to be avoided; if the complaints are presented too hysterically, the people will seem stupid and I don't want them to be stupid. It's difficult: I don't want them to be blasé either. It's a balance that's needed, that sense of having the character know it's childish to still be angry but to nonetheless still be angry.

A word or two about Diane's monologue. It is obviously meant very seriously, but though it has a high emotional content, the actress should be very careful in how much emotion she lets through and when. In auditions, some actresses ranted and raved and wept in the speech, and it was ungodly. Diane's speech is very verbal, and very methodically point-by-point; hysteria is an illogical interpretation of the tone and content of what she's saying.

The speech has so much charged material (the mother's death, the rape) that one must also be careful not to *ask* for sympathy.

It might be helpful in approaching the speech to remem-

ber that what she describes happened many years ago (not
that she's not traumatized, it's just that time has taken some
of the immediacy away at least); and also that Diane tries to
distance herself from the pain she feels by being analytic.
The tone of much of the speech, whatever underlying sadness might come through, should be factual, her attempt at
distancing herself: This happened to me, and then I thought
that, but that wasn't true, so then I thought this and
this, etc.

There is, though, probably a natural place (among other
possibilities) for the anger and pain to break through all this
distancing, and that's on "—this randomness seemed intolerable," which both follows a particularly futile attempt at
reasoning things out (her run-on, off-the-point comments
on what made the rapist a rapist) and is also the core of what
she hates Sister for: making her expect and desire order
where there doesn't seem to be any.

Some miscellaneous things:

At E.S.T. we cast Aloysius as an Italian street kid grown up,
and changed his last name to Busiccio. This seemed to work
fine, and is an option. The other option, I'd presume, is to
present him as tense, formal, uptight, and of undetermined
ancestry. (Note: With the latter option, be careful that the
interpretation does not imply homosexuality in any way,
which would throw the play's balance off.)

Gary is not meant to be effeminate. Sister's comment to
that effect is meant to show her prejudice, not reflect any
reality.

When Gary says, "definitely not" to Sister's query as to
whether he uses birth control, I don't mean for him to be
playing cat-and-mouse with her or to be making some
smirking allusion to being gay; it's simply that he indeed
doesn't use birth control and he says "definitely not"

quickly, without thinking what it might imply. The scene plays comically if she draws these facts out of him unwittingly; otherwise we're back in the "revenge plot" trap again.

"Celibate" does not rhyme with "celebrate," nor (in my mind) does Sister think it does. I prefer that she pronounce both words properly and then says they rhyme because she wants them to; it sort of extends her power to say blatantly false things when she feels like it, to make a point (as when she says Christ stoned many women taken in adultery).

Beyond Therapy

❦

Beyond Therapy was presented off-Broadway by the Phoenix Theater in January 1981. The production was directed by Jerry Zaks, setting by Karen Schulz, costumes by Jennifer von Mayrhauser, lighting by Richard Nelson, sound by David Rapkin. The cast was as follows:

BRUCE	Stephen Collins
PRUDENCE	Sigourney Weaver
DR. STUART FRAMINGHAM, psychiatrist	Jim Borelli
MRS. CHARLOTTE WALLACE, psychologist	Kate McGregor-Stewart
BOB	Jack Gilpin
ANDREW	Conan McCarty
PAUL RENNARD*	Nick Stannard

Beyond Therapy was presented on Broadway at the Brooks Atkinson Theater in May 1982 by Warner Theatre productions/Claire Nichtern and FDM productions/François de Menil and Harris Maslansky. The production was directed by John Madden, setting by Andrew Jackness, costumes by Jennifer von Mayrhauser, lighting by Paul Gallo, music coordination by Jack Feldman, stage management by Craig Jacobs. The cast was as follows:

BRUCE	John Lithgow
PRUDENCE	Dianne Wiest
DR. STUART FRAMINGHAM	Peter Michael Goetz
MRS. CHARLOTTE WALLACE	Kate McGregor-Stewart
BOB	Jack Gilpin
ANDREW	David Pierce

* The character of Paul, a previous suitor of Prudence, was written out of the final scene of the Broadway version.

ACT I

SCENE 1

A restaurant. BRUCE *is seated, looking at his watch. He is thirty to thirty-four, fairly pleasant-looking, probably wearing a blazer with an open shirt.*

Enter PRUDENCE, *twenty-nine to thirty-two, attractive, semi-dressed up in a dress or nice skirt and blouse. After hesitating a moment, she crosses to* BRUCE.

PRUDENCE: Hello.

BRUCE: Hello.

PRUDENCE (*referring to a newspaper in her hand*–The New York Review of Books): Are you the white male, thirty to thirty-five, 6'1", blue eyes, who's into rock music, movies, jogging, and quiet evenings at home?

BRUCE: Yes, I am. (*Stands.*)

PRUDENCE: Hi, I'm Prudence.

BRUCE: I'm Bruce.

PRUDENCE: Nice to meet you.

BRUCE: Won't you sit down?

PRUDENCE: Thank you. (*Sits.*) As I said in my letter, I've never answered one of these ads before.

BRUCE: Me neither. I mean, I haven't put one in before.

PRUDENCE: But this time I figured, why not?

BRUCE: Right. Me too. (*Pause.*) I hope I'm not too macho for you.

PRUDENCE: No. So far you seem wonderful.

BRUCE: You have lovely breasts. That's the first thing I notice in a woman.

PRUDENCE (*a bit uneasy*): Thank you.

BRUCE: You have beautiful contact lenses.

PRUDENCE: Thank you. I like the timbre of your voice. Soft but firm.

BRUCE: Thanks. I like *your* voice.

PRUDENCE: Thank you. I love the smell of Brut you're wearing.

BRUCE: Thank you. My male lover Bob gave it to me.

PRUDENCE: What?

BRUCE: You remind me of him in a certain light.

PRUDENCE: What?

BRUCE: I swing both ways actually. Do you?

PRUDENCE (*rattled, serious*): I don't know. I always insist on the lights being out. (*Pause.*)

BRUCE: I'm afraid I've upset you now.

PRUDENCE: No, it's nothing really. It's just that I hate gay people.

BRUCE: I'm not gay. I'm bisexual. There's a difference.

PRUDENCE: I don't really know any bisexuals.

BRUCE: Children are all innately bisexual, you know. If you took a child to Plato's Retreat, he'd be attracted to both sexes.

PRUDENCE: I should imagine he'd be terrified.

BRUCE: Well, he might be, of course. I've never taken a child to Plato's Retreat.

PRUDENCE: I don't think they let you.

BRUCE: I don't really know any children. (*Pause.*) You have wonderful eyes. They're so deep.

PRUDENCE: Thank you.

BRUCE: I feel like I want to take care of you.

PRUDENCE (*liking this tack better*): I would like that. My favorite song is "Someone to Watch over Me."

BRUCE (*sings softly*): "There's a somebody I'm longing duh duh . . ."

PRUDENCE: Yes. Thank you.

BRUCE: In some ways you're like a little girl. And in some ways you're like a woman.

PRUDENCE: How am I like a woman?

BRUCE (*searching, romantically*): You . . . dress like a woman. You wear eye shadow like a woman.

PRUDENCE: You're like a man. You're tall, you have to shave. I feel you could protect me.

BRUCE: I'm deeply emotional, I like to cry.

PRUDENCE: Oh I wouldn't like that.

BRUCE: But I *like* to cry.

PRUDENCE: I don't think men should cry unless something falls on them.

BRUCE: That's a kind of sexism. Men have been programmed not to show feeling.

PRUDENCE: Don't talk to me about sexism. You're the one who talked about my breasts the minute I sat down.

BRUCE: I feel like I'm going to cry now.

PRUDENCE: Why do you want to cry?

BRUCE: I feel you don't like me enough. I think you're making eyes at the waiter.

PRUDENCE: I haven't even seen the waiter.

(BRUCE *cries.*)

Please, don't cry. I don't know where to look. *Please*.

BRUCE (*stops crying after a bit*): I feel better after that. You have a lovely mouth.

PRUDENCE: Thank you.

BRUCE: I can tell you're very sensitive. I want you to have my children.

PRUDENCE: Thank you.

BRUCE: Do you feel ready to make a commitment?

PRUDENCE: I feel I need to get to know you better.

BRUCE: I feel we agree on all the issues. I feel that you like rock music, movies, jogging, and quiet evenings at home. I think you hate shallowness. I bet you never read *People* magazine.

PRUDENCE: I do read it. I write for it.

BRUCE: I write for it too. Free-lance actually. I send in letters. They printed one of them.

PRUDENCE: Oh, what was it about?

BRUCE: I wanted to see Gary Gilmore executed on television.

PRUDENCE: Oh yes, I remember that one.

BRUCE: Did you identify with Jill Clayburgh in *An Unmarried Woman*?

PRUDENCE: Uh, yes, I did.

BRUCE: Me too. We agree on everything. I want to cry again.

PRUDENCE: I don't like men to cry. I want them to be strong.

BRUCE: You'd quite like Bob then.

PRUDENCE: Who?

BRUCE: You know.

PRUDENCE: Oh.

BRUCE: I feel I'm irritating you.

PRUDENCE: No. It's just that it's hard to get to know someone. And the waiter never comes, and I'd like to order.

BRUCE: Let's start all over again. Hello. My name is Bruce.

PRUDENCE: Hello.

BRUCE: Prudence. That's a lovely name.

PRUDENCE: Thank you.

BRUCE: That's a lovely dress.

PRUDENCE: Thank you. I like your necklace. It goes nicely with your chest hair.

BRUCE: Thank you. I like your nail polish.

PRUDENCE: I have it on my toes too.

BRUCE: Let me see.

    (*She takes shoe off, puts foot on the table.*)

    I think it's wonderful you feel free enough with me to put your feet on the table.

PRUDENCE: I didn't put my feet on the table. I put one foot. I was hoping it might get the waiter's attention.

BRUCE: We agree on everything. It's amazing. I'm going to cry again. (*Weeps.*)

PRUDENCE: *Please,* you're annoying me.

    (*He continues to cry.*)

    What is the matter?

BRUCE: I feel you're too dependent. I feel you want me to put up the storm windows. I feel you should do that.

PRUDENCE: I didn't say anything about storm windows.

BRUCE: You're right. I'm wrong. We agree.

PRUDENCE: What kind of childhood did you have?

BRUCE: Nuns. I was taught by nuns. They really ruined me. I don't believe in God anymore. I believe in bran cereal. It helps prevent rectal cancer.

PRUDENCE: Yes, I like bran cereal.

BRUCE: I want to marry you. I feel ready in my life to make a long-term commitment. We'll live in Connecticut. We'll have two cars. Bob will live over the garage. Everything will be wonderful.

PRUDENCE: I don't feel ready to make a long-term commitment to you. I think you're insane. I'm going to go now.

BRUCE: Please don't go.

PRUDENCE: I don't think I should stay.

BRUCE: Don't go. They have a salad bar here.

PRUDENCE: Well, maybe for a little longer. (*She sits down again.*)

BRUCE: You're afraid of life, aren't you?

PRUDENCE: Well . . .

BRUCE: Your instinct is to run away. You're afraid of feeling, of emotion. That's wrong, Prudence, because then you have no passion. Did you see *Equus*? That doctor felt it was better to blind eight horses in a stable with a metal spike than to have no passion. (*Holds his fork.*) In my life I'm not going to be afraid to blind the horses, Prudence.

PRUDENCE: You ought to become a veterinarian.

BRUCE (*very offended*): You've missed the metaphor.

PRUDENCE: I haven't missed the metaphor. I made a joke.

BRUCE: You just totally missed the metaphor. I could never love someone who missed the metaphor.

PRUDENCE: Someone should have you committed.

BRUCE: I'm not the one afraid of commitment. You are.

PRUDENCE: Oh, dry up.

BRUCE: I was going to give you a fine dinner and then take you to see *The Tree of Wooden Clogs* and then home to my place for sexual intercourse, but now I think you should leave.

PRUDENCE: You're not rejecting me, buddy. I'm rejecting you. You're a real first-class idiot.

BRUCE: And you're a castrating, frigid bitch!

(*She throws a glass of water in his face; he throws water back in her face. They sit there for a moment, spent of anger, wet.*)

PRUDENCE: Absolutely nothing seems to get that waiter's attention, does it?

(BRUCE *shakes his head "no." They sit there, sadly. Lights fade.*)

SCENE 2

Psychiatrist's office. DR. STUART FRAMINGHAM. *Very masculine, a bit of a bully, wears boots, jeans, a tweed sports jacket, open sports shirt. Maybe has a beard.*

STUART (*speaking into intercom*): You can send the next patient in now, Betty.

(*Enter* PRUDENCE. *She sits. After a moment:*)

So, what's on your mind this week?

PRUDENCE: Oh I don't know. I had that Catherine the Great dream again.

STUART: Yeah?

PRUDENCE: Oh I don't know. Maybe it isn't Catherine the Great. It's really more like *National Velvet.*

STUART: What do you associate to *National Velvet?*

PRUDENCE: Oh I don't know. Childhood.

STUART: Yes?

PRUDENCE: I guess I miss childhood, where one could look to a horse for emotional satisfaction rather than a person. I mean, a horse never disappointed me.

STUART: You feel disappointed in people?

PRUDENCE: Well every man I try to have a relationship with turns out to be crazy. And the ones that aren't crazy are dull. But maybe it's me. Maybe I'm really looking for faults just so I won't ever have a successful relationship. Like Michael last year. Maybe he was just fine, and I made up faults that he didn't have. Maybe I do it to myself. What do you think?

STUART: What I think doesn't matter. What do you think?

PRUDENCE: But what do *you* think?

STUART: It's not my place to say.

PRUDENCE (*irritated*): Oh never mind. I don't want to talk about it.

STUART: I see. (*Makes a note.*)

PRUDENCE (*noticing he's making notes; to make up*): I did answer one of those ads.

STUART: Oh?

PRUDENCE: Yes.

STUART: How did it work out?

PRUDENCE: Very badly. The guy was a jerk. He talked about my breasts, he has a male lover, and he wept at the table. It was really ridiculous. I should have known better.

STUART: Well, you can always come back to me, babe. I'll light your fire for you anytime.

PRUDENCE: Stuart, I've told you you can't talk to me that way if I'm to stay in therapy with you.

STUART: You're mighty attractive when you're angry.

PRUDENCE: Stuart . . . Dr. Framingham, many women who have been seduced by their psychiatrists take them to court . . .

STUART: Yeah, but you wanted it, baby . . .

PRUDENCE: How could I have "wanted" it? One of our topics has been that I don't know what I want.

STUART: Yeah, but you wanted that, baby.

PRUDENCE: Stop calling me baby. Really, I must be out of my mind to keep seeing you. (*Pause.*) Obviously you can't be my therapist after we've had an affair.

STUART: Two lousy nights aren't an affair.

PRUDENCE: You never said they were lousy.

STUART: They were great. You were great. I was great. Wasn't I, baby? It was the fact that it was only two nights that was lousy.

PRUDENCE: Dr. Framingham, it's the common belief that it is wrong for therapists and their patients to have sex together.

STUART: Not in California.

PRUDENCE: We are not in California.

STUART: We could move there. Buy a house, get a Jacuzzi.

PRUDENCE: Stuart . . . Dr. Framingham, we're not right for one another. I feel you have masculinity problems. I hate your belt buckle. I didn't really even like you in bed.

STUART: I'm great in bed.

PRUDENCE (*with some hesitation*): You have problems with premature ejaculation.

STUART: Listen, honey, there's nothing premature about it. Our society is paced quickly, we all have a lot of things to do. I ejaculate quickly on purpose.

PRUDENCE: I don't believe you.

STUART: Fuck you, cunt.

PRUDENCE (*stands*): Obviously I need to find a new therapist.

STUART: Okay, okay. I lost my temper. I'm sorry. But I'm human. Prudence, that's what you have to learn. People *are* human. You keep looking for perfection, you need to learn to accept imperfection. I can help you with that.

PRUDENCE: Maybe I really should sue you. I mean, I don't think you should have a license.

STUART: Prudence, you're avoiding the issue. The issue is you, not me. You're unhappy, you can't find a relationship you like, you don't like your job, you don't like the world. You *need* my help. I mean, don't get hung up on who should have a license. The issue is I can help you fit into the world. (*Very sincerely, sensitively.*) Really I can. Don't run away.

PRUDENCE (*sits*): I don't think I believe you.

STUART: That's okay. We can work on that.

PRUDENCE: I don't know. I really don't think you're a good therapist. But the others are probably worse, I'm afraid.

STUART: They are. They're much worse. Really I'm very nice. I *like* women. Most men don't.

PRUDENCE: I'm getting one of my headaches again. (*Holds her forehead.*)

STUART: Do you want me to massage your neck?

PRUDENCE: Please don't touch me.

STUART: Okay, okay. (*Pause.*) Any other dreams?

PRUDENCE: No.

STUART: Perhaps we should analyze why you didn't like the man you met through the personal ad.

PRUDENCE: I . . . I . . . don't want to talk anymore today. I want to go home.

STUART: "You can never go home again."

PRUDENCE: Perhaps not. But I can return to my apartment. You're making my headache worse.

STUART: I think we should finish the session. I think it's important.

PRUDENCE: I just can't talk anymore.

STUART: We don't have to talk. But we have to stay in the room.

PRUDENCE: How much longer?

STUART (*looks at watch*): Thirty minutes.

PRUDENCE: Alright. But I'm not going to talk anymore.

STUART: Okay. (*Pause. They stare at each other.*) You're very beautiful when you're upset.

PRUDENCE: Please don't you talk either. (*They stare at each other; lights dim.*)

SCENE 3

The office of CHARLOTTE WALLACE. *Probably reddish hair, bright clothing; a Snoopy dog on her desk.*

*If there are walls in the set around her, they have
drawings done by children.*

CHARLOTTE (*into intercom*): You may send the next patient
in, Marcia. (*She arranges herself at her desk, smiles in
anticipation. Enter* BRUCE. *He sits.*) Hello.

BRUCE: Hello. (*Pause.*) Should I just begin?

CHARLOTTE: Would you like to begin?

BRUCE: I threw a glass of water at someone in a restaurant.

CHARLOTTE: Did you?

BRUCE: Yes.

CHARLOTTE: Did they get all wet?

BRUCE: Yes. (*Silence.*)

CHARLOTTE (*points to child's drawing*): Did I show you this
drawing?

BRUCE: I don't remember. They all look alike.

CHARLOTTE: It was drawn by an emotionally disturbed
three-year-old. His parents beat him every morning
after breakfast. Orange juice, toast, Special K.

BRUCE: Uh huh.

CHARLOTTE: Do you see the point I'm making?

BRUCE: Yes, I do, sort of. (*Pause.*) What point are you
making?

CHARLOTTE: Well, the point is that when a porpoise first
comes to me, it is often immediately clear . . . did I say
porpoise? What word do I want? Porpoise. Pompous.
Pom Pom. Paparazzi. Polyester. Pollywog. Olley olley

oxen free. Patient. I'm sorry, I mean patient. Now what was I saying?

BRUCE: Something about when a patient comes to you.

CHARLOTTE (*slightly irritated*): Well, give me more of a clue.

BRUCE: Something about the child's drawing and when a patient comes to you?

CHARLOTTE: Yes. No, I need more. Give me more of a hint.

BRUCE: I don't know.

CHARLOTTE: Oh I hate this, when I forget what I'm saying. Oh, damn. Oh, damn, damn, damn. Well, we'll just have to forge on. You say something for a while, and I'll keep trying to remember what I was saying. (*She moves her lips.*)

BRUCE (*after a bit*): Do you want me to talk?

CHARLOTTE: Would you like to talk?

BRUCE: I had an answer to the ad I put in.

CHARLOTTE: Ad?

BRUCE: Personal ad.

CHARLOTTE (*remembering, happy*): Oh, yes. Personal ad. I told you that was how the first Mr. Wallace and I met. Oh yes. I love personal ads. They're so basic. Did it work out for you?

BRUCE: Well, I liked her, and I tried to be emotionally open with her. I even let myself cry.

CHARLOTTE: Good for you!

BRUCE: But she didn't like me. And then she threw water in my face.

CHARLOTTE: Oh dear. I'm so sorry. One has to be so brave to be emotionally open and vulnerable. Oh, you poor thing. I'm going to give you a hug. (*She hugs him.*) What did you do when she threw water in your face?

BRUCE: I threw it back in her face.

CHARLOTTE: Oh good for you! Bravo! (*She barks for Snoopy and bounces him up and down.*) Ruff, ruff, ruff! Oh, I feel you getting so much more emotionally expressive since you've been in therapy, I'm proud of you.

BRUCE: Maybe it was my fault. I probably came on too strong.

CHARLOTTE: Uh, life is so difficult. I know when I met the second Mr. Wallace . . . you know, it's so strange, all my husbands have had the same surname of Wallace, this has been a theme in my own analysis. . . . Well, when I met the second Mr. Wallace, I got a filing cabinet caught in my throat . . . I don't mean a filing cabinet. What do I mean? Filing cabinet, frying pan, frog's eggs, faculty wives, frankincense, fornication, Folies Bergères, falling, falling, fork, fish fork, fish bone. I got a fish bone caught in my throat. (*Smiles. Long silence.*)

BRUCE: And did you get it out?

CHARLOTTE: Oh yes. Then we got married, and we had quite a wonderful relationship for a while, but then he started to see this fishwife and we broke up. I don't mean fishwife, I mean waitress. Is that a word, waitress?

BRUCE: Yes. Woman who works in a restaurant.

CHARLOTTE: No, she didn't work in a restaurant, she worked in a department store. Sales . . . lady. That's what she was.

BRUCE: That's too bad.

CHARLOTTE: He was buying a gift for me, and then he ran off with the saleslady. He never even gave me the gift, he just left me a note. And then I was so very alone for a while. (*Cries. After a bit, he gives her a hug and a few kisses from the Snoopy doll. She is suitably grateful.*) I'm afraid I'm taking up too much of your session. I'll knock a few dollars off the bill. You talk for a while, I'm getting tired anyway.

BRUCE: Well, so I'm sort of afraid to put another ad in the paper since seeing how this one worked out.

CHARLOTTE: Oh, don't be afraid! Never be afraid to risk, to risk! I've told you about *Equus*, haven't I? That doctor, Doctor Dysart, with whom I greatly identify, saw that it was better to risk madness and to blind horses with a metal spike, than to be safe and conventional and dull. Ecc, ecc, equus! Naaaaaaay! (*For Snoopy.*) Ruff ruff ruff!

BRUCE: So you think I should put in another ad?

CHARLOTTE: Yes I do. But this time, we need an ad that will get someone exceptional, someone who can appreciate your uniqueness.

BRUCE: In what ways am I unique? (*Sort of pleased.*)

CHARLOTTE: Oh I don't know, the usual ways. Now let's see. (*Writing on pad.*) White male, 30 to 35, 6'2", no—6'5", green eyes, Pulitzer Prize–winning author, into Kierkegaard, Mahler, Joan Didion, and sex, seeks similar-minded attractive female for unique encounters. Sense of humor a must. Write box whatever whatever. There, that should catch you someone excellent. Why don't you take this out to the office, and my dirigible will type it up for you. I don't mean dirigible, I mean Saskatchewan.

BRUCE: Secretary.

CHARLOTTE: Yes, that's what I mean.

BRUCE: You know, we haven't mentioned how my putting these ads in the paper for women is making Bob feel. He's real hostile about it.

CHARLOTTE: Who's Bob?

BRUCE: He's the guy I've been living with for a year.

CHARLOTTE: Bob. Oh dear. I'm sorry. I thought you were someone else for this whole session. You're not Thomas Norton?

BRUCE: No, I'm Bruce Lathrop.

CHARLOTTE: Oh yes. Bruce and Bob. It all comes back now. Well I'm very sorry. But this is a good ad anyway, I think, so just bring it out to my dirigible, and then come on back in and we'll talk about something else for a while. I know, I mean secretary. Sometimes I think I should get my blood sugar checked.

BRUCE: Alright, thank you, Mrs. Wallace.

CHARLOTTE: See you next week.

BRUCE: I thought you wanted me to come right back to finish the session.

CHARLOTTE: Oh yes, see you in a few minutes.

(*He exits.* CHARLOTTE *speaks into intercom.*)

Marcia, dear, send in the next porpoise please. Wait, I don't mean porpoise, I mean . . . pony, Pekinese, parka, penis, no not that. I'm sorry, Marcia, I'll buzz back when I think of it. (*She moves her lips, trying to remember. Lights dim.*)

SCENE 4

A restaurant again. BRUCE *waiting, looking at his watch. After a bit, enter* PRUDENCE.

PRUDENCE: Oh.

BRUCE: Hello again.

PRUDENCE: Hello.

BRUCE: Odd coincidence.

PRUDENCE: Yes.

BRUCE: Are you answering an ad again?

PRUDENCE: Well, yes, I am.

BRUCE: Me too. I mean I put one in again.

PRUDENCE: Yes. Well . . . I think I'll wait over here. Excuse me. (PRUDENCE *sits at another table. After a bit* BRUCE *comes over to her.*) Yes?

BRUCE: I'm afraid it's crossed my mind that you answered my ad again.

PRUDENCE: I would not be so stupid as to answer the same ad twice.

BRUCE: I changed my ad.

(*She stares at him.*)

I was hoping to get a different sort of person.

PRUDENCE: Are you then the Pulitzer Prize–winning author, 6'5", who likes Kierkegaard, Mahler, and Joan Didion?

BRUCE: Yes I am. Sorry.

PRUDENCE: I see. Well that was a ludicrous list of people to like anyway, it serves me right. I feel very embarrassed.

BRUCE: Don't be embarrassed. We're all human.

PRUDENCE: I see no reason not to be embarrassed at being human.

BRUCE: You should be in therapy.

PRUDENCE: I am in therapy.

BRUCE: It hasn't worked.

PRUDENCE: Thank you very much. Do you think we're the only two people who answer these ads?

BRUCE: I doubt it. Maybe we're fated.

PRUDENCE: Jinxed seems more like it.

BRUCE: You think you're unlucky, don't you? In general, I mean. (*He sits down.*)

PRUDENCE: You're going to sit down, are you?

BRUCE: Well what else should I do? Go home to Bob?

PRUDENCE: Oh yes. How is Bob?

BRUCE: He's kind of grumpy these days.

PRUDENCE: Perhaps he's getting his period.

BRUCE: I don't know much about menstruation. Tell me about it.

PRUDENCE (*stares at him*): Yes I do think I'm unlucky.

BRUCE: What?

PRUDENCE: In answer to your question. I mean, I am attractive, aren't I? I mean, without being conceited, I know I'm *fairly* attractive. I mean, I'm not within the world's two percent mutants . . .

BRUCE: I don't think you're a mutant at all. I mean, I think you're very attractive.

PRUDENCE: Yes? Well, I don't know if I can really credit your opinion. You're sort of a crackpot, aren't you?

BRUCE: You really don't like me, do you?

PRUDENCE: I don't know you really. Well, no, I probably don't like you.

BRUCE: Well I don't like you either.

PRUDENCE: Well fine. It was delightful to see you again. Goodbye. (*She starts to leave. He starts to cry, but tries to muffle it more than usual.*) I really hate it when you cry. You're much too *large* to cry.

BRUCE: I'm sorry, it's not you. Something was just coming up for me. Some childhood something.

PRUDENCE: Yes, I miss childhood.

BRUCE: I thought you were leaving.

PRUDENCE (*sits*): Alright, I want to ask you something. Why did you put that ad in the paper? I mean, if you're living with this person named Bob, why are you trying to meet a woman?

BRUCE: I want to be open to all experiences.

PRUDENCE: Well that sounds all very well, but surely you can't just turn on and off sexual preference.

BRUCE: I don't have to turn it on or off. I prefer both sexes.

PRUDENCE: I don't know, I just find that so difficult to believe.

BRUCE: But why would I be here with you if I weren't interested in you?

PRUDENCE: You might be trying to murder me. Or punish your mother.

BRUCE: Or I might just be trying to reach out and touch someone.

PRUDENCE: That's the slogan of Coke or Dr Pepper, I think.

BRUCE: The telephone company actually. But it's a good slogan. I mean, isn't that what we're all trying to do, reach out to another person? I mean, I put an ad in a newspaper, after all, and you answered it.

PRUDENCE: I know. It's very hard to meet people. I mean I do meet people at the magazine, but they're never right. I met Shaun Cassidy last week. Of course, he's too young for me.

BRUCE: Bob really likes Shaun Cassidy.

PRUDENCE: Oh, I'll have to try to set them up.

BRUCE: I don't think your therapist is helping you at all.

PRUDENCE: Well I think yours must be a maniac.

BRUCE: My therapist says you have to be willing to go out on a limb, to risk, to risk!

PRUDENCE: My therapist says . . . (*at a loss*) I have to settle for imperfection.

BRUCE: I know it's unconventional to be bisexual. My wife Sally didn't deal with it at all well.

PRUDENCE: You were married?

BRUCE: For six years. I married this girl Sally I knew all through grammar school and everything. She was runner-up for the homecoming queen.

PRUDENCE: I didn't go to the prom. I read *Notes from Underground* instead.

BRUCE: You should have gone to the prom.

PRUDENCE: I don't like proms. Why did you and Sally break up?

BRUCE: Well, I didn't understand about bisexuality back then. I thought the fact that I wanted to sleep with the man who came to read the gas meter meant I was queer.

PRUDENCE: I'm never home when they come to read the gas meter.

BRUCE: And so then Sally found out I was sleeping with the gas man, and she got real angry, and we got a divorce.

PRUDENCE: Well I guess if you're homecoming queen runner-up you don't expect those sorts of problems.

BRUCE: You haven't been married, have you?

PRUDENCE (*uncomfortable*): No.

BRUCE: Has there been anyone serious?

PRUDENCE: I have two cats. Serious, let's see. Well, about a year and a half ago I lived for six months with this aging preppie named Michael.

BRUCE (*pleased—a connection*): I'm an aging preppie.

PRUDENCE: Yes I know. Michael was a lawyer, and . . .

BRUCE: I'm a lawyer.

PRUDENCE (*registers this fact, then goes on*): And he was very smart, and very nice; and I should've been happy with him, and I don't know why I wasn't. And he was slightly allergic to my cats, so I broke it off.

BRUCE: And you haven't gone out with anyone since?

PRUDENCE: Well I do go out with people, but it never seems to work out.

BRUCE: Maybe you're too hard on them.

PRUDENCE: Well should I pretend someone is wonderful if I think they're stupid or crazy?

BRUCE: Well no, but maybe you judge everybody too quickly.

PRUDENCE: Well perhaps. But how many nights would you give David Berkowitz?

BRUCE: You went out with David Berkowitz?

PRUDENCE: No. It was a rhetorical question.

BRUCE: You must ask yourself what you want. Do you want to be married?

PRUDENCE: I have no idea. It's so confusing. I know when I was a little girl, Million Dollar Movie showed this film called *Every Girl Should Be Married* every night for seven days. It was this dumb comedy about this *infantile* girl played by Betsy Drake who wants to be married to a pediatrician played by Cary Grant who she sees in a drugstore. She sees him for two minutes, and she wants to move in and have babies with him. And he finds her totally obnoxious. But then at the end of the movie suddenly he says, "You're right, you're adorable," and then they get married. (*Looks baffled by the stupidity of it all.*)

BRUCE: Well it was a comedy.

PRUDENCE: And what confused me further was that the actress Betsy Drake did in fact marry Cary Grant in real life. Of course, it didn't last, and he married several other people, and then later Dyan Cannon said he was insane and took LSD and so maybe one wouldn't want to be married to him at all. But if it's no good being married to Cary Grant, who is it good being married to?

BRUCE: I don't know.

PRUDENCE: Neither do I.

BRUCE: Well you should give things time. First impressions can be wrong. And maybe Dyan Cannon was the problem. Maybe anyone married to her would take LSD. Maybe Cary Grant is still terrific.

PRUDENCE: Well he's too old for me anyway. Shaun Cassidy's too young, and Cary Grant's too old.

BRUCE: I'm the right age.

PRUDENCE: Yes I guess you are.

BRUCE: And you haven't left. You said you were leaving but then you stayed.

PRUDENCE: Well it's not particularly meaningful. I was just curious why you put the ad in the paper.

BRUCE: Why did you answer it?

PRUDENCE: I don't wish to analyze my behavior on the issue.

BRUCE: You're so afraid of things. I feel this overwhelming urge to help you. We can look into the abyss together.

PRUDENCE: Please don't say pretentious things. I get a rash.

BRUCE (*depressed*): You're right. I guess I am pretentious.

PRUDENCE: Well I really am too hard on people.

BRUCE: No you're probably right to dislike me. Sally hates me. I mean, sometimes I hear myself and I understand why no one likes me.

PRUDENCE: Please don't be so hard on yourself on my account. Everyone's stupid, so you're just like everyone else.

(*He stares at her.*)

I'm sorry, that sounded terrible, I'm stupid too. We're all stupid.

BRUCE: It's human to be stupid. (*Sings romantically.*) There's a somebody I'm longing duh duh, duh duh duh duh, duh duh duh duh . . .

PRUDENCE (*sings*): Someone to watch . . . (*Realizes she's singing alone.*) Oh I didn't realize you were stopping.

BRUCE: Sorry. I didn't realize you were . . . starting.

PRUDENCE: Yes. Stupid of me to like that song.

BRUCE: It's a pretty song.

PRUDENCE: Well I guess it is.

BRUCE: I want to say something. I like you.

PRUDENCE (*surprised anyone could like her*): You do?

BRUCE: I like women who are independent-minded, who don't look to a man to do all their thinking for them. I like women who are persons.

PRUDENCE: Well you sound like you were coached by Betty Friedan, but otherwise that's a nice sentiment. Of course, a woman who was independent-minded wouldn't like the song "Someone to Watch over Me."

BRUCE: We have to allow for contradictions in ourselves. Nobody is just one thing.

PRUDENCE (*serious*): That's very true. That wasn't a crackpot comment at all.

BRUCE: I know it wasn't. And just because I'm a crackpot on some things doesn't mean I'm a total crackpot.

PRUDENCE: Right. You're a partial crackpot.

BRUCE: You could be a crackpot too if you let yourself go.

PRUDENCE: That wasn't what I was attempting to do when I got up this morning.

BRUCE: To risk, to risk! Do you like me?

PRUDENCE: Well I don't know. I don't really know you yet.

BRUCE: Do you want to get to know me?

PRUDENCE: Well, I don't know. Maybe I shouldn't. I mean, we did meet through a personal ad, you don't have a Pulitzer Prize . . .

BRUCE: I have a membership in the New York Health and Racquet Club.

PRUDENCE: Well similar, but not the same thing.

BRUCE: As a member I can get you a discount.

PRUDENCE: I don't know if I'm ready to exercise yet. I'm thinking about it, but I'm cautious still.

BRUCE: We're getting on, aren't we?

PRUDENCE: Well yes, in a way. (*She smiles warmly. He smiles back. She then looks around.*) Do you think maybe they don't have waiters in this restaurant?

BRUCE: Maybe they're on strike. Why don't we go to another restaurant? I know a good Mexican one.

PRUDENCE: I don't like Mexican food, I'm afraid.

BRUCE: Japanese?

PRUDENCE: Well no.

BRUCE: Chinese?

PRUDENCE: Well more than Japanese, but not really.

BRUCE: Where do you want to go?

PRUDENCE: Well could we go to an American restaurant? I know I'm very dull, but I didn't even like vanilla ice cream when I was a child. I was afraid of it.

BRUCE: That's a significant statement you've just made.

PRUDENCE: It does sound pathological, doesn't it?

BRUCE: Don't be afraid to sound pathological. That's what I've learned from my therapy so far.

PRUDENCE: I don't think I've learned much from mine yet.

BRUCE: Maybe I can help you. We can look into the abyss together. Oh that's right, you didn't like it when I said that before.

PRUDENCE: That's alright. I'll look into the abyss for one evening.

BRUCE: Oh you're becoming more open. Good for you. Ruff, ruff, ruff!

PRUDENCE (*very taken aback*): I'm sorry?

BRUCE (*very embarrassed*): Oh, my therapist barks. For encouragement.

PRUDENCE: Ah, of course.

BRUCE: Now tell me about your fear of vanilla ice cream.

PRUDENCE (*as they exit*): Well, I had gotten very used to baby food, and I also liked Junket, but there was something about the texture of vanilla ice cream . . .

(*They exit.*)

SCENE 5

DR. STUART FRAMINGHAM's *office again.*

STUART (*on phone*): Hiya, babe, it's me. Whatcha doin'? Oh, I'm just waiting for my next patient. Last night was great, wasn't it? It was great. What? So quickly. What is it with you women? You read some goddamned sex manual and then you think sex is supposed to go on for hours or something. I mean, if you're so frigid you can't get excited in a couple of minutes, that's not my problem. No it isn't. Well, fuck you too. (*Hangs up.*) Jesus God. (*Into intercom:*) Betty, you can send in the next patient.

(*Enter* PRUDENCE. *She sits.*)

Hello.

PRUDENCE: Hello.

STUART: What's on your mind this week?

PRUDENCE: Nothing.

STUART: Goddamn it. I don't feel like dragging the words out of you this week. Talk, damn it.

(*She stares at him.*)

You pay me to listen, so TALK!

PRUDENCE: What?

STUART: I'm sorry, I'm on edge today. And all my patients are this way. None of them talk. Well this one guy talks, but he talks in Yiddish a lot, and I don't know what the fuck he's saying.

PRUDENCE: Well you should tell him that you don't understand.

STUART: Don't tell me how to run my business! Besides, we're here to talk about you. How was your week? Another series of lonely, loveless evenings? I'm still here, babe.

PRUDENCE: Don't call me babe. No, I've had some pleasant evenings actually.

STUART: You have?

PRUDENCE: Yes I have.

STUART: You been answering ads in the paper again?

PRUDENCE: Well, yes actually.

STUART: That's a slutty thing to do.

PRUDENCE: As a therapist you are utterly ridiculous.

STUART: I'm just kidding you. You shouldn't lose your sense of humor, babe, especially when you're in a promiscuous stage.

PRUDENCE: I am not promiscuous.

STUART: There's nothing wrong with being promiscuous. We're all human.

PRUDENCE: Yes, we are all human.

STUART: So who is this guy? Have you slept with him?

PRUDENCE: Dr. Framingham . . .

STUART: Really, I gotta know for therapy.

PRUDENCE: Yes, we have slept together. Once. I wasn't really planning to, but . . .

STUART: Is he better than me?

PRUDENCE: Stuart . . .

STUART: No really. You liked him better? Tell me.

PRUDENCE: Yes I did. Much better.

STUART: I suppose he took his time. I suppose it lasted just hours. That's sick! Wanting sex to take a long time is sick!

PRUDENCE: Well he was attentive to how I felt, if that's what you mean.

STUART: So this fellow was a real success, huh?

PRUDENCE: Success and failure are not particularly likeable terms to describe sexual outings, but if you must, yes, it was successful. Probably his experiences with men have made him all that better as a lover.

STUART: What?

PRUDENCE: He's bisexual.

STUART (*starting to feel on the winning team again*): Oh yeah?

PRUDENCE: So he tells me. Masters and Johnson say that homosexuals make much more responsive sex partners anyway.

STUART: BULLSHIT! You are talking such bullshit! I understand you now. You're obviously afraid of a real man, and so you want to cuddle with some eunuch who isn't a threat to you. I understand all this now!

PRUDENCE: There's no need to call him a eunuch. A eunuch has no testicles.

STUART: I GOT BALLS, BABY!

PRUDENCE: I am so pleased for you.

STUART: You're afraid of men!

PRUDENCE: I am not afraid of men.

STUART: You're a fag hag. I gotta write that down. (*Writes that down, makes further notes.*)

PRUDENCE: Look, I admit I find this man's supposed bisexuality confusing and I don't quite believe it. But what are my options? A two-minute roll in the hay with you, where you make no distinction between sexual intercourse and push-ups, and then a happy evening of admiring your underarm hair and your belt buckles? (*Irritated.*) What are you writing?

STUART (*reading from his pad*): I'd like to give this patient electroshock therapy. I'd like to put this patient in a clothes dryer until her hair falls out. I'd like to tie her to the radiator and . . . (*Stops, hears himself, looks stricken.*)

PRUDENCE: I think this is obviously my last session.

STUART: No, no, no. You're taking me seriously. I'm testing you. It was a test. I was just putting you on.

PRUDENCE: For what purpose?

STUART: I can't tell you. It would interfere with your therapy.

PRUDENCE: You call this therapy?

STUART: We're reaching the richest part of our therapy. And already I see results. But I think you're entering a very uncharted part of your life just now, and so you must stay with your therapy. You're going out with homosexuals, God knows what you're going to do next. Now I'm very serious. I'm holding out the lifeline. Don't turn away.

PRUDENCE: Well I'll think about it, but I don't know.

STUART: You're a very sick woman, and you mustn't be without a therapist even for a day.

PRUDENCE (*not taken in by this; wanting to leave without a scene*): Is the session over yet?

STUART: We have thirty more minutes.

PRUDENCE: Could I go early?

STUART: I think it's important that we finish out the session.

PRUDENCE: I'd like to go.

STUART: Please, please, please, please . . .

PRUDENCE: Alright, alright. For God's sake.

(*They settle down, back in their chairs.*)

STUART: When are you seeing this person again? I'm asking as your therapist.

PRUDENCE: Tonight. He's making dinner for us.

STUART: *He's* making dinner?

PRUDENCE: He says he likes to cook.

STUART: I don't think I need say anything more.

PRUDENCE: I don't think you do either.

(*They stare at one another; lights dim.*)

SCENE 6

BRUCE's *apartment.* BRUCE *fiddling with pillows on couch, looking at watch, etc. Doorbell.*

BRUCE (*letting in* PRUDENCE. *They kiss.*): Hi. Come on in.

PRUDENCE: Hello. I brought some wine.

BRUCE: Oh thanks.

PRUDENCE: You have a nice apartment.

BRUCE: Thanks.

PRUDENCE: It looks just like my apartment.

BRUCE: Yeah, I guess it does.

PRUDENCE: And like my therapist's office. And like the lobby of my bank. Everything looks alike.

BRUCE: Yes, I guess it does.

PRUDENCE: I'm sorry, I'm just rattling on.

BRUCE: That's alright. Sit down. (*They sit.*) Can I get you a drink?

PRUDENCE: Ummm, I don't know.

BRUCE: Do you want one?

PRUDENCE: I don't know. Do you want one?

BRUCE: Well I thought I might have some Perrier.

PRUDENCE: Oh that sounds good.

BRUCE: Two Perriers?

PRUDENCE: Well, do you have Poland water?

BRUCE: I think I do. Wait here. I'll be right back.

(BRUCE *exits. After a moment* BOB *enters.* BOB *sees* PRUDENCE, *is rattled, ill at ease.*)

BOB: Oh. You're here already. I . . . didn't hear the bell ring.

PRUDENCE: Oh. Hello. Are you Bob?

BOB: Yes. (*At a loss, making an odd joke.*) And you must be Marie of Roumania.

PRUDENCE: I'm Prudence.

BOB: Yes, I know. (*At a loss how to get out of room.*) Is Bruce in the kitchen?

PRUDENCE: Yes.

BOB: Oh. (*Starts to go there, stops.*) Oh, well, never mind. When he comes out would you tell him I want to see him in the other room?

PRUDENCE: Alright.

BOB: Excuse me.

(*Exits back to bedroom presumably. Enter* BRUCE *with two glasses of water.*)

BRUCE: Well here we are. One Perrier, and one Poland water.

PRUDENCE: I thought you said Bob was away.

BRUCE: Oh, you met Bob already? Yes, he *was* going away, but then he changed his mind and I'd already bought the lamb chops.

PRUDENCE: You mean he's going to be here all through dinner?

BRUCE: Oh I don't think so. He said he was going to his mother's for dinner. He has a very funny mother. She's sort of like Auntie Mame.

PRUDENCE: Oh, yes?

BRUCE: Now don't let Bob upset you.

PRUDENCE: Well he seemed very uncomfortable. He asked me if I was Marie of Roumania.

BRUCE: Oh he always says that. Don't take it personally. (*Raising drink.*) Well, cheers.

PRUDENCE (*remembering*): Oh. He said he wanted to see you in the other room.

BRUCE: Oh. Well, alright. I'll just be a minute. Here, why don't you read a magazine?

PRUDENCE: *People*, how nice.

BRUCE: Be right back.

(*Exits.* PRUDENCE *reads magazine uncomfortably, and tastes his Perrier water to compare it with her Poland water. We and she start to hear the following offstage argument; initially it's just a buzz of voices, but it grows into anger and shouting.* PRUDENCE *looks very uncomfortable.*)

BRUCE (*offstage*): This isn't the time to talk about this, Bob.

BOB (*offstage*): Well, when is the time?

BRUCE (*offstage*): We can talk about this later.

BOB (*offstage*): That's obviously very convenient for you.

BRUCE (*offstage*): Bob, this isn't the time to talk about this.

BOB (*offstage*): Well when *is* the time?

BRUCE (*offstage*): Come on, Bob, calm down. (*Softer.*) Now I told you this doesn't have anything to do with us.

BOB (*offstage, very angry*): Oh God!

BRUCE (*offstage*): I'm sick of this behavior, Bob!

BOB (*offstage*): Well I'm sick of it too!

(*There is a crash of something breaking. Pause. Then reenter* BRUCE.)

BRUCE: Everything's fine now. (*Pause.*) We broke a vase. Well Bob broke it.

PRUDENCE: Maybe I should go.

BRUCE: No, everything's fine now. Once Bob vents his anger then everything's fine again.

PRUDENCE: I thought you told me that Bob didn't mind about your seeing me, and that the two of you had broken up anyway.

BRUCE: Well, I lied. Sorry. Some members of Bob's group therapy wrote me a note saying they thought if I wanted to see women, I should just go on and see women, and so I just sort of presumed they'd convince Bob eventually, but I guess they haven't yet.

PRUDENCE: They wrote you a letter?

BRUCE: It's a very intense group Bob is in. They're always visiting each other in the hospital and things.

PRUDENCE: But what shall we do about this evening?

BRUCE: I think you and Bob will really like one another once you get past this initial discomfort. And besides, I'm sure he'll be going to his mother's in a little while.

PRUDENCE: Maybe we should go to a restaurant.

BRUCE: No, really, I bought the lamb chops. It'll be fine. Oh my God, the rice. I have to go see about the rice. It's wild rice; well, Rice-A-Roni. I have to go see about browning it. I won't be a minute.

PRUDENCE: No, no, don't leave . . .

BRUCE: It's alright. (*As he leaves.*) Bob will come talk to you . . .

(*Exits.*)

PRUDENCE (*as she sees he's gone*): I know . . . Oh dear.

(*Enter* BOB.)

BOB: Hello again.

PRUDENCE: Oh hi.

BOB: I didn't mean to make you uncomfortable about Marie of Roumania. It's just something I say.

PRUDENCE: Oh that's alright.

BOB (*offering it as information*): I just broke a vase.

PRUDENCE (*being pleasant*): Oh yes, I thought I heard something.

BOB: Bruce says that I will like you if I can just get past my initial hostility.

PRUDENCE: Oh. Well I hope so.

BOB: Bruce is really a very conflicted person. I really suffer a lot dealing with him.

PRUDENCE: Oh I'm sorry.

BOB: And now this latest thing of having women traipse through here at all hours.

PRUDENCE: Ah.

BOB: Did you ever see the movie *Sunday Bloody Sunday*?

PRUDENCE: No I didn't. I meant to.

BOB: Well I sure wish Bruce had never seen it. It had a big effect on him. It's all about this guy played by Murray Head who's having an affair with Peter Finch *and* with Glenda Jackson.

PRUDENCE: Oh. Good actors.

BOB: Yes, well the point is that it's a very silly movie because I don't think bisexuality exists, do you?

PRUDENCE: Well it's hard to know really.

BOB: I mean, I think that Bruce is just trying to prove something with all these ads in the paper for women. That's what my mother says about Bruce. She tells me I should just be patient and understanding and that it's just a phase Bruce is going through. I've put a lot of work into this relationship. And it's so difficult meeting new people, it's just thoroughly intimidating.

PRUDENCE: It is hard to meet people.

BOB: I think everyone is basically gay, don't you?

PRUDENCE: Well, no, not really.

BOB: You just say that because you haven't come out yet. I know lots of lesbians who'd like you a lot. I'd be happy to give them your number.

PRUDENCE: Thank you, but no.

(*Enter* BRUCE.)

BRUCE: Well I burned the rice. Sorry. We'll just have more salad.

PRUDENCE: Oh that's alright.

BRUCE: So have you two been getting to know one another?

PRUDENCE: Yes.

BOB (*truly being conversational, not trying to be rude; to* BRUCE): Don't you think Prudence would be a big hit in a lesbian bar?

BRUCE: Yes, I guess she would.

BOB: I know Liz Skinner would certainly like her.

BRUCE: Yes, she is Liz's type.

PRUDENCE: Bruce, could I speak to you for a moment, please? (*To* BOB:) I'm sorry, excuse me. (BRUCE *and* PRUDENCE *cross to side of room.*) Bruce, I'm getting very uncomfortable. Now, you told me that Bob wasn't going to be here and that he wasn't jealous about your seeing women, and I don't want to be told which lesbians would like me. So I think maybe I should forget the whole thing and go home.

BRUCE: No, please, don't go. Bob needs help to get over his feelings about this, and I'm sure he'll go to his mother's in a little while. So please just be nice to him for a little longer. For our sake.

PRUDENCE: I don't know.

BRUCE: Really, it'll be fine.

PRUDENCE (*deciding to try*): Alright. Alright. (*On returning; to* BOB:) Sorry.

BOB: Don't be sorry. I realize I make you uncomfortable.

PRUDENCE: No, no, really it's not that.

BRUCE: Prudence likes you, Bob. She isn't like the other women you know.

PRUDENCE: Yes, I do . . . I like lots of men. (*Laughs nervously.*)

BOB: We have that in common.

PRUDENCE: Yes . . . (*Laughs, very uncomfortable.*)

BRUCE (*making big transition into "conversation"*): So, Prudence, did you finish writing your interview with Joyce De Witt?

PRUDENCE (*trying to be very friendly*): Oh, she's the brunette actress on the TV show "Three's a Crowd." (*Pause; looks mortified.*) I mean, "Three's Company." (*Long pause. They all feel awful.*)

BRUCE: So, did you finish the article?

PRUDENCE: Yes. I did. Right on time. (*Pause; to* BOB:) Bruce tells me your mother is like Auntie Mame.

(BOB *glares at* BRUCE.)

Oh, I'm sorry. Was that a bad thing to say?

BOB: It depends on what you mean by Auntie Mame.

PRUDENCE: I don't know. Bruce said it.

BOB: My mother has a certain flair, if that's what he means.

BRUCE: Your mother acts like a transvestite. I'm sorry, she does.

BOB: Just because my mother has a sense of humor is no reason to accuse her of not being feminine. (*To* PRUDENCE:) Don't you agree that women *theoretically* can have senses of humor?

PRUDENCE: Yes indeed.

BRUCE: Sense of humor isn't the issue.

PRUDENCE (*trying to help conversation*): I've always hated transvestites. It's such a repugnant image of women.

(BOB *looks disapproving.*)

I'm sorry, I don't mean to imply anything about your mother. I . . . I liked Jack Lemmon as a woman in *Some Like It Hot.*

BOB: My mother does not resemble Jack Lemmon in *Some Like It Hot.*

PRUDENCE: I'm sure she doesn't. I didn't mean to imply . . . I don't know what I meant to imply . . .

BRUCE: Change the subject, Prudence. This is getting us nowhere.

PRUDENCE: Oh, alright. (*Thinks.*) What does Bob do for a living?

BOB: I'm still in the room.

PRUDENCE: Oh, I'm sorry. I know you are. (*Mortified pause.*) What do you do for a living, Bob?

BOB: I'm a pharmacist.

PRUDENCE: Oh really?

BOB: Do you need any pills?

PRUDENCE: No thank you. (*Pause.*) Maybe later.

BRUCE (*to* PRUDENCE): Can I freshen your Poland water?

PRUDENCE: No thank you. I'm fine. (*Pause.*) So you're a pharmacist.

BOB: Yes.

BRUCE: I wish I hadn't burned the rice. (*Whispers to* PRU-
DENCE:) Say something to him, he's starting to sulk.

PRUDENCE: Ummmm . . . What exactly is in Di-Gel, I
wonder.

BOB: That's alright. I realize I'm making everyone uncomfortable. Excuse me.

(*Exits.*)

PRUDENCE: Really, Bruce, this isn't very fair to me. This is a
problem the two of you should work out together.

BRUCE: Well you're right, actually. You're always right.
That's why I like you so much. (*Moves closer, puts arm
around her.*)

PRUDENCE: Maybe I should go.

BRUCE: Oh you're too sensitive. Besides, he'll be leaving
soon.

(BOB *reenters.*)

BOB: My mother's on the phone.

BRUCE: I didn't hear it ring.

BOB: I called her. (*To* PRUDENCE:) She wants to speak to you.

PRUDENCE: I don't understand. I . . .

BOB (*hands her the phone*): Here.

PRUDENCE (*it's happening too fast to stop*): Hello. Who is
this? Oh, hello. Yes. (*Laughs uncomfortably.*) Yes,
thank you. What? No, I don't want to ruin your son's
life. What? No, really, I'm not trying to . . .

BRUCE (*takes phone away from* PRUDENCE; *talks into it*):

Now, look, Sadie, I've told you not to meddle in my life. It doesn't do anybody any good when you do, including Bob. Don't sing when I'm talking to you, that's not communication to sing when someone is talking to you. Sadie . . . Sadie! (*Hands phone to* BOB.) She's singing "Rose's Turn" from *Gypsy*, it's utterly terrifying.

BOB: Hello, Mother.

BRUCE (*to* PRUDENCE): She's an insane woman.

BOB: Mother, it's me, you can stop singing now. Okay, well, just finish the phrase. (*Listens.*)

PRUDENCE: Where's Bob's father?

BRUCE: She killed him.

BOB: That's not funny, Bruce. Okay, Mother, wrap the song up now. Yes, I'm alright. Yes, I'll tell them. (*To the two of them:*) My mother thinks you're both very immature. (*Back to phone:*) Yes, I think she's a lesbian too.

PRUDENCE: I'm going to go home now.

BRUCE: No, no, I'll fix this. (*Takes phone away from* BOB.) Finish this conversation in the other room, Bob. Then please get out of here, as we agreed you would do earlier, so Prudence and I can have our dinner. I mean, we agreed upon this, Bob.

BOB: You mean you agreed upon it.

BRUCE: I've finished with this conversation, Bob. Go in the other room and talk to your mother. (*Listens to phone.*) What's she singing now, I don't recognize it?

BOB: That's "Welcome to Kanagawa" from *Pacific Overtures*.

BRUCE: Keep singing, Sadie. Bob is changing phones. It was good hearing from you.

BOB: I just don't understand your behavior. I just don't.

(*Exits.*)

PRUDENCE: Bruce, I can't tell you how uncomfortable I am. Really, I must go home, and then the two of you should go to a marriage counselor or something.

BRUCE: I am sorry. I should have protected you from this. (*Listens to phone, hangs it up.*)

PRUDENCE: I mean we're only seeing one another casually, and you and Bob have lived together, and his mother calls up and she sings . . .

BRUCE: I'm not feeling all that casual anymore. Are you?

PRUDENCE: Well I don't know. I mean, probably yes, it's still casual.

BRUCE: It needn't be.

PRUDENCE: Bruce, I just don't think your life is in order.

BRUCE: Of course it's not. How can life be in order? Life by its very nature is disordered, terrifying. That's why people come together, to face the terrors hand in hand.

PRUDENCE: You're giving me my rash again.

BRUCE: You're so afraid of feeling.

PRUDENCE: Oh, just put the lamb chops on.

BRUCE: I feel very close to you.

(*Enter* BOB *with suitcase. Phone rings.*)

BOB: Don't answer it. It's just my mother again. I told her I was checking into a hotel and then jumping out the window. There's just no point in continuing. (*To* PRU-DENCE, *sincerely:*) I hope you're both very happy. Really.

PRUDENCE (*startled, confused*): Thank you.

BRUCE: Bob, come back here. (*Answers phone.*) Sadie, we'll call you back. (*Hangs up.*) Bob.

BOB: No, go back to your evening. I don't want to stand in your way.

BRUCE: You're just trying to get attention.

BOB: There's just no point in continuing.

(*Phone rings;* BRUCE *answers it.*)

BRUCE: It's all right, Sadie, I'll handle this. (*Hangs up.*) Bob, people who announce their suicide are just asking for help, isn't that so, Prudence?

PRUDENCE: I really don't know. I think I should leave.

BOB: No, please, I don't want to spoil your dinner.

BRUCE: You're just asking for help.

(*Phone rings.*)

Let's let it ring. Bob, look at me. I want you to get help. Can you hear me? I want you to see my therapist.

BOB: I have my own group therapy.

BRUCE: You need better help than that. Doesn't he, Pru-dence? (*Answers phone.*) It's all right, Sadie, I'm going to call up my therapist right away. (*Hangs up.*) Now you just sit down here, Bob, and we're going to call Mrs. Wallace right up. (*To* PRUDENCE:) Unless you think your therapist is better.

PRUDENCE: No! Yours would have to be better.

BOB: I don't know what you have against my group therapy. It's been very helpful to me.

BRUCE: Bob, you're trying to kill yourself. That proves to me that group therapy is a failure.

BOB: Suicide is an innate human right.

(*Phone rings.*)

BRUCE (*answers; hands phone to* PRUDENCE): Will you tell her to stop calling?

PRUDENCE: Hello?

BRUCE: You're not acting logically.

PRUDENCE: No, I don't want to see him dead.

BOB: I simply think I should end my life now. That's logical.

PRUDENCE: Please don't shout at me, Mrs. Lansky.

BRUCE: We have to talk this through.

PRUDENCE: Bruce.

BOB: I don't want to talk it through. (*Sings:*) Frère Jacques, Frère Jacques, dormez-vous? dormez-vous? (*Etc., continues on.*)

PRUDENCE: Bruce.

BRUCE: Don't sing when I'm talking to you.

PRUDENCE: Bruce.

BRUCE: What is it, Prudence?

PRUDENCE: Please, Mrs. Lansky is yelling at me.

BRUCE: Well she can't hurt you. Yell back.

BOB (*takes phone*): Mother, it's alright, I want to die. (*Hands phone back to* PRUDENCE, *goes back to song:*) Ding dong ding ding dong ding. Frère Jacques . . . (*continues.*)

BRUCE: Bob, you're acting like a baby.

PRUDENCE: No, he's still alive, Mrs. Lansky.

BRUCE (*irritated, starts to sing at* BOB): Seventy-six trombones led the big parade, with a hundred and ten cornets close behind . . . (*continues.*)

PRUDENCE: Mrs. Lansky, I'm going to hang up now. Goodbye. Stop yelling. (*Hangs up.*)

BOB (*stops singing*): Did you hang up on my mother? (BRUCE *stops too.*)

PRUDENCE: OH WHY DON'T YOU JUST GO KILL YOURSELF?

(BOB *sits down, stunned. Phone rings.*)

PRUDENCE (*answers it*): Oh shut up. (*Hangs up.*) I am very uninterested in being involved in this nonsense. You're both just making a big over-dramatic mess out of everything, and I don't want to watch it anymore.

BRUCE: You're right. Bob, she's right.

BOB (*looks up*): She is?

BRUCE: Yes, she is. We're really acting stupid.

(*Phone rings.* BRUCE *picks it up, and hangs up imme-diately. Then he dials.*)

I'm calling Mrs. Wallace now. I think we really need help.

PRUDENCE: You have her home number?

BRUCE: Yes. She's a really wonderful woman. She gave me her home number after our second session.

PRUDENCE: I slept with my therapist after our second session.

BRUCE: Hello? Uh, is Mrs. Wallace there? Thank you. (*To them:*) I think that was her husband.

BOB (*not defiantly; just for something to do, sings softly*): Frère Jacques, Frère Jacques, dormez-vous . . . (*etc.*)

BRUCE (*suddenly hearing it*): What do you mean you slept with your therapist?

PRUDENCE: I don't know, I . . .

BRUCE (*to* BOB, *suddenly, as Mrs. Wallace is now on the phone*): Sssssh. (*Into phone.*) Hello. Mrs. Wallace? Mrs. Wallace, this is Bruce, we have a bit of an emergency, I wonder if you can help. . . . We're in desperate need of some therapy here . . .

ACT II

MRS. WALLACE's *office, twenty minutes after the end of Act I.* MRS. WALLACE *present, enter* BRUCE *and* BOB.

BRUCE: Hi, it's us.

CHARLOTTE: Hello.

BRUCE: Really, it's so nice of you to see us right away.

CHARLOTTE: That's alright.

BRUCE: Mrs. Wallace, this is Bob Lansky.

CHARLOTTE: Hello.

BOB: Hello.

BRUCE: Well I'm going to leave you two and go have dinner with Prudence.

BOB: You're not going to stay?

BRUCE: Bob, you're the one who's not handling this situation well. Now I haven't eaten all day, and this hasn't been fair to Prudence. (*To* MRS. WALLACE:) Now if he gets totally out of control, we're going to be at the

Squire Restaurant. I mean I could be paged. Otherwise, I'll just see you back at the apartment.

BOB: I thought you wanted her to talk to us together.

BRUCE: Not for the first session. Now you listen to what Mrs. Wallace has to say, and I'll see you later tonight. (*Gives* BOB *an affectionate hug, then exits.* BOB *and* MRS. WALLACE *stare at one another for a while.*)

BOB: Should I sit down?

CHARLOTTE: Would you like to sit down?

(*He sits. She sits, holds her Snoopy doll.*)

BOB: Why are you holding that doll?

CHARLOTTE: Does it bother you that I hold the doll?

BOB: I don't know.

CHARLOTTE: Were you allowed to have dolls as a child?

BOB: Yes I was. It was trucks I wasn't allowed to have.

CHARLOTTE: Great big trucks?

BOB: Toy trucks. (*Silence.*)

CHARLOTTE: Now, what seems to be the matter?

BOB: Bruce seems to be trying to end our relationship.

CHARLOTTE: What do you mean?

BOB: He's been putting these ads in the paper for women. And now he seems a little serious about this new one.

CHARLOTTE: Women?

BOB: Women.

CHARLOTTE: And why does this bother you?

BOB: Well, Bruce and I have been living together for a year. A little more.

CHARLOTTE: Living together?

BOB: Yes.

CHARLOTTE: As roommates?

BOB: Well, if that's the euphemism you prefer.

CHARLOTTE: I prefer nothing. I'm here to help you.

BOB: But you can see the problem.

CHARLOTTE: Well if Bruce should move out, surely you can find another roommate. They advertise in the paper. As a matter of fact, my son is looking for a roommate, he doesn't get on with the present Mr. Wallace. Maybe you could room with him.

BOB: I don't think you've understood. Bruce and I aren't just roommates, you know. I mean, doesn't he talk to you about me in his own therapy?

CHARLOTTE: Let me get his file. (*Looks through her drawers, takes out rope, binoculars, orange juice carton, folders, messy clipboard. Laughs.*) No, it's not here. Maybe my dirigible knows where it is. (*Pushes button.*) Marcia. Oh that's right, she's not in the office now. (*To intercom:*) Never mind. Well, I'll have to rely on memory.

BOB: Dirigible?

CHARLOTTE: I'm sorry, did I say dirigible? Now what word did I want?

BOB: Blimp?

CHARLOTTE (*not understanding*): Blimp?

BOB: Is the word blimp?

CHARLOTTE (*irritated*): No, it's nothing like blimp. Now you've made me forget what I was saying. (*Holds her head.*) Something about apartments. Oh yes. Did you want to meet my son as a possible roommate?

BOB: I don't understand what you're talking about. Why do you want me to meet your son? Is he gay?

CHARLOTTE (*offended*): No he's not gay. What an awful thing to suggest. He just wants to share an apartment with someone. Isn't that what you want?

BOB: No it isn't. I have not come to you for real estate advice. I've come to you because my lover and I are in danger of breaking up.

CHARLOTTE: Lover?

BOB: Your patient, Bruce! The person who was just here. He and I are lovers, don't you know that?

CHARLOTTE: Good God, no!

BOB: What do you mean, Good God, no!

CHARLOTTE: But he doesn't seem homosexual. He doesn't lisp.

BOB: Are you kidding?

CHARLOTTE: Well, he doesn't lisp, does he? Now what was I thinking of? Be quiet for a moment. (*Holds her head.*) Secretary. The word I was looking for was secretary.

BOB: I mean, didn't Bruce talk about us? Am I that unimportant to him?

CHARLOTTE: I really can't remember without access to the files. Let's talk about something else.

BOB: Something else?

CHARLOTTE: Oh, tell me about your childhood. At what age did you masturbate?

BOB: I don't want to talk about my childhood.

CHARLOTTE: Very well. We'll just sit in silence. (*She hugs Snoopy.*) New patients are difficult, aren't they, Snoopy? (*She nods Snoopy's head, glares at* BOB *significantly.*)

BOB: May I see your accreditation, please?

(CHARLOTTE *starts to empty drawer again.*)

Never mind.

CHARLOTTE: So you and Bruce are an item, eh? Odd, that I didn't pick that up.

BOB: Well we may be an item no longer.

CHARLOTTE: Well the path of true love never doth run smoothly.

BOB: I mean, suddenly there are all these women.

CHARLOTTE: Well if you're homosexual, I guess you don't find me attractive then, do you?

BOB: What?

CHARLOTTE: I guess you don't find me attractive, do you?

BOB: I don't see what that has to do with anything.

CHARLOTTE: Very well. We'll drop the subject. (*Pause.*) Not even a teensy weensy bit? Well, no matter. (*Pause.*) Tell me. What do you and Bruce do exactly?

BOB: What do you mean?

CHARLOTTE: You know what I mean. Physically.

BOB: I don't care to discuss it.

CHARLOTTE: Tell me.

BOB: Why do you want to know?

CHARLOTTE: Patients act out many of their deepest conflicts through the sexual act. Women who get on top may wish to feel dominant. Men who prefer oral sex with women may wish to return to the womb. Couples who prefer the missionary position may wish to do anthropological work in Ghana. Everything people do is a clue to a trained psychotherapist. (*Pause.*) Tell me! Tell me!

BOB: I don't care to talk about it.

CHARLOTTE: Very well. We'll move on to something else. (*Sulks.*) I'm sure I can guess what goes on anyway. (*Sulks.*) I wasn't born yesterday. (*Pause; screams:*) COCKSUCKER!

BOB: What?

CHARLOTTE: Oh, I'm sorry. It was just this terrible urge I had. I'm terribly sorry. (*Gleefully.*) COCKSUCKER! (*Screams with laughter, clutches Snoopy, rocks back and forth.*) Oh my goodness, I'm sorry, I'm sorry. COCKSUCKER! Whoops! Sorry. Oh God, it's my blood sugar. Help, I need a cookie. Help, a cookie! COCKSUCKER! Wait, don't leave, I think I have a cookie in one of the drawers. Oh, I'm going to say it again, oh God! (*Screams the word as she stuffs cookie into her mouth; the word is muffled. Her body shakes with laughter and pleasure.*) Mmmm, cookie, cookie. Oh God. (*Collapses, lets arms dangle, leans back in chair.*) Oh, God. (*Lies on floor, laughs lightly.*) Oh, that was wonderful.

BOB (*stands, takes out a gun*): It's people like you who've oppressed gay people for centuries. (*Shoots her several times.*)

CHARLOTTE (*startled; then*): Good for you! Bravo! I like that. You're expressing your feelings, people have got to express their feelings. Am I bleeding? I can't find any blood.

BOB: It's a starting pistol. I bought it a couple of days ago, to threaten Bruce with.

CHARLOTTE: Good for you!

BOB: I don't want to go to prison. That's the only reason it's not a real gun.

CHARLOTTE: Good reason. You know what you want, and what you don't want. Oh I like this directness, I feel I'm starting to help you. I mean, don't you see the similarity? Now why don't I have ulcers? Do you know?

(BOB *sits on floor next to her.*)

BOB: I don't know what you're talking about.

CHARLOTTE: I don't have ulcers because I don't repress things. I admit to all my feelings. Now a few minutes ago when I wanted to hurl anti-homosexual epithets at you, I didn't repress myself, I just let 'em rip. And that's why I'm happy. And when you were mad at me, you took out your toy gun and you shot me. And *that's* the beginning of mental health. I mean, do you understand what I'm saying?

BOB: Well I follow you.

CHARLOTTE: Oh we're making progress. Don't you see? And you said it yourself. You didn't buy the gun to shoot me, you bought it to shoot Bruce and that floozie of his. Right?

BOB: Yes.

CHARLOTTE: So you see what I'm getting at?

BOB: You mean, I should follow through on my impulse and go shoot Bruce and Prudence.

CHARLOTTE (*stands, staggers to her desk, overwhelmed with how well the session is going*): Oh I've never had such a productive first session!

BOB: But should I get a real gun, or just use this one?

CHARLOTTE: That would be up to you. You have to ask yourself what you *really* want.

BOB: Well I don't want to go to jail, I just want to punish them.

CHARLOTTE: Good! Punish them! Act it out!

BOB: I mean, I could go to that restaurant right now.

CHARLOTTE: Oh yes! Oh good!

BOB: Will you come with me? I mean, in case someone tries to stop me you can explain it's part of my therapy.

CHARLOTTE (*agreeably*): Okay. Let me just get another cookie. Oh, I'm so glad you came to me. Now, should I bring Snoopy with me, or leave him here?

BOB: Well, which do you really *want?*

CHARLOTTE: Oh you're right. That's the issue, good for you. Okay, now . . . I don't know which I want. Let me sit here for a moment and figure it out.

(*She sits and thinks, weighing pro-and-con-Snoopy ideas in her head; lights dim.*)

SCENE 2

The restaurant again. BRUCE, PRUDENCE.

PRUDENCE: Why have we come back to this restaurant? We've been here twice before and never got any service.

BRUCE: You're upset about Bob, aren't you?

PRUDENCE: No. I understand. It's all difficult.

BRUCE: Bob will get used to the idea of us. I just tried to make it happen too soon. He's innately very flexible.

PRUDENCE: Then maybe the two of you should stay together.

BRUCE: Will you marry me?

PRUDENCE: Bruce, this is inappropriate.

BRUCE: Prudence, I believe one should just *act*—without thought, without reason, act on instinct. Look at the natives in Samoa, look at Margaret Mead. Did they think about what they were doing?

PRUDENCE: Important life decisions can't be made that way.

BRUCE: But they can, they must. Think of people who become heroes during emergencies and terrible disasters—they don't stop to fret and pick things apart, they just *move,* on sheer adrenaline. Why don't we think of our lives as some sort of uncontrollable disaster, like *The Towering Inferno* or *Tora! Tora! Tora!* and then why don't we just *act* on instinct and adrenaline. I mean, put that way, doesn't that make you just want to go out and get married?

PRUDENCE: But shouldn't I marry someone *specific*?

BRUCE: I'm specific.

PRUDENCE: Well, of course. But, what about the gas man? I mean, do I want the children saying I saw Daddy kissing the gas man?

BRUCE: We'd get electric heat.

PRUDENCE: Oh, Bruce!

BRUCE: Besides, I don't want lots and lots of people—I want you, and children, and occasionally Bob. Is that so bad?

PRUDENCE: Well it's not the traditional set-up.

BRUCE: Aren't you afraid of being lonely?

PRUDENCE: Well, I guess I am.

BRUCE: And aren't all your girlfriends from college married by now?

PRUDENCE: Well, many of them.

BRUCE: And you know you should really have children *now,* particularly if you may want more than one. I mean, soon you'll be at the end of your childbearing years. I don't mean to be mean bringing that up, but it is a reality.

PRUDENCE: Can we talk about something else?

BRUCE: I mean time is running out for you. And me too. We're not twenty anymore. We're not even twenty-six anymore. Do you remember how old thirty used to seem?

PRUDENCE: Please don't go on, you're making me hysterical.

BRUCE: No, but these are realities, Prudence. I may be your last chance, maybe no one else will want to marry you until you're forty. And it's hard to meet people. You already said that Shaun Cassidy was too young. I mean, we have so little time left to ourselves, we've got to grab it before it's gone.

(STUART *enters, sees them, hides behind a table.*)

PRUDENCE: Oh stop talking about time, please. I mean, I know I'm thirty, it doesn't mean I'm dead.

BRUCE: I didn't say dead. I just said that our time on this earth is limited.

PRUDENCE: Stop talking, stop talking. (*Covers her ears.*)

BRUCE: Prudence, I think you and I can make each other happy. (*Looks behind her; sees* STUART.) Do you see someone over there? Is that a waiter *hiding*?

PRUDENCE: Oh for God's sake.

BRUCE: What is it?

PRUDENCE: It's my therapist.

BRUCE: Here?

PRUDENCE: I thought we were being followed. (*Calling.*) Dr. Framingham, we see you.

BRUCE: What's he doing here?

(STUART *comes over to them.*)

STUART: I want you to leave here with me this instant.

PRUDENCE: Why are you following me?

STUART: I'm going to give you a prescription for a sedative, and then I'm going to drive you home.

PRUDENCE: I can't believe that you've been following me.

STUART: I care about my patients. (*To* BRUCE:) She's really *very* sick. The work we have to do together will take years.

PRUDENCE: Dr. Framingham, I've been meaning to call you since our last session. I'm discontinuing my therapy with you.

STUART: That would be very self-destructive. You'd be in Bellevue in a week.

PRUDENCE: I really don't want to see you ever again. Please go away now.

STUART: You don't mean what you say.

BRUCE: Do you want me to hit him?

PRUDENCE: No, I just want him to go away.

BRUCE: The lady wants you to leave, mister.

STUART (*to* PRUDENCE): So this is the degenerate you told me about?

BRUCE: What did she tell you about me?

PRUDENCE: Bruce, don't talk to him, please. Stuart, leave the restaurant. I'm tired of this.

STUART: Not until we set up our next appointment.

PRUDENCE: But, Stuart, I *told* you I'm discontinuing our therapy.

STUART: You haven't explained why to me.

PRUDENCE: Then I will. BECAUSE YOU ARE A PREMATURE EJACULATOR AND A LOUSY THERAPIST. NOW BEAT IT!

STUART (*very hurt, very mad*): Okay, Miss Sensuous Woman. But do you know what's going to happen to you without therapy? You're going to become a very pathetic, very lonely old maid. You know what's going to happen to you? You're going to break off with this clown in a few days, and then you're not going to go out with men anymore at all. Your emotional life is going to be tied up with your cats! (*To* BRUCE:) Do you know what she does in her apartment? She keeps cats! Some guy she almost married last year wanted to marry her but he was allergic to cats and so *she* chose the cats!

PRUDENCE: That's not why we broke up at all!

STUART: You're gonna end up taking little boat cruises to Bermuda with your *cats* and with spinster librarians when you're fifty unless you decide to kill yourself before then! And all because you were too cowardly and self-destructive and stupid to keep yourself from being an old maid by sticking with your therapy!

PRUDENCE: You are talking utter gibberish. Michael was only *slightly* allergic to cats and we didn't get married because we decided we weren't really in love. And I'm not going to end up an old maid, I'm going to get married. In fact, I may even marry Bruce here. And if I do, Bruce and I will send you a picture of our children every Christmas to the mental institution where you'll be locked up!

STUART (*hysterical*): You're a terrible, terrible patient!

PRUDENCE: And you're a hideous doctor! I hate you!

(*They throw water at each other. Enter* BOB *and* MRS. WALLACE.)

CHARLOTTE: Hello, everybody!

STUART: Who are these people?

CHARLOTTE: Go ahead, Bob, tell them.

BOB: I want to tell you how you've made me feel. I feel very angry.

(*He takes out his gun;* PRUDENCE, BRUCE, *and* STUART *look terrified. He fires the gun at them six or seven times. They are terribly shocked, stunned; are trying to figure out if they've been hit and are dying. Enter a young* WAITER.)

WAITER: I'm sorry. We're going to have to ask you people to leave.

BRUCE: But we haven't even seen menus.

WAITER: I'm sorry. We can't have shootings in here.

STUART: Oh my God. Oh my God. (*Feels himself all over for wounds; just coming out of his fear.*)

PRUDENCE (*taking the gun from* BOB): Give me that. (*Points the gun at the* WAITER.) Now look here, you. I am sick of the service in this restaurant. *I am very hungry.* Now

I want you to bring me a steak, medium rare, no potato, two vegetables, a small salad with oil and vinegar, and a glass of red wine. (*Angry, grouchy.*) Anyone else want to order?

CHARLOTTE: I'd like to see a menu.

PRUDENCE (*waving the gun*): And bring these other people menus. And make it snappy.

WAITER: Yes, ma'am.

(*Exits in a hurry.*)

CHARLOTTE (*to* PRUDENCE): Oh I *like* your directness. Bravo!

STUART (*feeling for bullet holes*): I don't understand. Did he miss all of us?

PRUDENCE: Shut up and sit down. I'm going to eat some dinner, and I want everyone to shut up.

CHARLOTTE: Oh, I think she's marvelous.

PRUDENCE (*aims the gun at her*): Shut up.

CHARLOTTE: Sorry.

(*Everyone sits quietly.* WAITER *brings menus, which people look at, except for* PRUDENCE, *who glares, and* STUART, *who's shaken.*)

WAITER: Our specials today are chicken Marsala, cooked in a garlic and white wine sauce, roast Long Island duckling, cooked in . . .

(*Lights dim to black.*)

SCENE 3

The restaurant still. They've finished their dinners: PRUDENCE, BRUCE, BOB, MRS. WALLACE, STUART. *The* WAITER *is clearing the dishes.*)

CHARLOTTE: Mmmmm, that chocolate mousse was delicious. I really shouldn't have had two.

WAITER (*to* PRUDENCE): Will there be anything else?

PRUDENCE: Just the check, please.

(WAITER *exits.*)

STUART (*who's still in a sort of shock; to* BOB): I thought you'd killed us all. You should be locked up.

BOB: Well all's well that ends well.

CHARLOTTE: Please, I thought we'd exhausted the whole topic of the shooting. No harm was done.

STUART: What if I'd had a heart condition?

CHARLOTTE: That would have been your responsibility. We must all take responsibility for our own lives.

STUART: I think you're a terrible therapist.

CHARLOTTE: Sounds like professional jealousy to me.

PRUDENCE (*to* STUART): I would not bring up the subject of who's a terrible therapist, if I were you.

CHARLOTTE (*to* BRUCE): She's so direct, I just find her wonderful. Congratulations, Bruce.

PRUDENCE: What are you congratulating him on?

CHARLOTTE: Aren't you getting married?

BRUCE: Yes.

PRUDENCE (*simultaneously*): No.

> (*Reenter* WAITER *with the check.*)

WAITER: Here's the check.

> (MRS. WALLACE *calls for the check.*)
>
> The second chocolate mousse was on the house, Mrs. Wallace.

CHARLOTTE: Thank you, honey.

> (*Kisses him on the cheek;* WAITER *exits.*)
>
> He's one of my patients too.

BOB: He's quite attractive.

BRUCE: I thought you were going to kill yourself.

BOB: Mrs. Wallace helped me express my anger and now I don't feel like it anymore.

STUART: If one runs around shooting off guns, blank or otherwise, just because one is angry, then we'll have anarchy.

BOB: No one is interested in your opinion.

BRUCE: I think Prudence and I are a good match. I think we should get married as soon as possible.

PRUDENCE: I never want to get married, ever. I'm going to quit my job, and stay in my apartment until they evict me. Then I'm going to become a bag lady and live in the tunnels under Grand Central Station.

(*They all stare at her.*)

BRUCE (*to* PRUDENCE): If you marry me, I'll help you want to live again.

BOB: What am I supposed to do?

BRUCE: You seemed too busy with the waiter a minute ago.

BOB: For God's sake, I just looked at him. You're trying to go off and marry this woman. Really, you're just impossible. I thought after I shot at you, you'd get over this silly thing about women.

BRUCE: I need the stability of a woman.

BOB: You think she's stable? She just said she was going to become a bag woman.

BRUCE: She was speaking metaphorically.

BOB: What kind of metaphor is becoming a bag woman?

BRUCE: She meant she was depressed.

BOB: So I'm depressed too. Why don't you marry me? We'll go find some crackpot Episcopal minister somewhere, and then we'll adopt children together.

BRUCE: And that's another thing. I want to have my own children. I want to reproduce. She can give me children.

PRUDENCE: Please stop talking about me that way. I don't want to have your children. I want to be left alone. I want to become a lesbian and move in with Kate Millett.

BOB: Now she's making sense.

BRUCE: Don't make fun of her. She's upset.

BOB: I'm upset. No one worries about me.

BRUCE: Prudence, don't cry. We'll live in Connecticut. Everything will be fine.

STUART: Why doesn't she marry me? I make a good living. Prudence, as your therapist, I think you should marry me.

BRUCE: Prudence would never marry a man who didn't cry.

STUART: What?

BRUCE: You're too macho. Prudence doesn't want to marry you.

STUART: There's no such thing as macho. There's male and female; and then there's whatever you are.

(BRUCE *cries*.)

Oh, I'm sorry. Was it what I said?

CHARLOTTE: Bruce cries all the time. I encourage him to.

BRUCE (*having stopped crying; to* PRUDENCE): Why won't you marry me?

STUART: She should marry me.

PRUDENCE: No. I don't want to marry either of you. You're both crazy. I'm going to marry someone sane.

BOB: There's just me left.

PRUDENCE: No. I'll marry the waiter. Waiter!

CHARLOTTE: Oh dear, poor thing. Fear of intimacy leading

to faulty reality testing. Prudence, dear, you don't know the waiter.

PRUDENCE: That doesn't matter. Bruce said it's better to know nothing about people when you get married.

BRUCE: But I meant you should marry me.

PRUDENCE: But I know too much about you and I know nothing about the waiter. Waiter!

(*Enter* WAITER.)

WAITER: Is something the matter?

PRUDENCE: Yes. I want you to marry me.

WAITER: I don't understand. Did I add the check wrong?

PRUDENCE: No. I want you to marry me. I only have a few more years in which it's safe to have children.

WAITER: I don't understand.

CHARLOTTE: It's alright, Andrew. She's in therapy with me now.

PRUDENCE (*takes out the blank gun, aims it at him*): Marry me! Marry me! (*Starts to giggle.*) Marry me!

CHARLOTTE: It's alright, Prudence; you're my patient now. Everything's going to be alright.

PRUDENCE: I don't want any more therapy! I want tennis lessons!

CHARLOTTE: Now, dear, you're not ready for tennis yet. You must let me help you.

STUART: She's my patient.

CHARLOTTE: I think you've already failed her. I think I shall have to take her on.

PRUDENCE (*screams*): I don't want either of you! I don't want any more therapy! I've been to see several therapists, and I'm sick of talking about myself!

(CHARLOTTE *throws a glass of water in* PRUDENCE's *face.*)

CHARLOTTE: Enough of this self-destructive behavior, young woman!

(PRUDENCE, *furious, picks up another glass of water to throw back at* CHARLOTTE, *hesitates momentarily, then throws it in* STUART's *face instead.*)

Bravo, good for you!

STUART: Why did she do that?

CHARLOTTE: She's getting in touch with her instincts. Prudence, you're making progress in my care already.

PRUDENCE: I HATE THIS RESTAURANT!

CHARLOTTE: Prudence, the restaurant isn't the problem. You're looking for perfection. Prudence, you know the song "Someday My Prince Will Come"? Well, it's shit. There is *no* prince. Everyone in this world is limited, and depending on one's perspective is either horrible or okay. Don't you agree, Dr. Framingham?

STUART (*just noticing*): I'm all wet.

CHARLOTTE: Ah, the beginnings of self-awareness, bravo, ruff ruff ruff! Oh that's right, I left Snoopy home. Well, that was a wrong decision. Prudence, I'm making a point here. We're all alone, everyone is crazy, and you have no choice but to be alone or to be with someone in what will be a highly imperfect and probably eventually unsatisfactory relationship.

PRUDENCE: I don't believe that's true.

CHARLOTTE: But you do. That's exactly why you act the way you do, because you believe that.

PRUDENCE: I believe there's more chance for happiness than that.

CHARLOTTE: YOU DON'T! And why should you? Look at Chekhov! (*She has surprised herself with her own thought, but forges on.*) Masha loves Konstantin, but Konstantin only loves Nina. Nina doesn't love Konstantin, but falls in love with Trigorin. Trigorin doesn't love Nina, but sort of loves Madame Arkadina, who doesn't love anyone but herself. And Medviedenko loves Masha, but she only loves Konstantin, which is where we started out. And then at the end of the play, Konstantin kills himself! Don't you see?

PRUDENCE: What's your point?

CHARLOTTE: I've forgotten. Oh damn. Oh yes! My point is that everyone thinks that Chekhov's plays are tragedies, but he called them comedies. (*Momentarily not sure this is germane, but charges on.*) It's all how you look at it. If you take psychological suffering in the right frame of mind, you can find the humor in it. And so *that's* how you should approach your relationship with Bruce!

BRUCE: This is getting too complicated.

PRUDENCE: My stomach feels queasy.

BRUCE: Never mind that. Prudence, remember what I said about acting on instinct, like you do in a crisis?

CHARLOTTE (*happily*): Like when I threw the water!

BRUCE: Right.

PRUDENCE: Yes, I remember.

BRUCE: Okay, I want you to answer quickly now, on instinct, don't think about it, alright?

PRUDENCE: Alright.

BRUCE: Is your stomach queasy?

PRUDENCE: Yes.

BRUCE: Is your name Prudence?

PRUDENCE: Yes.

BRUCE: Is your dress wet?

PRUDENCE: Yes.

BRUCE: Will you marry me?

PRUDENCE: Yes.

CHARLOTTE: Well, I'm glad that's settled.

STUART: You're not going to say yes like that, are you?

PRUDENCE: I guess so. All the other answers were yes. I have to go to the ladies' room to throw up. Excuse me.

(*Exits.*)

BRUCE: I'm so happy! (*Hugs* CHARLOTTE.) Not that she's sick, but that we're getting married.

BOB (*discontent*): Well, everybody's happy then.

STUART: All my patients leave their therapy. It's very upsetting.

CHARLOTTE: Would you like to talk about it?

BOB (*to* ANDREW): Hi. I don't think we've actually met yet. My name is Bob.

ANDREW: Hi. I'm Andrew.

BOB: You look awfully familiar.

ANDREW: You've probably just seen my type.

BOB: Ah, well . . .

ANDREW: I get off in five minutes.

BOB: Need any help?

(*Everyone looks a bit aghast, especially* BRUCE.)

ANDREW: Could be.

(*Exits.*)

BRUCE: What are you doing?

BOB: Well if you expect me to live over the garage and let you carry on with that woman whenever you feel like it, then I'm allowed an occasional waiter.

STUART: Good God, he's not really going to live over the garage, is he?

CHARLOTTE: Well, it depends on the zoning laws, I guess. (*Holds both sides of her head.*) Uh, I'm getting a rush from all that mousse. Anyone feel like going to a disco?

BOB: I'm game. Bruce?

BRUCE: Not particularly. (*Testy.*) Maybe the waiter will want to go.

CHARLOTTE: Oh, Andrew is an excellent dancer! He's been to reform school.

BOB: Oh, he's sulking now.

BRUCE: I feel jealous about you and the waiter.

BOB: That's not very fair. What about you and Prudence?

BRUCE: You're right. But I still feel the emotion. And that's alright, isn't it, Mrs. Wallace?

CHARLOTTE: It's alright with me.

BRUCE: I feel happy about Prudence, and unhappy about the waiter. And I think I may want to cry. (*Tries.*) No. False alarm.

(*Enter* ANDREW *in leather jacket.*)

STUART: He certainly cries a lot.

CHARLOTTE: Don't you ever cry, Dr. Framingham?

STUART: Only when things fall on me.

CHARLOTTE: Oh yes! Do you all remember Skylab—that space thing that fell from the sky? That upset my porpoises very much.

STUART: You have porpoises?

CHARLOTTE: I'm sorry. Did I say porpoises? Andrew, what word do I want?

ANDREW: Patients.

CHARLOTTE: Yes, thank you. Patients.

ANDREW: We had this guy in reform school that we didn't like much. So we took this big heavy metal bird bath, and we dropped it on him. *He* didn't cry.

CHARLOTTE: That's interesting, Andrew.

ANDREW: He went into a coma.

CHARLOTTE (*stern*): Andrew, I've told you, I want you to have *empathy* for other people.

ANDREW: Oh right. I forgot. We felt real bad for him.

CHARLOTTE: Andrew has a real sensitivity in him; we just haven't seen any of it yet.

BOB: How long were you in reform school?

ANDREW: About three years. (*Grins.*) Till it burned down.

BOB: Ah. (*Starting to think* ANDREW *may be a bad idea.*) Great.

BRUCE: I hope Prudence isn't ill.

CHARLOTTE: Oh who cares? Let's go dancing!

BOB: Bruce, would you prefer I didn't go?

BRUCE: No, it's okay. I guess you're allowed waiters. We'll talk later. Have a nice time.

BOB: Thanks.

BRUCE: I think I better go check on Prudence. Good night, everybody.

(*Gives* BOB *and* CHARLOTTE *hugs, exits.*)

CHARLOTTE: He's so nice. Well, the music is calling all of us, I think.

ANDREW (*to* BOB): My motorcycle's out this way.

BOB: My mother doesn't like me to ride motorcycles.

ANDREW (*shrugs*): Fuck her.

STUART (*to* CHARLOTTE): I don't think I want to go. I don't like discos.

CHARLOTTE: Nonsense. You must learn to like them.

STUART: There'll be too many women. I shouldn't tell you this, but I have troubles relating to women.

CHARLOTTE: Not to me. I think you're delightful.

STUART: You do?

CHARLOTTE: You know what I think? I think I could help you. I think you should come into therapy with me. I don't mean therapy, I mean thermidor.

ANDREW: No, you mean therapy.

CHARLOTTE: Do I? It doesn't sound right. Thermidor. Thorazine. Thermometer.

BOB: No, he's right, you mean therapy.

CHARLOTTE: Therapy. Therapy? Thackeray. Thespian. The Second Mrs. Tanqueray. Ftatateeta. Finickulee, finickula. Well let's just go. It'll come to me. (*She starts to go.*) Ovaltine! Orca, the killer whale. Abba dabba dabba dabba dabba dabba dabba. Oh, now I've really lost it.

(CHARLOTTE, STUART, BOB, *and* ANDREW *exit. Enter* BRUCE *and* PRUDENCE.)

PRUDENCE: Please, don't ever come into the ladies' room after me again, alright? It's very disconcerting.

BRUCE: I was worried.

PRUDENCE: Where is everybody?

BRUCE: They went to a disco.

PRUDENCE: Why?

BRUCE: Something about the mousse Mrs. Wallace ate.

PRUDENCE: Never mind. I don't want to know.

BRUCE: Okay, now, answer on instinct again. Where in Connecticut do you think we should live? Quick, instinct!

PRUDENCE: Bridgeport.

BRUCE: Oh, God, have you ever been to Bridgeport?

PRUDENCE: No, I meant Westport.

BRUCE: No, you said Bridgeport. There may be some psychic reason it's right we live in Bridgeport.

PRUDENCE: No, please, we can't keep making decisions like this.

BRUCE: There are probably some lovely parts of Bridgeport.

PRUDENCE: Please, I don't want to live in Bridgeport. Bruce, why do you want to marry me? Answer on instinct.

BRUCE: I wrote it down earlier. (*He takes out typed piece of paper; reads:*) "I want to marry Prudence because all my life I keep fluctuating between being traditional and being insane. For instance, marrying Sally was my trying to be traditional, while sleeping with the gas man or that time I took my clothes off in the dentist's office were my going to the opposite extreme. But I'm not *happy* at either extreme. And that's where Prudence fits in. I feel she's very traditional, like Sally, but Sally has no imagination, she's too stable. And I think that even though Prudence is very traditional, she's very *un*stable and because of that I think we could be very happy together." Do you understand what I'm saying?

PRUDENCE: I don't understand what happened at the dentist's office.

BRUCE: Well, I needed root canal . . .

PRUDENCE (*getting upset*): And that wasn't on instinct. You'd written that down.

BRUCE: Well, I know. But it was an instinct to *read* it.

PRUDENCE: How can I marry someone who takes his clothes off at the dentist's office?

BRUCE: I don't take them off as a general rule. It just happened once.

PRUDENCE (*very upset*): I must be out of my mind.

BRUCE: Oh God, you're changing your mind, aren't you? Oh my God, oh my God.

(*Sits down, weeps.* PRUDENCE *sits down, calm at first, then she too starts to cry. Then she starts to sob.* BRUCE *stops crying, looks up.*)

BRUCE: Prudence, you're crying. Don't cry. (*Holds her.*) What's the matter?

PRUDENCE (*through weeping*): I don't know. I'm upset you took your clothes off at the dentist's office because that means you must be insane, and I thought maybe you weren't insane but just sort of . . . lively. (*Cries some more.*)

BRUCE (*trying to comfort her*): I'm lively.

PRUDENCE: No, you're too lively. I wouldn't be able to cope.

BRUCE (*desperate to please her, keep her, comfort her*): Mrs. Wallace could give me lithium, she could give you speed. We might meet in the middle.

PRUDENCE: I don't want speed. I want an Alka-Seltzer. Do you think the waiter could get me one?

BRUCE: The waiter went to the disco with Bob.

PRUDENCE: Well, there must be another waiter, don't you think?

BRUCE: Well, it is a restaurant. (*Calls:*) Oh waiter! Waiter! I don't see anybody.

PRUDENCE: I don't either. (*Calls:*) Waiter!

BRUCE: I'm really honored you cried in front of me. Thank you.

PRUDENCE: You're welcome. Waiter!

BRUCE: I bet you don't cry very frequently.

PRUDENCE: No. Not in front of anyone at least.

BRUCE: I'm really honored.

PRUDENCE: I'll try to cry for you again sometime. Waiter!

BRUCE: Thank you. Waiter!

PRUDENCE: Waiter. Waiter.

BRUCE: Waiter. Waiter. This is a very existential restaurant.

PRUDENCE (*a little woozy, a little sad, a little cheerful*): Yes, that's why I like it here so much.

BRUCE: You like it here?

PRUDENCE: Yes. Sort of. It's very comforting. They leave you alone here. It's conducive to conversation.

BRUCE (*very friendly, a basis for hope again*): Yes, it's a great place to talk.

PRUDENCE (*smiles; then futilely calls again*): Waiter! Waiter!

BRUCE (*makes a joke, sings*): There's a waiter that I'm longing to see, duh duh duh duh . . .

BRUCE and PRUDENCE (*sing together, a little ruefully*): Duh duh duh duh. Dum dum dum dum, over me.

BRUCE (*smiles at her*): Silly song.

PRUDENCE (*smiles at him*): Very silly.

(**Lights dim to black.**)